Friendship as a Way of Life

Friendship as a Way of Life

Foucault, AIDS, and the
Politics of Shared Estrangement

TOM ROACH

Hervé Guibert, *"L'ami,"* 1980. B/W photograph. Reproduced with the permission of Christine Guibert.

David Wojnarowicz, "A Painting to Replace the British Monument in Buenos Aires," 1984. Acrylic on street poster. Reproduced with the permission of the Estate of David Wojnarowicz and P.P.O.W., New York.

Published by State University of New York Press, Albany

For information, contact State University of New York Press, Albany, NY
www.sunypress.edu

Production by Kelli W. LeRoux
Marketing by Anne M. Valentine

Library of Congress Cataloging-in-Publication Data

Roach, Tom.
   Friendship as a way of life : Foucault, AIDS, and the politics of shared estrangement / Tom Roach.
      p. cm.
   Includes bibliographical references and index.
   ISBN 978-1-4384-4000-2 (pbk. : alk. paper)
   ISBN 978-1-4384-3999-0 (hardcover : alk. paper)
   1. Friendship. 2. Friendship—Philosophy. 3. Gay and lesbian studies.
4. Foucault, Michel, 1926–1984   I. Title.
   BF575.F66R587 2012
   177.6'2—dc22   2011010771

10 9 8 7 6 5 4 3 2 1

For Gary

Wonder at the sight of a cornflower, at a rock, at the touch of a rough hand—all the millions of emotions of which I'm made—they won't disappear even though I shall. Other men will experience them, and they'll still be there because of them. More and more I believe I exist in order to be the terrain and proof which show other men that life consists in the uninterrupted emotions flowing through all creation. The happiness my hand knows in a boy's hair will be known by another hand, is already known. And although I shall die, that happiness will live on. "I" may die, but what made that "I" possible, what made possible the joy of being, will make the joy of being live on without me.

—*Jean Genet,* Prisoner of Love

Contents

Acknowledgments

Like all intellectual endeavors, this is a collaborative work. First and foremost, I would like to thank my doctoral dissertation advisor, Cesare Casarino, for his support, guidance, and challenge. At every stage of this project he instilled in me the necessary confidence and determination to see it through. I am also indebted to my doctoral dissertation committee—Robin Brown, Lisa Disch, and John Mowitt—whose advice and input shaped the contours of this work. Richard Leppert, Tom Pepper, Michelle Stewart, Elizabeth Walden, Nicholas De Villiers, Cecily Marcus, and Roni Shapira Ben-Yoseph likewise played significant roles as interlocutors. Indeed, I am grateful for the generosity and camaraderie of the entire faculty and graduate student body of the Department of Cultural Studies and Comparative Literature at the University of Minnesota as well as my colleagues in the Department of Literary and Cultural Studies at Bryant University. Special thanks to Jason Weidemann at the University of Minnesota Press for his sage counsel in matters of academic publishing.

This work would not have been possible without the financial support of Bryant University's Summer Research stipend, and the University of Minnesota's Harold Leonard Memorial Film Studies Fellowship, Graduate Research Partnership Program, and Doctoral Dissertation International Research Grant. These awards afforded me time, that most precious of all commodities, to conduct archival research at *l'Institut mémoires de l'édition contemporaine* in Paris and Caen, the AIDS Activist Video Preservation Project in the New York Public Library, and the David Wojnarowicz Papers in New York University's Fales Library. My special thanks to José Ruiz-Funes and Catherine Josset at IMEC, Ann Butler and the helpful staff at the Fales Library, Christine Guibert for permission to reprint Hervé Guibert's photograph, "*L'ami*," and to Jamie Sterns from the Estate of David Wojnarowicz and the P.P.O.W. Gallery for permission to reprint David Wojnarowicz's painting, "A Painting to Replace the British Monument in Buenos Aires."

An alternate version of Chapters 1 and 2 was published as a single essay, "Impersonal Friends: Foucault, Guibert, and an Ethics of Discomfort," in *new formations: A Journal of Culture/Theory/Politics* 55 (Spring 2005): 54–72. Portions of Chapters 2 and 3 appear in "Murderous Friends: Homosocial Excess in Alfred Hitchcock's *Rope* (1948) and Gus Van Sant's *Elephant* (2003)" in *The Quarterly Review of Film and Video* 29.2, 2012. A truncated version of Chapters 4 and 5 was published as "Sense and Sexuality: Foucault, Wojnarowicz, and Biopower" in *Nebula: A Journal of Multidisciplinary Scholarship* 6.3, 2009. Also appearing in Chapter 4 is an extract of a book review of Michael Hardt and Antonio Negri's *Empire*. This review can be found in *Cultural Critique* 48 (Winter 2001): 253–54.

I am beholden to my editors at SUNY Press, Andrew Kenyon and Larin McLaughlin, for believing in this project and helping steer it to completion. Additionally, the careful reading and productive suggestions of the manuscript's anonymous reviewers doubtless improved the quality of this book. Leo Bersani, Tim Dean, and William Haver likewise provided insight and encouragement in the project's final stages. I am humbled by and immensely appreciative of their support.

Finally, to Gary Thomas, to my friends, and to my family: You inspired me, put up with me, and cheered me on throughout. Thank you.

Introduction

Between Friends

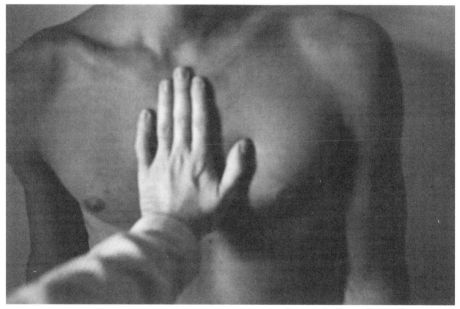

Hervé Guibert, *"L'ami,"* 1980.

> The philosopher is the concept's friend; he is potentiality of the concept. . . . Does this mean that the friend is the friend of his own creations? Or is the actuality of the concept due to the potential of the friend, in the unity of the creator and his double?
>
> —*Deleuze and Guattari* (What is Philosophy? 5)

A concept is created in the intellectual interstices of two philosophers, two friends. It is not rightfully *their* concept, of course; it is, as Deleuze and Guattari note, their friend, the doubling (even quadrupling) of their friendship. The property of neither, the potentiality of both, the concept emerges as a third term between two. Its arrival enacts the principal features of its conceptual persona: the relational terms of a lived friendship

1

and the theoretical implications of each thinker's work on friendship are actualized in this event. It is thus a singular concept generated in common; this in itself is its purpose, its *raison d'être*. Although the result of a profound intimacy (between thinkers and thought, between individuals), it resists assimilating its originary differences into an identity. It holds these friends at remove, in suspension, nurturing and continuously soliciting their individual and shared power. As such, this concept of friendship bears the imprint of a historical relationship yet points toward a posthumous political project with a life of its own. Michel Foucault provides the textual components, Hervé Guibert the visual, and I venture a name: friendship as shared estrangement.[1]

The title of this book, respectfully borrowed from a 1981 Foucault interview of the same name, and the photograph gracing the cover, Hervé Guibert's *"L'ami"* (1980), perhaps say as much about this concept of friendship as the words contained herein. Although each thinker certainly offers a unique understanding of friendship, I am interested here in articulating a concept that emerges in between. In terms of the physical space of this book's cover, then, I suppose I am charting the territory amid the title and the photo, creating overlays and drawing form lines to make legible and navigable that fertile zone between two oeuvres. In that common space lies this book's primary concept, friendship as shared estrangement. In that common space the concept's very formulation enacts its political strategy. Friendship as shared estrangement is a communal invention (of Foucault and Guibert, between myself and the two, and, most importantly, as I argue, among caregivers, activists, and Persons with AIDS [PWAs] throughout the AIDS crisis), dead set against the privatization of its constituent excesses. It is political by its very nature and it points to a sexual politics quite different from what we know today as "gay rights." What follows, then, is not only an attempt to chart the conceptual terrain between two thinkers, but to read the resulting map so as to forge a course out of the quagmire of sexuality, sexual identity, and contemporary sexual politics.

As the bulk of these pages is devoted to close analyses of Foucault's late work, I wish to begin my exploration of friendship as shared estrangement by giving Guibert's photography its due. *"L'ami"* is one of Guibert's most renowned photos, anthologized many times over and used as cover art for a number of books, including the Gallimard collection of his photography.[2] It welcomed visitors into the Galerie Agathe Gaillard in 1984, where Guibert exhibited the series that would become his first book of photography, *Le seul visage*. It is the first photo in that book.[3] As such, *"L'ami"* is in many respects representative of Guibert's visual style and bears some of its hallmarks: black-and-white stock, subject-centered, self-inclusive, with strong emphasis on the interplay of shadow and light, blurry and focused surfaces. Although both figures in the photo are faceless and fragmented, we can surmise from biographical and textual context that the hand belongs to Guibert and the chest to one of his closest confidants/lovers, Thierry.[4] Compositionally, Guibert's arm juts into the photographic space from the bottom-left corner. His hand touches the sternum of Thierry, whose bare chest and shoulders dominate the frame. With the exception of Thierry's right pectoral, each element is out of focus, fuzzy, lending a dreamy if not spectral quality to the shot. Darkness threatens to engulf Thierry from his left: In certain spots he is nearly indistinct from the wall behind, his left bicep and pectoral barely visible at all. Although this shadowy figure is a forceful and ominous presence, he is simultaneously motionless, passive, even vulnerable. Guibert's more brightly lit hand, the photo's (just-left-of) centerpiece, is similarly multivalent: Is it actively pushing Thierry away? Is it restraining him from moving closer? Is it supporting a forward-leaning body? Or, is it gently caressing Thierry, touching him where love "resides"? Like Thierry's presence, the meaning of Guibert's gesture is ambiguous. In view of that, and taking into account the title of the piece, what type of friend and what form of friendship is offered here?

One might be, and many have been, tempted to read this image as specifically and politically "gay." Given the historical context of gay liberation, the fact that Guibert self-identified as homosexual, and the assimilationist political desire to identify and collect "positive images" of homosexuality, such an interpretation is reasonable, if reductive.[5] Even if we accept that this text has something to do with "being gay," even if the subjects are in fact Guibert and Thierry, and, forgetting names, dates and biographies for the moment, even if the extended arm is in fact attached to a male body, the photo remains a quite peculiar, a not unequivocally "positive" display of homoeroticism.[6] The hand gesture, for starters, communicates a number of conflicting messages: (1) "STOP! Stay where you are; don't come any closer" in the language of the traffic cop (or even "in the name of love," à la Diana Ross and the Supremes); (2) "Don't go, please stay, I want you here" in the language of the lover; and (3) "Leave me alone, goodbye" or, anachronistically, "talk to the hand," in the language of the departing and/or dismissing. Indeed, as noted earlier, the gesture is simultaneously tender and commanding, accommodating and rejecting; the hand pushes, restrains, supports, and caresses. To build the mystery further, it remains unclear to which figure the title refers: Is the singular friend the restrainer or the restrained, the toucher or the touched? Is the title itself an abbreviated, perhaps coded, reference to "boyfriend" (*un petit ami*)? Although we can be certain that this is a male friend (*L'ami*, not *L'amie*), we cannot say without doubt that *the* friend is Thierry (who is the named subject of other portraits titled "Thierry, 1979" and "T., 1976"), as it may well be Guibert himself. For these reasons, the photo demands an interpretation beyond the details of biography, history, and sexual identity. For all of its ambiguity, I assert that this text is not merely photographic evidence of a lived friendship, but, rather, an early attempt by Guibert to articulate a concept of friendship as shared estrangement—a concept he will elaborate a decade later in his fictionalized AIDS memoir, *To the Friend Who Did Not Save My Life.*

Thus, if we understand this photo not only as a representation of a singular friend but also as a nascent theory of friendship itself, four facets of this theory are immediately evident: friendship involves a relation between one and another (or between one and oneself), anonymity, bodily contact, and, somewhat paradoxically, physical distance. The friend is held at arm's length, refused a certain access to the other; yet the gesture that separates simultaneously unites.[7] The touch, the lighting, the closed framing, and the softened edges of body parts all work to create a tenderly lurid atmosphere, suggesting, as some critics would have it, a postcoital, preparting moment in a romantic narrative.[8] The arguably forceful hand gesture, however, complicates this narrative by calling attention to the discrete boundaries and willed movements of each character. The existential push and pull of individuality versus community is possibly at play here; friendship, not necessarily romance, becomes the stage on which this drama is enacted. But *Tristan und Isolde* this is not. Rather than a fusing of body and soul, we have here an intimacy that resists amalgamation—a seemingly *impersonal* intimacy that comprehends, perhaps counterintuitively, a sensual component. The nameless, fragmented, even abstracted bodies seem more at home in a Kenneth Anger film than in a Wagner opera, their intimacy more akin to the Judas kiss of betrayal than a love beyond the grave.[9] The subjects' lack of features heightens the impersonality of the scene: we see merely gestures and postures, no facial expressions, no windows to the soul. These could be any bodies whatever, any two pale-skinned men in any interior space. The scene is rife with potentiality, uncertainty—anything could have happened, could be happening, could happen; its polyvalence confounds. We are, however, guided by the title to "*the* friend," or, the more comprehensive, "friend": This is not simply *a* friend (*un ami*) but either a specific one or the very idea of "friend" itself. If we take seriously the latter interpretation, as I clearly do, we have already a preliminary definition of Guibertian friendship: a complex, even contradictory, relation involving attraction and resistance, intimacy and separation, sensuality and frigidity; a relation that resists dialectical fusion in favor of nondialectical mingling; a friendship that by no means excludes the sensual but remains, perhaps, indifferent to the sexual.

To more clearly explicate this last claim, it is important to note that the photo's sensuality does not immediately translate to sexuality, especially in its antinomial modern conception. Granted, one clothed, seemingly male arm touches another man's bare chest, but in the semiotics of contemporary erotic gestures, this hardly constitutes "homosexuality." Again, it is by and large the biographical, historical, and textual context that urges us to interpret the photo as specifically "gay." If we allow it to read more openly, we see instead what Ralph Sarkonak has designated Guibert's "sensuality of surfaces," a sensuality "not lodged in the muscle tissue beneath the skin, in the rock hard flesh that seeks to force its way out . . . [but, instead] . . . located in the touch and the feel of the body's outer envelope" ("Traces and Shadows" 187). The faceless anonymity of the figures adds force to an interpretation that emphasizes surface. If this photo concerns homosexuality at all, then, sexual "depth" is hardly at issue. Countering the biopolitical demand to understand sexuality as the inner locus of self-truth, Guibert frees his subjects here from the shackles of identity and interiority. This liberation from the sexual "soul" is a key feature of both Foucault's and Guibert's understandings of friendship. Both prefer to explore the surface pleasures of the flesh over the internal workings of desire.[10] As we shall see, for Foucault this move is politically strategic: to put faith in the "sexuality" of the *scientia sexualis* is to remain forever entangled in a discursive game that has been rigged from the outset. Such trust in the liberatory powers of sexuality, in Foucault's estimation, represses actual practices of freedom.[11] His, then, is a friendship not determined or limited by King Sexuality; no longer the fulcrum around which interpersonal relations are defined, sexuality loses its constituting force. The implementation of this insight alone, I argue throughout, might go some way in enriching the relational mosaic and, consequently, toward the fabrication of genuine alternatives to the administered life.[12] With this in mind, we can safely say that the "truth" of Guibert's sensual subjects in "*L'ami*" does not lie in some interior sexual essence. Indeed, the traditionally impassable barrier between friend and lover seems to collapse—the potentially sexual act of touching does not establish divisive relational parameters or determine for good these men's identities. The terms of this relationship remain open: An impersonal intimacy holds them in suspension between desire and restraint, between proximity and distance. Although one is, or both are, "the friend," this designation now connotes a protean malleability, even a becoming-exogenous. Such boundlessness encourages an active practice of friendship: It requires attention and care, a mutual trust, and, bizarre as it sounds, betrayals.

Comprehending the latter, quite unusual feature of friendship as shared estrangement requires a brief detour through some biographical details of Guibert and Foucault's lived relationship. Ralph Sarkonak, Guibert's principal biographer, describes their rapport as follows:

> the mutual attraction that these two men felt for each other's company, conversations at once casual and serious, narcissistic betrayals, and the telling of secrets typical of the life of gay bars, as well as the braiding together of life's daily rituals—including illness and death—with the outrageous *jouissances* of sex and the creative act. It is the truth of a friendship of two kindred spirits, each caught up in his own original manner in a web of words, yet still full of admiration for his friend's unique literary form of praxis. (185)

Emphasizing the friendship's intellectual, conversational, catty, and creative aspects, Sarkonak's rendering reads almost like an "out" gay update of the cryptically queer bond between another pair of famous French intellectuals, Montaigne and la Boétie.[13] With the exception of the "narcissistic betrayals," a behavior not typically sought after in a potential friend, their rapport comes across as quite traditional: supportive, inspirational, perhaps a bit competitive, but rounded out with a mutual admiration for each others' work. So, whence come the betrayals? Sarkonak is referring here to two publications in which Guibert disclosed private aspects of Foucault's life: The first, *To the Friend*, in which Guibert transforms Foucault into the fictional character, Muzil, and supposedly "tells all" about Foucault's struggle with AIDS—a matter Foucault did not discuss in public; and the second, a short story, "A Man's Secrets," written the day after Foucault's funeral, in which Guibert relays three of Foucault's childhood memories that apparently had a significant effect on the philosopher's development. Such revelations scandalized the French literary world, which consequently accused Guibert of exploiting Foucault's legacy for personal gain. Guibert, who called his treason an "amorous crime," countered his critics by claiming "complete authority" in breaching confidentiality because, as persons with AIDS, he and Foucault were united by a "common thanatological destiny,"[14] and that "it wasn't so much my friend's last agony I was describing as it was my own" (*To the Friend* 91–92). Although these betrayals have been variously interpreted as vengeful acts of a jilted lover, "narcissistic," as above, and opportunistic,[15] all of which may certainly apply, it seems to me that they also foreground the importance of betrayal to the mutual theory of friendship articulated and practiced by these men. A third instance of betrayal, not mentioned by Sarkonak or others, compounds the treachery as it concerns Guibert betraying Foucault betraying Guibert. In a quite personal letter sent to Guibert in 1983, Foucault more or less informs his friend that he is an afterthought, an aside, in the philosopher's daily life (Betrayal One). Designating this letter a "gift" and a "true text," Guibert publishes the potentially embarrassing epistle in *L'Autre Journal* in 1985 (Betrayal Two).[16] Foucault's deceit comes after a lush poetic description of his morning ritual spying on a man across the alley from his apartment. The last line of the letter reads: "This morning the [man's] window is closed; instead I am writing to you."[17] Until this final phrase, Guibert remains unaddressed and unacknowledged. If the window across the way had been open, he is told, the anonymous beauty would have occupied his friend's morning. Voyeuristic pleasure, in essence, takes precedence over friendship. At once intimate in its candid rendering of possibly unsavory behavior and cold in its lack of personal sentiment, this letter, the point of departure for Chapter 1, not only gives a sense of their unusual rapport but also demands that we take seriously betrayal as crucial to their friendship praxis. More interesting than mere narcissism (or, if it is narcissism, it is one so unbounded it cannot distinguish self from friend), betrayal if nothing else works to prevent a dialectical fusion: As an anti-intersubjective practice, it refuses to assimilate self to other, other to self; by cutting a transverse line through the friend–enemy opposition, it complicates binary logic and provokes a productive tension between friends. In short, betrayal demands a rethinking of the traditional ethical terms of friendship.

Chapter 1, then, begins with a close reading of Foucault's letter in order to highlight five features of his theory of friendship: anti-confessional discourse; parrhesia; ascetics; impersonality; and estrangement. Reading the letter in relation to *The Hermeneutics of the Subject*, one of Foucault's last seminars at the *Collège de France*, as well as other late works, especially interviews and invited lectures, gives context to its themes and foregrounds their sexual-political stakes. Because friendship has been so idealized in the Western philosophical canon—forming the bedrock of Aristotle's *polis*, surpassing romantic love for Montaigne—it is no surprise that gays and lesbians have likewise valorized it as a respite from social ostracism as well as an alternative to compulsory heterosexuality and heteronormativity. If one's very being and its attendant relations are deemed inferior if not pathological, why not align that self and its community with a superior relational form?[18] Foucault's concept of friendship, however, is anything but utopian: Betrayal, distance, brutal honesty, indeed, an impersonal intimacy founded in estrangement are its makings. This is, to be blunt, the shit of friendship. When the most troubling aspects of relationships become the very foundation of a friendship, however, new subjective, communal, and political forms can be imagined.

In the interview, "Friendship as a Way of Life," Foucault designates friendship the becoming of queer relationality: "the development towards which the problem of homosexuality tends is the one of friendship" (*Essential, V1: Ethics* 136). Chapter 2, then, seeks to analyze this "problem" and its "development," which requires, as Foucault insinuates, the construction of a new ethics. Revisiting the encounter between Foucault and Guibert, I mine Foucault's late work and Guibert's *To the Friend* to articulate an ethics of discomfort that gives direction to friendship as a *mode de vie.* The community of friends in Guibert's novel, for example, is founded on an acceptance of finitude; it emphasizes that which cannot be shared and intensifies alienation between friends. At the same time, these friendships encourage the mutual cultivation of an immanent impersonal self, calling into question traditional, dialectical conceptions of subjectivity, community, and belonging. The ethics of discomfort guiding these friends opens onto communal forms that cannot be contained by sadistic social hierarchies of identitarian difference.

Returning to the cover for a moment, an ethics of discomfort can likewise be glimpsed in "*L'ami.*" As we have seen, Guibert's friends inhabit the gray area in a black-and-white world, wandering the zone between anyone-whomever/someone-in-particular, intimacy/distance, and yearning/restraint. With an understanding of betrayal as integral to Guibertian–Foucaultian friendship, the anonymity of the photo's subjects now becomes even more significant. Namelessness and facelessness—that is, identityless-ness—provide a blank slate for the invention of new subjective forms. Raymond Bellour focuses on this aspect of Foucault and Guibert's rapport in the following passage:

> It was not just homosexuality that brought them together. They shared a profound, indomitable understanding, an understanding that one supposes was at the root of the mutual fascination inherent in their friendship, and the understanding was, specifically, of fiction, of the invention of the self as a fiction, with all the risks that that entails in life as well as in writing and philosophy. ("H.G./F." 78)

Betrayals are one such risk in the formation of new personas and fictive selves. Guibert's disclosure of Foucault's secrets works toward the creation of a different Foucault, and hence the friend breathes again in a new form. This itself is part of the ethics of discomfort: The friend's role is actively to enhance the other's potential, to push the friend to become-other. Betrayal is one practice through which this occurs; it instigates an ethical relation that cares little for historically determined identity. In fact, it seems that Foucault and Guibert treated each other's public personas as characters to be written, molded, and manipulated, regardless of consequence to self or other. Furthermore, considering Guibert made a career of blurring lines between fact and fiction in his novels, his treachery is both a literary allusion and a literary creation. Jean Genet, the great theorist of betrayal, the master of friendly enmity, the saintly despiser of homosexual identity, is the key literary referent here, and he too comes to life again through Guibert's actions.[19] Guibert-Genet creates Foucault-Muzil and the ethical imperative to annihilate identity, to transform the self and the friend, is fulfilled. The practice of betrayal, then, is an experiment in an antirelational ethics that points toward a politics beyond identity.[20]

Moreover, secrets are, of course, meant to be shared: As Guibert writes in *The Fantom Image*: "Secrets must necessarily circulate."[21] What gives a secret its power is its potential to expose; without this, it is nothing. Because, according to Foucault, sexuality in modernity has been discursively constructed as *the* secret, as that which reveals the self, undercutting the secret's power becomes a strategy for operating beyond the constricting limits of biopolitical rationality. The friend–enemy dichotomy, which holds considerable sway in the philosophical canon from Aristotle through Carl Schmitt, is shattered when the betrayal of secrets is part and parcel of friendship. In this sense, the true friend— the friend who will push one beyond historically determined identity, the friend who will help another think and relate differently—is the betrayer. Guibert hints at this insight in the following passage from "A Man's Secrets": "These secrets [Foucault's secrets] would have vanished with Atlantis—so patiently, so sumptuously sculpted only to be destroyed in an instant by a thunderbolt—had an avowal of friendship not also suggested a vague and uncertain hope of passing them on" (67). This hope, "vague and uncertain," for betrayal, what Emily Apter calls an "avowed disavowal" (85), gives lie to the title of the story: A secret told with the expectation that all will, and perhaps should, be revealed is not a secret at all.[22] Or, if it is still a secret, it can only be an *open* secret—that discursive formation bedeviling homosexuality since its invention.[23] Here, then, is the rub: toying with betrayals, self-exposures, and open secrets, Foucault and Guibert in their friendship praxis undermine not only the logic of the closet and the in/out mentality of gay liberation, but also the very idea of sexuality itself.

In Chapter 3 I explore the ontological foundations of Foucaultian friendship so as to argue that the friend only emerges once the sexological category of homosexual is overcome. Just as Monique Wittig obliterates the always-already patriarchal category "woman" in order to create her "lesbian," Foucault too uses a Nietzschean conception of radical negation to create an autonomous friend. This chapter completes my sketch of the philosophical context for Foucault's friendship model. A careful look at his late writings on power, biopower, and resistance, as well as an assessment of Foucault's relationship to Hegelian dialectics, offer a glimpse of friendship's potential political forms. I assert moreover that in his exploration of friendship Foucault solidifies his status as a philosopher of immanence. His antidialectical turn, coincident with, if not a consequence of, his studies in ontology and friendship in Antiquity, demands that his theories of power, subjectivity, and sexuality be re-evaluated. Only with the recent publication of *The Hermeneutics of the Subject* can we adequately assess how a Foucaultian immanentist ontology bears not only on his theories of friendship and sexuality but also on Foucaultian political strategy itself. For this reason I revisit two Foucault-inspired thinkers who energized queer theory in the 1990s, namely Judith Butler and David Halperin, to reassess their interpretation of Foucaultian subjectivity and resistance. Using these thinkers' work both as a building block and a point of contrast, I contend that Foucault's final turn away from Hegelian conceptions of being engenders new conceptions of community and politics that hold the capacity to revitalize queer studies.

One such important insight from Foucault's late work concerns the delinking of sexuality and truth in friendship (as witnessed in the betrayals, the open secrets, and mutual invention of fictitious selves) and the consequent relinking of self-knowledge and self-transformation. Foucault designates this process, surprisingly, a spiritual practice. Indeed, it is startling to find in Foucault's *Hermeneutics* an insistence on the necessity of spirituality for both the care of the self and for progressive political action. He argues that the separation of spirituality from philosophy represents not only the historical point of rupture between ancient and modern Western thought but also the great schism in the genealogy of subjectivity and truth. He hesitantly designates the "Cartesian moment" as the instant at which erudition subsumes praxis, whence access to truth requires merely self-knowledge, not self-transformation. A subject always already capable of truth irrespective of way of life, then, is Descartes' Platonic legacy. Such an insight raises some important questions: Is truth by self-knowledge alone perhaps the navel-gazing ruse that has brought us the deployment of sexuality, identity politics, even biopower *tout court*? Is Foucault's late turn toward the care of the self an attempt to reopen a space for a thoroughly *materialist* spirituality in philosophical thought?[24] One thing is clear from *Hermeneutics*: For Foucault, what we lost in the divorce of philosophy and spirituality is tantamount to the foreclosure of subjective and relational becomings. However irrecoverable spirituality in its ancient forms might be, philosophy today is worthless if not undertaken as a quest to reunite knowledge with practice, thought with ways of life. Philosophy today must effect the transition from *stultitia* to *sapientia*, or it is nothing.

"We are in this condition of *stultitia*," Foucault writes, "when we have not yet taken care of ourselves" (*Hermeneutics* 131). In Stoic thought, the *stultus* (literally "the fool") is restless, flighty, distracted—too affected by external representations and internal turbulence to will freely, too dispersed in the world to be concerned with the then imperative project of self-care. The *stultus* has no authentic relationship with himself and thus requires the help of a philosopher to reach a state of *sapientia*. The *sapiens*, by contrast, displays self-control and self-mastery and is capable of taking pleasure in himself because he has worked hard to will freely. He has harmonized thought and behavior and in the process has become the true subject of his actions. The role of the guide in self-transformation is more than the simple imparting of theoretical knowledge and practical know-how: He must speak frankly concerning the *stultus*'s bad choices and harmful habits and take an active, daily, therapeutic role in correcting them. Although the concrete form of the philosopher-guide shifts in Antiquity (from the Epicurean and Pythagorean schools to Marcus Aurelius's private counselors), one characteristic remains more or less constant through the first and second centuries: The philosopher-guide must be a friend.[25]

Although Hellenistic and Roman models for friendship are instructive and enticing, their masculinist, racist, and classist dimensions have no place in a contemporary context—we definitely cannot go home again. All the same, the Ancient precept of the care of the self, filtered through Foucault's exegeses, is this project's guiding force. His late work offers a powerful model for reimagining male friendship in particular. By jettisoning sexuality as the truth-telling fulcrum distinguishing friend from lover, it explodes the coercive and impoverishing codes of homosocial male bonding so crucial to patriarchal social hierarchies. In the spirit of Lillian Faderman's *Surpassing the Love of Men*, Adrienne Rich's "Compulsory Heterosexuality and Lesbian Existence," and Monique Wittig's *The Straight Mind*, my project molds Foucault's concept of friendship into one that simultaneously reinvests it as a political relation, confounding gender and sexual categorization and giving lie to the very concept of sexuality as we know it. The primary subcategories through which we understand

sexuality—principally homo- and heterosexuality—have provided an all
too efficient framework for classifying and evaluating human affection.
The modern byproduct of our centuries-old investment in sexuality as
a window into human personality, behavior, psychology, and identity
becomes an oppressive command to locate, express, and speak of our
sexual desires while paradoxically policing their every permutation. As
Foucault repeatedly points out, the sexological invention of an essential,
bifurcated sexuality not only impoverishes our relational world but also,
and more insidiously, provides a useful tool for the social management of
individuals—heterosexuals and homosexuals alike—in the maintenance
of patriarchal, heteronormative power structures.

For Foucault, the friend as we know it—from the Western literary
canon, from the reified representations offered by the culture industry—
can no longer be trusted. In order for friendship to be viable, meaningful,
again, it must metamorphose into something altogether different. AIDS
ushers in this metamorphosis with poignant urgency. For the communities
hit hardest by AIDS in the early days of the crisis, finitude—that most
singular and most common fact of existence—becomes ubiquitous and
unavoidable. For Foucault's queer audience, friendship as a way of life
mutates into friendship as a way of death. The impersonal intimacy
glimpsed in Foucault and Guibert's friendship foregrounds an acceptance
of finitude that emerges so strikingly in AIDS friendships. Indeed, Guibert's
forceful hand gesture in "*L'ami*" can be read as a futile attempt to bridge
the infinite distance, the estrangement, between friends. And yet, when
a nontranscendent estrangement in the form of finitude becomes the
bedrock of friendship, a respect for the absolute alterity and singularity
of the self and other is encouraged. A relation founded on a finitude
so radically unsharable can be the cornerstone of a community that
coheres not in identity but in a more radical being-in-common. In the
gaping crevasse between friends, a politics of shared estrangement lies
in wait. Therefore, I analyze in the latter half of the book the politics of
friendship at the heart of organizations such as the AIDS Buddy system
and ACT UP. Such groups transform friendships of shared estrangement
into a mode of biopolitical resistance that breaches boundaries of gender,
race, class, and generation and that encourages radically democratic
forms of citizenship and civic participation. Indeed, the politicization of
friendship as shared estrangement in AIDS caregiving and activism offers
a powerful model for biopolitical formations unwedded to the dialectic
of identity and difference—precisely the model needed to combat the
social management of life in the age of Empire.

After developing the ontological and ethical implications of Foucault's
spare but suggestive writings on friendship in Chapters 1 to 3, then, I set

out in Chapter 4 to assess the political salience of this friendship model in light of recent developments in the political economy. Broadly, Chapters 4, 5, and the epilogue aim to return biopolitics to its "home" in sexuality studies, to bring queer theory up to speed with biopolitical debates, and to articulate a concept of shared estrangement as biopolitical strategy. Although Foucault underscores the decisive role sexuality plays in the development of biopower, recent elaborations of the concept, especially in contemporary Marxist and neo-Heideggerean critiques of globalization and sovereign power, de-emphasize, if not ignore, the importance of sexuality for biopolitical regimes. Specifically, whereas Foucault designates sexuality as biopower's central *dispositif*, Michael Hardt and Antonio Negri argue in the *Empire* trilogy that sexuality in the post-Fordist era is no longer the privileged site of biopolitical control. When human affect, language, and cooperation are subsumed into the productive processes of capital, they argue, the very thoughts, gestures, and expressions of the social body become capital's principal commodity. Although I take seriously Hardt and Negri's analysis of biopower's enmeshment with labor and capital, I question their failure to define a specific concept of sexuality in the biopolitical context. When AIDS, a subject that receives no serious discussion in Hardt and Negri's work, is understood as a primary locus of biopolitical struggle, sexuality simply cannot be ignored or folded into a generalized concept of *bios*. So overdetermined by the category of sexuality, so enmeshed in the struggle over life administration, AIDS must be at the forefront of any and all analyses of global biopolitics. I thus focus on AIDS service organizations and activist movements that work to delink sexuality from truth by transforming a concept of friendship as shared estrangement into biopolitical resistance.

Friendship, as I understand it and as I argue throughout, bespeaks the anarchical contingency of all relationality. In its very nature it is *anti-institutional*, indeed it cannot congeal into an epistemological object known as "society." It is excessive of self-identity, and hence contrary to Aristotle's claim, structurally incapable of grounding social forms. I find it nonetheless necessary to run the risk of seeking out communal and political forms that approximate friendship: ones that acknowledge the impossibility of the social as such, ones that embrace the contradiction of relating at the point of unrelatability. It is only in such forms that we might think and live beyond the inherently inequitable hierarchies of identitarian difference. In Chapter 5, then, I locate in the work of David Wojnarowicz a concept—what he calls "sense"—that reveals the political potential of an ethics of antirelationality. His memoirs, written from the frontlines of the AIDS activist battlefield in the 1980s and 1990s, are instructive here in that they remind us of our continued failure to understand HIV as distinct from sexual identity and of our incapacity to disentangle sexuality from subjective truth. Consonant with Foucault's insight that the discursive link between sexual desire and self-truth is a formidable tool of control, Wojnarowicz's "sense" ruptures this link by deterritorializing sexual affect and putting it to work in a politics of shared estrangement. The "sense" he gleans from his various sexual escapades involves a breakdown of intersubjectivity, a delinking of sexual desire and truth, and an understanding of death's immanence to life. In the recognition of the "common thanatological destiny" he shares with a multitude of AIDS casualties, in acknowledging the nonidentical sameness of the other, Wojnarowicz transforms his alienated, nihilistic rage into collective resistance. Aiding in my articulation of Wojnarowicz's political vision are the various thinkers comprising "the antisocial turn" in queer studies. Coined by Judith Halberstam, this term refers to the work of Leo Bersani, Heather Love, Tim Dean, Lee Edelman, William Haver, and others, which resists the increasing hetero- and homonormativity of queer culture.[26] Anti-assimilationist to the core, these projects embrace the abject social position homosexuality historically has been obliged to occupy and explore the political potential, if any, of negativity, hopelessness, and antirelationality. Although Foucault's concept of friendship as shared estrangement certainly falls under the "antisocial" rubric, I find its approximation in the AIDS Buddy network and ACT UP a hope of sorts for mapping sites of resistance to biopolitical administration in the present. My project seeks to theorize and reclaim this politics of friendship for queer activism today.

The recent legalization of gay marriage in Canada, Spain, and an increasing number of U.S. states reveals the effectiveness of gay, lesbian, bisexual, and transgendered (GLBT) identity politics for institutional legitimacy. Although such victories are hard won and worthy of celebration, the legalization of gay marriage should not, contrary to conservative critic Andrew Sullivan's insistence, put an end to queer politics.[27] I assert, with Foucault, that the progress made by reproducing the marriage bond is slight. A radical queer politics would fight *against* the institutional impoverishment of the social fabric, and *for* the creation of unconventional forms of union and community. Friendship, as a formless relation without telos, provides a counterpoint to a GLBT political agenda seeking social legitimacy in the right to marry. Friendship is an immanent alternative to an institutionalized—hence concretized, deadened—form of union. Whereas marriage enacts the privatization of relational pleasures and practices, friendship remains properly communal, in common. Leela Gandhi teases out this aspect of friendship in her important work, *Affective Communities.* Friendship for her is "the most comprehensive philosophical signifier for all those invisible, affective gestures that refuse alignment along the secure axes of filiation to seek expression outside, if not against, possessive communities of belonging."[28] Gandhi's understanding of friendship's inherent homelessness, its uncanniness, mirrors my earlier articulation of the emergence of the concept of friendship as shared estrangement. This concept is the property of neither Foucault nor Guibert nor myself; the idea and the relation are generated in common and regenerate the common. The friend is neither possessive nor possessed, neither owner nor owned. If, for Foucault, the becoming of homosexuality is friendship, it is because friendship is always a becoming; if homosexuality is a "problem," it is precisely because it arrests the becoming of being-in-common. The friend is the fleeting placeholder of an asubjective affectivity moving through ontologically variegated singularities; it is the figure that intuits and enacts the common, that which seethes beneath and is excessive of relations and communities founded on identitarian difference. Indeed, coming back to the cover photograph, perhaps what Guibert best captures in "L'ami" is not only the space of the in-between, but also a zone of unbelonging, a property of the property-less. It is no small feat to traverse such terrain, adrift in the great wide open, ceaselessly threatened and delegitimated by landed, private interests. It is the goal of the coming pages, however, to discover where such wandering might lead us.

Chapter 1

A Letter and Its Implications

About eleven months before his death, Michel Foucault wrote Hervé
Guibert a letter describing a morning ritual of watching a man opposite
his apartment. The letter appears in Guibert's quasi zine, "*L'Autre Journal
d'Hervé Guibert*," a collection of musings, photographs, and fiction
turning on the theme of friendship, published in a 1985 issue of the arts/
literature/politics magazine, *L'Autre Journal*. Under the heading *Cadeau*
(gift), Guibert writes: "On the 28th of July, 1983, Michel wrote me a real
text (*un vrai text*) in a letter." It reads:

> *J'avais envie de te raconter le plaisir que je trouve à regarder,
> sans bouger de ma table, un garçon qui chaque jour vient à
> la même heure s'accouder à une fenêtre de la rue d'Alleray. À
> neuf heures, il ouvre sa fenêtre, il a une petite serviette bleue,
> ou un slip bleu également, il penche la tête sur son bras, enfouit
> son visage dans son coude; il ne bouge pas, sauf de temps en
> temps, rarement et lentement pour aller tirer une bouffée de la
> cigarette qu'il tient de l'autre main; mais il est si fatigué qu'il
> ne peut ni bouger (ou presque) la main qui tient la cigarette,
> ni se redresser; il se lasse glisser sur l'appui du balcon, sa tête
> roulant d'un bras à l'autre; puis il reprend sa première position,
> enfouit à nouveau son visage dans son coude, va y chercher
> des rêves extrêmement forts, intenses, épuisants, qui le laissent
> dans un grand (flûte, plus de papier bleu) abattement; des fois
> il a un grand geste du bras qui reste libre, ou même de tout
> le corps; ce n'est pas qu'il se détende ou cherche à se réveiller;
> on voit bien qu'il se drape encore dans la nuit; et s'il vient
> au bord de son balcon ce n'est pas pour dissiper à la lumière
> les dernières ombres où il est pris, c'est pour montrer à tous,
> à personne (puisqu'il n'y a que moi qui le regarde) qu'il n'y
> a pas de jour qui puisse vaincre l'obstination douce qui reste
> sur lui et le maîtrise souverainement. Il manifeste à la face du
> jour la puissance molle de sommeil. Ma myopie me protège de*

connaître son visage: il est donc beau. Et puis brusquement, il se redresse, il s'assoit à un table où il doit lire? Écrire? Taper à la machine? Je ne sais pas; je ne vois que le coude et l'épaule nus; et je me demande quels rêves ses yeux ont puisés dans le pli de son bras, quels mots ou quels dessins peuvent naître; mais je me dis que je suis le seul à avoir vu, de l'extérieur, se former et se déformer la chrysalide gracieuse où ils sont nés. Ce matin la fenêtre reste fermée; en lieux et place de quoi je t'écris.

—M.F.

[I have been wanting to tell you about the pleasure I take in watching, without moving from my table, a guy who leans out of a window on the rue d'Alleray at the same time every morning. At nine o'clock he opens his window; he wears a small blue towel or underpants, also blue; he leans his head on his arm, buries his face in his elbow; he does not move, apart from making occasional, rare, slow movements when he takes a puff of the cigarette he is holding in his other hand; but he is so tired that he is (almost) neither able to move the hand that holds the cigarette, nor to prop himself up; he gets tired moving along the railing of the balcony, his head rolling from one hand to the other; he then takes up his initial position, tucking his face back again in his elbow to look there for strong, intense, and powerful dreams, which leave him in a great (darn, [I need] more blue paper) depression; sometimes he makes a grand gesture with his arm that hangs freely or even his whole body; it is not that he is resting or trying to wake up; one can see that he is draping himself again in the night; and if he comes to the edge of his balcony it is not to cast light on the last shadows where he is caught, it is to show to everyone, to no one (since it is only me who is watching him) that there is no day that can overthrow the gentle obstinacy that remains with him and sovereignly masters him. He shows to the face of daytime the tender power of sleep. My shortsightedness protects me from knowing what his face looks like: he is thus beautiful. And then, brusquely, he straightens up, he sits down at a table where he might read? Write? Type? I don't know: I see only his naked elbow and shoulder; and I wonder what dreams his eyes found in the fold of his arms, what words or drawings are being born; but I tell myself that I am the only one to have seen from the outside the gracious chrysalis in which they were born, take shape, and lose shape. This morning the window is closed; instead I am writing to you.—M.F.[1]]

Guibert's inclusion of the letter in the journal's "Friendship" issue produces some salient questions. Is the text meant to suggest something about Guibert's friendship with Foucault? If so, what type of friendship is it? What are its stakes, its habits, its limits? Moreover, why does Guibert consider this both a gift and a "real text?" An atypical gift to a friend, the letter contains neither personal sentiment nor any direct expression of love or concern. Similarly atypical in the context of Foucault's other "real texts"—known for their erudition, meticulous wording, their dense yet playful style—this one is darkly poetic, introspective, more like a diary entry, or even a Peeping Tom's play-by-play commentary. That the letter is written to Guibert, or has anything at all to do with Guibert, seems at first incidental. Foucault addresses him only twice, in the first and last sentences, using the informal second-person pronoun. If the "you" of the first sentence is the recipient of happy news from an excited intimate ("I have been wanting to tell you about the pleasure I take"), the same "you" in the final line takes on a slightly chilly tone: "This morning the window is closed; instead I am writing to you." Foucault makes known in this backhandedly affectionate gesture that the letter is written only because his cherished boy is absent. Guibert is summoned as a replacement or a substitute for Foucault's voyeuristic ritual. Although the letter is revealing—what Foucault sees through a window becomes a window into his life—are its author's somewhat dismissive conclusion and its recipient's near invisibility nonetheless indicative of the impersonal, even unfriendly, nature of their rapport? Moreover, given Guibert's fondness for betraying his friends (as discussed in the introduction), might Foucault be writing with the knowledge that this is not merely a letter to a friend but a future publication on a theory of friendship?

Although surely a "lesser" work in Foucault's oeuvre, the letter opens onto some key themes and ideas concerning his late writings on friendship. These include

1. Anticonfessional discourse,

2. *Parrhesia,*

3. Ascetics,

4. Impersonality,

5. Estrangement.

At the risk of oversimplifying these complex themes, I merely introduce them here through a close reading of the letter. My first three points concern the letter's form and context: reading the letter in relation to Foucault's other late work, showing the ways the letter references ideas that occupied Foucault shortly before his death, asking what the letter enacts and performs. The latter two deal specifically with the letter's content from which I tease out some of the ethical terms of Foucaultian friendship. I recognize the irony, perhaps the blasphemy, of schematizing the thought of a decidedly antisystematic and detail-oriented philosopher. My reasons for doing so are purely logistical: Highlighting key themes and providing philosophical context here allow me to conduct a more rigorous analysis of Foucault's concept of friendship in the ensuing chapters. However widely discussed,[2] the implications—ontological, ethical, political—of this concept have not to my knowledge been sufficiently elaborated.

Anticonfessional Discourse

While the letter's subject, voyeurism, might be seen as scandalous if not unethical, its tone is neither guilty nor confessional. One could well imagine a very different voyeur's account, told in a style more libertine, sexy, tell-all, replete with shamefaced disclaimers or defensive proclamations that open the floodgates of confessional discourse. But this is not de Sade nor is it the anonymous author of *My Secret Life*.[3] As Foucault makes clear in *History of Sexuality, Volume One,* these authors are part of a more generalized historical imperative to speak of sex, their "shocking" words perfectly consonant with a psycho-sexological discourse that links self-truth with sexuality. In his late interviews, Foucault argues that in order to resist the biopolitical administration of life this link must be broken. He writes in "The End of the Monarchy of Sex":

> They [sexologists, doctors, vice squads] basically tell us: "You have a sexuality, this sexuality is both frustrated and mute, hypocritical prohibitions repress it. So, come to us, show us, confide in us your unhappy secrets. . . ." This type of discourse is in fact a formidable tool of control and power. As always, it uses what people say, feel and hope for. It exploits their temptation to believe that to be happy, it suffices to cross the threshold of discourse and remove a few prohibitions. It ends up in fact repressing and controlling movements of revolt and liberation. (*Foucault Live* 217)

And later, in the same interview:

A movement seems to be taking shape today which seems to be reversing the trend of "always more sex," of "always more truth in sex," a trend which has doomed us for centuries: it's a matter, I don't say of rediscovering, but rather of fabricating other forms of pleasure, of relationships, coexistences, attachments, loves, intensities. (218)

Foucault's sole example of this tendency to reverse the "truth in sex" imperative is none other than the letter's recipient, Hervé Guibert.[4] This "real text" of Foucault's could be read, then, as an experiment conducted with Guibert in producing an anticonfessional, postsexuality discourse of friendship. If the delinking of truth and sexuality involves the creation of antinormative forms of pleasure and relationships, such creation is taking place here both in Foucault's sexographical poetics and his emerging discourse of impersonal friendship.

Although axiomatic and perhaps overindulged in queer studies, *History of Sexuality, Volume One* is key to understanding why Foucault in his friendships avoids the confessional register. When in the nineteenth century sexuality was constituted as a problem of truth, the confession became the lynchpin between sexuality and truth, the discursive rite that provided a subject with a knowable, manageable self. Historically rooted in the Christian pastoral,[5] the ritual has become so familiar in modern Western life that "we no longer perceive it as the effect of a power that constrains us" (*HoS, V1* 60). We view confessions instead as liberatory, redeeming, and purifying rather than as systems of regulation and surveillance. Although a normalizing rite, the confession comes replete with its own system of pleasure. In seeking the truth of desire—knowing it, controlling it, exposing it, withholding it, goading it—we have created "a specific pleasure of the true discourse on pleasure" (71). The search for such truth, from the penitent's chair to the therapist's couch, creates "intrinsic modifications in the person who articulates it"(62). The ensuing transformation binds the confessor to his expelled truth and creates a dependence on an often manipulative Other who promises salvation.

Foucault's genealogy of the confession includes modern discourses of sexual liberation. Such discourses, above all the Freudo-Marxian liberationist rhetoric of Marcuse and Reich, are part and parcel of Foucault's "repressive hypothesis" and ultimately reinforce the shackling link between sexuality and truth. By extension, the gay liberationist act of coming out, as David Halperin has noted,[6] likewise secures the gay confessor to her or his sexual truth and prompts an epistemological double bind. Initially authorizing a truth-producing discourse ("I am gay"), the gay confessor is simultaneously reconstituted by the limits of that discourse (i.e., the sexual truth becomes the essence of the confessor's being), and subjected to the interpretations and "superior knowingness" of (straight) listeners. Coming out further entails coming *into* a predetermined identity, rife with stereotypes and pathologies, which effectively constrains self-identified lesbians and gays to the uniform truths of the historico-discursive construct of "homosexuality," repressing rather than instigating, in Foucault's words, "movements of revolt." Forever nodding to an absent heteronormative authority, coming out might, in the last instance, merely reiterate a script that hearkens back to one of the most familiar systems of control within Western history.

If Foucault finds worth in "fabricating other forms of pleasure, of relationships, coexistences, attachments, loves, intensities," he is critical, although never disparaging, of a politics founded on a confession that links truth and sexuality. Deploying the terms *gay* and *lesbian* in the political arena runs the risk of reifying the very categories and typologies that have historically disciplined same-sex desire. In terms of garnering rights and changing laws, however, the use of such identity markers has proven quite successful. The recent legalization of same-sex marriage in an increasing number of countries and states is evidence of the potency of identity politics. However, as Foucault notes in "The Social Triumph of the Sexual Will," such politics will only affirm extant and quite limited relational forms:

> . . . if you ask [gay and lesbian] people to reproduce the marriage bond for their personal relationship to be recognized, the progress made is slight. We live in a relational world that institutions have considerably impoverished. Society and the institutions which frame it have limited the possibility of relationships because a rich relational world would be very complex to manage. We should fight against the impoverishment of the relational fabric. (*Essential, V1: Ethics* 158)

Fighting for a richer relational world entails the creation of new ways of communicating and new forms of community. Operating under the confessional imperatives of "out" politics, gay and lesbian couples have earned state recognition. But armed with Foucault's critique of the confession and his historicization of the link between sexuality and truth, queers could open doors to different, perhaps queerer, worlds. Foucault's experiment in anticonfessional discourse in his letter to Guibert offers a model of sorts for corresponding and relating differently. Resisting a confessional tone even in describing an erotically charged scene, he brushes against the very grain of the biopolitical production of subjectivity—a subject required to speak his sexual truth, a subject identified, classified, and managed by this truth. Although the thrills garnered from post-kiss tellings, from provocative admissions of shameful fantasies or perverse inclinations, are titillating and satisfying, Foucault is simply asking more of friendship. Operating in a different discursive mode from the *scientia sexualis* and by extension the biopolitical state, Foucault's tone in this letter suggests that friendship can offer a respite from our confessional lives, from identities founded on sexuality.

But respite is only half the picture: Friendship must play a part in enriching that "relational fabric" or it is worthless. While Foucault's anticonfessional tone might seem merely a reactive snub to more conventional forms of friendly confessional exchange, it is at the same time, active, creative, and productive of new discursive pleasures. Foucault shares with Guibert the philosophical-sexual pleasure he derives from inventing a beautiful stranger's dreams. Not unlike Roland Barthes' perverse relation to texts,[7] Foucault's pleasure emerges in the atypically perverse recounting of a typically perverse situation. That is to say, it is not so much, or not only, the sexual act of looking that produces pleasure here, but the discursive invention of the interior life of the watched boy. The act of sharing with a friend the projected thoughts and feelings of a stranger multiplies and communizes such pleasure. In the spirit of Diogenes, the Cynic philosopher who publicly masturbated so as to call into question the distinction between public and private spheres and to snub ancient Greek codes of decency, Foucault exposes himself. A private, onanistic ritual is transformed into a public, rather banal pleasure. In the process, Foucault becomes somebody else: He is neither the distinguished professor at the *Collège de France* nor the activist on the frontlines, but a melancholy poet of the sexual imaginary. In reclaiming the reified category of voyeurism from the clutches of psychoanalytic discourse—divesting it of its pathology and using it as a springboard for new discursive pleasures—Foucault, with the help of a friend, transforms himself. His mention of the "gracious chrysalis" out of which "new words and drawings . . . [are] born, take shape, and lose shape" becomes a metaphor for Foucaultian friendship. An anticonfessional discourse of friendship entails a mutual striving toward new selves, a death of sorts for the confessional friend whose truth is linked to sex, and a metamorphosis from confession to *parrhesia*.

Parrhesia

> We also find the obligation to be frank with one's friends and
> to say everything one has on one's mind. However, all these
> elements seem to me to be profoundly different from what we
> should call "confession" in the strict, or anyway, spiritual sense
> of the word. . . . To confess is to appeal to the indulgence of
> the gods or judges. (*Hermeneutics* 365)

In his final lectures and writings, Foucault takes great care to distinguish
Ancient philosophical principles and procedures from Christian ones. A
less rigorous intellectual historian might trace an unwavering, continuous
line between Greco-Roman and Christian practices of the self—ascetics
becomes monasticism, care of the self becomes self-renunciation,
parrhesia becomes confession, and so on—but Foucault calls attention
to the historical singularity of Hellenistic/Roman thought. For example,
in contrast to confession, "the verbal act by which the subject, in an
affirmation about what he is, binds himself to this truth, places himself in
a relation of dependence with regard to the other person and at the same
time modifies the relationship he has with himself" (370), *parrhesia*, also
a speech act, requires neither an affirmation of self-truth nor a relation of
dependence. By definition the act of telling all, speaking openly, speaking
frankly, *parrhesia* produces, somewhat counterintuitively, a subject of
silence. Although Christian doctrine requires the "putting into discourse"
of sins and self-truths, a student of Hellenist philosophy could, in fact
should, keep one's mouth shut en route to being "saved." The student strives
throughout his life to become a subject of veridiction in order to achieve
an immanent salvation in old age. The elder *parrhesiastes* speaks the truth
because he learned it from listening quietly to others; he embodies the
truth only after the achievement of an adequate self-relation. Although the
social practice of *parrhesia* has taken various forms—conducted among
friends (Epicureans), in public crowds (Cynics), and one-on-one, between
master and student (Stoics)—its goal remains consistent: to aid the listener
and speaker alike in developing "an autonomous, independent, full and
satisfying relationship to himself" (379). The *parrhesiastes* simultaneously
guides himself and another: Advice to a friend, for example, serves the
dual purpose of reminding the speaker of his own quest for self-mastery.

In his comparative analysis of the Christian and Hellenist/Roman
eras, Foucault notes a turning point in the history of Western subjectivity:
Speaking about one's truth (confession) displaces the practice of becoming
a subject of truth (subjectivation). In this displacement self-knowledge

is detached from and privileged over practices of the self and self-transformation. Philosophy is ultimately severed from spirituality and immanent salvation in old age gives way to transcendent salvation in an afterlife. For Foucault, *parrhesia* and the confession not only denote different discursive practices, they produce antipodal subjects operating under different modalities of knowledge and different relations to truth.

Foucault thus excavates the *parrhesiatic* subject to bring to light the uncanny Other of Western subjectivity. In *The Hermeneutics of the Subject* he argues that the Hellenist model of care of the self is overshadowed by "the two other great models" of Platonism and Christianity (254). In the Platonic model, self-care begins when the subject awakens to his own ignorance: once we realize that we know nothing of ourselves, we set about the task of understanding it. Self-care and self-knowledge thus collapse in this model (in getting to know the self we are taking care of the self), and the point at which these practices meet is recollection. "The soul discovers what it is by recalling what it has seen" (255), which is to say, the soul "re-members" its divine essence, and understands its place as a particularity in a rational totality. In the Christian monastic tradition, by contrast, self-knowledge is linked to comprehending the Word of God: One must know one's soul and purify it in preparation for divine revelation. This purification involves self-exegesis. Deciphering the soul's secret illusions and representations and subsequently confessing its sinful truth are necessary to achieve the ultimate goal—self-renunciation. Both of these forms of self-care—recollective and exegetical—should seem quite familiar today: They find their modern, secular analogs in essentialized, "New-Age" understandings of identity, in pop psychological quests for the "whole," true self, and even, unfortunately, in the confessional obligations of sexual liberation movements. The linking of sex and truth in modern biopolitics is in part a result of this triumphant duo: In insisting on the objectification of the self in true discourse, these models pave the way for the deployment of sexuality and the quagmire of identity politics. Both emphasize self-knowledge over self-transformation and force the latter to occur only as a flight into transcendence.

The Hellenistic model, by contrast, privileges self-transformation over self-knowledge/decipherment. It takes as its objective neither self-exegesis/renunciation nor the recovery of a lost, whole identity, but rather the self-to-self relation. In this tradition the self is purely relational: it emerges between and through subjection (sociohistorical determinants, moral codes, norms, etc. that produce a self) and subjectivation (various exercises and practices designed to modulate forces of subjection to produce an autonomous self, a subject of truth). Self-knowledge is of value only when it can produce an *ethos*, a change in the subject's being.

Foucault designates the self's relation to truth in this model as *ethopoetic*: true speech that immediately translates into sound action (237). Knowledge is measured only in its practicality, in its ability to move the body, to make decisions, or, to respond to various challenges. Self-knowledge should advance the subject toward a more autonomous relation to the self; it is truthful to the extent to which it becomes ethical action. If both the Platonic and Christian models of subjectivity require a moment of transcendence—a recollection of divine totality, a preparation for an afterlife—Foucault discovers in the Hellenists an immanentist conception of subjectivity. He writes:

> I have therefore tried to explore the possibilities of a genealogy of the subject while knowing that historians prefer the history of objects and philosophers prefer the subject who has no history. This does not stop me from feeling an empirical kinship with those who are called historians of "mentalities" and a theoretical debt towards a philosopher like Nietzsche who raised the question of the subject's historicity. It was a matter then for me of getting free from the ambiguities of a humanism that was so easy in theory and so fearsome in reality; it was also a matter of replacing the principle of the transcendence of the ego with research into the subject's form of immanence. . . . The self with which one has the relationship is nothing other than the relationship itself . . . [I]t is, in short, the immanence, or better, the ontological adequacy of the self to the relationship. (533)

Foucault finds an antidote to transcendent conceptions of subjectivity, including psychoanalytic conceptions, in immanent practices of self-care. The immobilizing effects of subjection and normalization explored in *Discipline and Punish* find a self-transformative counterpart in Foucault's late concept of subjectivation. Frederic Gros, commentator on Foucault's lectures in *Hermeneutics*, explains the course of action: "It is the fold of processes of subjectivation over procedures of subjection, according to more or less overlapping linings subject to history" (526). The self thus exists *only as* a relation between subjection and subjectivation: identities are formed in the immanence of history and through history they can be de- and re-formed.

Understanding the self-to-self relation in this manner is crucial to understanding Foucault's concepts of relationality across the board. For example, his theorization of power in *History of Sexuality, Volume One* as force relations in which resistance is immanent to domination conceptually mirrors his theorization of male friendship in "Friendship as a Way of Life"—that is, as a relation in which immanent affective intensities forever threaten normative homosociality. More pertinent to this discussion, Foucault's embrace of immanentist conceptions of subjectivity runs parallel to his exploration of Ancient practices of friendship. Significantly, the embrace is arguably *the result* of the exploration: Foucault's immanentist turn is coincident with, if not the consequence of, his study of friendship. If the self is only a relation between subjection and subjectivation, then the true friend, the *parrhesiastes*, pushes the subject beyond historical determinants in encouraging "processes of subjectivation over procedures of subjection." The friend is thus the *sine qua non* of self-transformation and immanent salvation. An adequate assessment of Foucault's concept of subjectivity therefore requires a detailed analysis of the ontological implications of his late work on friendship. I explore this in detail in Chapter 3.

For now, it is important to note that the Hellenist concern with the self is not simply a game of philosophical navel-gazing; rather, it forces the subject to understand both himself and the world in a relational manner. Foucault learns from Seneca's *Natural Questions*, for example, that in Hellenist ascetics knowledge of the self and of nature are absolutely linked. That is, we can only come to an adequate relation with the self after realizing our place in the human community and our inconsequentiality in the face of the geological laws of time. The study of nature involves getting free of oneself, it "reveals to us that we are no more than a point whose interiority is clearly not a problem" (278). Here, again, we are very far from a form of knowledge in which the monitoring and the objectifying of an interiority takes precedence. Although the Hellenistic emphasis on self-transformation might seem from a modern vantage point solipsistic or individualistic at best, when placed next to its Christian confessional counterpart, its "selfishness" pales in comparison. Moreover, Foucault emphasizes the importance of the self-to-self relation in the political arena:

> [I]f we take the question of power, of political power, situating it in the more general question of governmentality understood as the strategic field of power relations in the broadest and not merely political sense of the term, if we understand by governmentality a strategic field of power relations in their mobility, transformability, and reversibility, then I do not think that reflection on this notion of governmentality can avoid passing through, theoretically and practically, the element of a subject defined by the relationship of self to self. Although the theory of political power as an institution usually refers to

a juridical conception of the subject of right, it seems to me that the analysis of governmentality—that is to say, of power as a set of reversible relationships—must refer to an ethics of the subject defined by a relationship of self to self. (252)

In addition to laying bare his reasons for shifting focus to a genealogy of subjectivity and truth, Foucault in this quotation reveals the fundamental link between the self-to-self relation and politics. The distinction between the *parrhesiatic* self and the confessional self, then, is not only important to the history of philosophy but to the history of politics, for *parrhesia* offers an alternative model of subjectivity and relationality. If the confession engenders dependence on another and requires the objectification of the self to speak its truth, *parrhesia* operates along more immanentist lines: The self is not objectified but subjectivated, the self becomes the subject of true discourse and is transformed in the truth's enunciation. Whereas what we might call a "confessional friendship" requires friends to act as supplicant and judge, fostering a guilty interdependence, a *parrhesiatic* friendship is an experiment in truth-telling that provokes a productive tension. Foucault writes: "When, for example, you see a friend doing something wrong and you risk incurring his anger by telling him he is wrong, you are acting as a *parrhesiastes*. In such a case, you do not risk your life, but you may hurt him by your remarks, and your friendship may consequently suffer for it" (*Fearless Speech* 16). Danger is thus involved in a *parrhesiatic* friendship: encouraging the friend to become self-sufficient through criticism runs the risk of losing him.

Although it might seem a stretch to deem Foucault's letter *parrhesiatic* (there is neither blatant critical evaluation of Guibert's behaviors nor sagely instructions about how he might become a subject of veridiction), it is nonetheless infused with a *parrhesiatic* sensibility. To begin, Foucault holds his friend at a critical distance: the lack of personableness and the somewhat cutting parting gesture alone indicate as much. *Fearless Speech*, Foucault's 1983 lecture at University of California, Berkeley, gives some clues as to what this distance might mean. Foucault points out that the two great adversaries of *parrhesia* are flattery and rhetoric. Flattering friends does them an injustice in abetting a deceptive relationship of self-to-self; the flattered can never be alone with themselves, can never possess a full, adequate self-relation as they are forever dependent on another's praise to think well of themselves. Rhetoric, the second enemy, is the art of persuasion—not necessarily truth. The exercise of *parrhesia* must be dictated by generosity toward the other, not manipulation or opportunism. To encourage a friend to develop self-sovereignty in a form he finds most suitable is neither to impose one's will nor to influence that development through eloquent, convincing instructions. Keeping Guibert at an arm's length, then, Foucault performs the role of a *parrhesiastes*: His tone avoids flattery and rhetoric in favor of a frankness with a subtly instructive edge. Working outside the parameters of confessional discourse, Foucault seeks not the causes of his voyeuristic desires, nor does he bore or burden his friend with a remorseful examination of conscience. Rather he presents his "self-truth" in the form of a forthright description about a quotidian ritual.

And yet the dismissive gesture at the end of the letter ("This morning window is closed, instead I am writing to you.") is still puzzling. What is Guibert to make of this? Does Foucault's self-absorption signal a disinterest in his friend's well-being? What type of self-absorption is this? Akin to entries from Seneca's "On Tranquility of Mind," a text in which the philosopher-teacher chronicles his daily actions for the benefit of both himself and his student friend, Foucault's "self-absorption" again enacts a *parrhesiatic* game. In this case, Guibert's role is that of the listener: neither flattered with small talk, nor persuaded to change his ways, nor goaded to speak his truth, he is summoned only to sit back and silently take in his "master's" discourse. If the goal of *parrhesia* is to aid the friend in developing an autonomous relationship to the self, the distance Foucault puts between him and his friend in this letter could be an attempt to encourage such self-sufficiency. Guibert's description of the letter as "un vrai text" now becomes more interesting. A colloquial translation of the phrase as "a real text" seems appropriate; philosophically, however, "a *true* text" might be more accurate. As an intimate, Guibert was well aware of Foucault's intellectual pursuits and took great interest in his work.[8] In calling this letter a "true text" is he acknowledging Foucault's investment in *parrhesia*? Is this text an indication of the way these friends resuscitated *parrhesiatic* practices? With a closer look at Foucault's interest in ancient ascetics, the letter becomes ever more different—and the terms of Foucaultian friendship come into clearer focus.

Ascetics

You make your examination of conscience to a friend, to someone dear to one and with whom you have intense affective relations. You take him as your spiritual director, and it is quite normal to take him as a guide regardless of his qualification as a philosopher . . . simply because he is a friend. (*Hermeneutics* 163)

Although in this quote Foucault is describing Seneca's and Marcus Aurelius' respective practices of sharing self-evaluations with friends, in a different context he might be revealing his reasons for writing Guibert his "true text." If I suggested earlier that in the letter Foucault plays the truth-telling master to Guibert's silent listener, it becomes clear in Foucault's analysis of ancient ascetics that the roles are reversible: sage becomes student and vice versa. In this regard, Guibert becomes Foucault's ethical sounding board. Through sharing a self-analysis of his daily routine, Foucault might be asking, "Is my voyeurism ethical? Is my pleasure exploitative? Are my actions in harmony with my truth?" Such questions hover over the lines. They imply not only the importance of the friend in the care of the self, but also the necessity of maintaining a strong link between self-knowledge and self-transformation.

In *Hermeneutics*, Foucault asks why the notion of "know thyself" (*gnothi seautou*) holds such a privileged place in histories of Western philosophy. He argues that this supposedly fundamental principle is merely part of a larger system of thought best designated "care of the self" (*epimeleia heautou*). This attribute—caring for oneself, finding one's pleasure in oneself, being the friend of oneself—was the actual basis of morality in Antiquity, self-knowledge just one tenet of it. So why has caring for oneself been overshadowed by the imperative to know thyself? Foucault offers a few hypotheses. First, as a foundation for morality the care of the self disturbs us "moderns": It signifies either an egoistic "moral dandyism" or a "somewhat melancholy and sad expression of the withdrawal of the individual who is unable to hold on to . . . a collective morality . . . and who, faced with the disintegration of this collective morality, has naught else to do but attend to himself" (13). In both *The Use of Pleasure* and *The Care of the Self* Foucault challenges these assumptions, arguing that the care of the self in Antiquity comprised a set of practices that crystallize social relations. As a way of life, the care of the self was not an egoistic or resigned retreat into individualism. The self-transformation sought was not a narcissistic endeavor conducted in solitude, but a social practice occupying a whole set of daily activities undertaken in philosophical communities, aristocratic households, and friendships. Intensifying social relations as opposed to alienating citizen from citizen, these practices of the self were hardly the Socratic search for the essence of being (or, for that matter, a pop-psychological "self-realization"). The free men privileged enough to practice such an art constructed and created a self as they advanced together through exercises of self-discipline. These aestheticians of existence understood the self not as the core of the individual, not as something essential to be discovered, but, rather, as something to be cultivated: an always-becoming self with which one could and must experiment (*HoS, V3* 42–55).

Second, the principle of *epimeleia heautou* mutated into the austere rules of self-care found in Christian monastic practices, "taking the form either of self-renunciation or of a 'modern' obligation towards others— whether this be other people, the collectivity, the class, or the fatherland" (*Hermeneutics* 13). Aligning Christianity, Marxism, and Fascism, discovering at their roots the same will to renounce the self in order to become identical or unified, Foucault implies in this sweeping gesture that a very different and untapped will to historical transformation—to revolution—lies buried beneath the historical weight of Christianity. He marks a clear distinction between Ancient ascetics and Christian asceticism, as the latter term has "quite specific connotations and refers to an attitude of renunciation, mortification, etcetera" (416). Ascetics, by contrast, involves a set of given exercises used by individuals to achieve "a definite spiritual objective, . . . a certain transformation of themselves as subjects, as subjects of action and as subjects of true knowledge" (416). The goal of these exercises lies in linking self-knowledge with self-transformation: ascetics relies on philosophy and spirituality to work together to create a new, more beautiful self in which actions and words harmonize.

Finally, in answering the question "Why 'know thyself' over 'care of the self?,' " Foucault points a finger at Descartes. In placing self-evidence at the foundation of philosophical inquiry, Descartes privileges self-knowledge over self-care. The "Cartesian moment," as Foucault tentatively calls it, requalifies the *gnothi seautou* by discrediting the *epimeleia heautou*: Self-knowledge alone determines the conditions for access to truth. Consequently, the various ascetic exercises that at one time prepared the subject for such access are disregarded. In Foucault's reading, the Cartesian subject ultimately signals an unfortunate shift in the genealogy of subjectivity and truth: After Descartes, the link between philosophy and spirituality is severed. But how does this change the subject's relation to truth? to himself? Foucault writes:

> We will call, if you like, "philosophy" the form of thought that asks, not of course what is true and what is false, what determines that there is and can be truth and falsehood and whether or not we can separate the truth and the false. We will call "philosophy" the form of thought that asks what it is that enables the subject to have access to the truth and which attempts to determine the conditions and limits of the

subject's access to the truth. If we call this "philosophy," then
I think we could call "spirituality" the search, practice and
experience through which the subject carries out the necessary
transformation on himself in order to have access to the truth.
We will call "spirituality" then the set of these researches,
practices, and experiences, which may be purifications, ascetic
exercises, renunciations, conversions of looking, modifications
of existence, etc., which are, not for knowledge but for the
subject, for the subject's very being, the price to be paid for
access to the truth. (15)

Modern philosophy begins when the subject is essentially,
ontologically, capable of truth—and yet this truth can no longer save
the subject. The various spiritual exercises of subjectivation that once
promised a transfiguration of being in old age are replaced by an
infinite accumulation of forms of knowledge that do not guarantee self-
transformation or enlightenment. "If we define spirituality as being the
form of practices which postulate that, such as he is, the subject is not
capable of the truth, but that, such as it is, the truth can transfigure and
save the subject, then we can say that the modern age of the relations
between the subject and truth begin when it is postulated that, such
as he is, the subject is capable of truth, but that, such as it is, the truth
cannot save the subject" (19). According to Foucault, Aristotle is the
true founding father of modern philosophy: For him, the question of
spirituality was least important. His thought paves the way for Aquinas
(who referred to Aristotle simply and tellingly as "the philosopher")
and a theological tradition that posits a knowing subject that must seek
fulfillment in an omniscient God. For when philosophy and spirituality
are severed, salvation comes only from above.
     But Aristotle is the exception to—not the exemplar of—ancient
philosophy. Leaving "the philosopher" aside, Foucault unearths a moral
universe in which the question of "how to have access to truth" *is
inseparable from* self-transformation. His meticulous analyses of ancient
ascetics can ultimately be understood as an attempt to resuture self-
knowledge and self-exercises, philosophy and spirituality, ontology and
ethics—perhaps especially for modern sexual liberation movements.
Descartes' "simplified" theory of the subject, taking into account only
half the concern of Hellenist theorizations, finds its logical conclusion in
the subject of sexuality. "I think therefore I am" and "I am what I desire"
operate on similar ontological grounds: Access to truth is guaranteed in
knowing thyself, not necessarily in the process of transforming that self.
With the subject ontologically capable of truth, with self-care optional,

ethics is an afterthought: The subject of right action emerges subsequent to the subject of truth.

The question of access and action however are coextensive and inseparable for Foucault's Ancients—becoming a subject capable of truth hinges upon an ethical conversion to truth. Foucault's insistence in his late interviews that gay liberation movements find an ethics based not in a scientific objectification of the self, but rather a self-stylization—that is to say, an aesthetics of self-transformation—makes more sense in this respect. The delinking of sexuality and truth involves the relinking of self-knowledge and self-transformation. In "An Interview with Stephen Riggins," he offers himself as an example of the knowledge/transformation/ethics conjunction:

> I am not interested in the academic status of what I am doing because my problem is my own transformation. . . . This transformation of one's self by one's own knowledge is, I think, something rather close to the aesthetic experience. Why should a painter work if he is not transformed by his own painting? (*Essential, V1: Ethics* 131)

And, later, when asked if there is an ethics of sex implicit in *History of Sexuality, Volume One*:

> If you mean by ethics a code that would tell us how to act, then of course *The History of Sexuality* is not an ethics. But if by ethics you mean the relationship you have to yourself when you act, then I would say that it intends to be an ethics, or at least to show what could be an ethics of sexual behavior. It would be one that would not be dominated by the problem of the deep truth of the reality of our sex life. The relationship that I think we need to have with ourselves when we have sex is an ethics of pleasure, of intensification of pleasure. (131)

Although I examine in detail this "ethics of pleasure" in Chapter 2, for now its mention helps elucidate the opening proclamation of Foucault's letter: "I have been meaning to tell you about the pleasure I take. . . ." To readers of Foucault, privileging pleasure—over, specifically, desire—is nothing new, and yet in this letter we see that an ethics of pleasure emerges through ascetics. Writing like a Seneca or a Marcus Aurelius, Foucault shares with a friend the process and progress of his quest toward an adequate relation with the self. Read in the context of his other writings on friendship, the letter signifies the importance of friendship for re-connecting self-knowledge with self-transformation, philosophy with spirituality. In this sense, friendship becomes not merely a relation but a *practice*: part of a regimen of self-care through which one can attain an immanent salvation. The stakes of friendship for Foucault are thus quite high: Can this practice, working in conjunction with other spiritual exercises, replace the need for a flight into transcendence? If so, an ethics of friendship—the ways friendship will be practiced and lived—are paramount. Looking closer now at the content of the letter, I tease out some of the ethical terms of Foucault's concept of friendship.

Impersonality

To reiterate, the letter begins not with a conventional "Cher Hervé" but with a declaration of pleasure—aesthetic, philosophical, perhaps sexual pleasure. In analyzing its tone, I have argued that the text is neither an attempt to shock nor a masochistic plea for admonishment: It is, rather, an experiment in anticonfessional, *parrhesiatic* discourse; an ascetic exercise shared with a friend. But what type of sharing is this, and with whom? It seems the letter could have been written to anybody: Guibert remains unnamed, aspects of his personhood, his life, are never mentioned. It is almost unclear who Foucault's real friend is here: Is it the invisible Guibert or the intensely observed man across the way? This somnolent figure is presented as a collection of body parts—an elbow here, a shoulder there—a cinematic montage of close-ups and jump-cuts. In classic pornographic fashion, Foucault's gaze objectifies and fragments a body rather than humanizing or personalizing an individual. And yet in his anonymity, in his object-ness, the man seems to become, at least in this letter, a closer friend than Guibert. His very "facelessness" attracts Foucault: "My shortsightedness protects me from knowing what his face looks like: he is thus beautiful." Shielded from his identity, Foucault is allowed to enter into the man's life with an intensity that an actual meeting might never engender. His nonidentity motivates Foucault to invent this stranger, and, in the process, another strange self. Anonymity and nonidentity thus offer the opportunity for desubjection and subjectivation—in other words, the undoing of socially, historically determined selves and the creation of new ones. Foucault writes the following about anonymity in sexual encounters:

> I think it is politically important that sexuality be able to function the way it functions in saunas, where, without [having to submit to] the condition of being imprisoned in one's own identity, in one's own past, in one's own face, one can meet

people who are to you what one is to them: nothing else but bodies with which combinations, fabrications of pleasure will be possible. These places afford an exceptional possibility of desubjectivization, of desubjection, perhaps not the most radical but in any case sufficiently intense to be worth taking note of. [Anonymity is important] because of the intensity of the pleasure that follows from it. It's not the affirmation of identity that's important, it's the affirmation of non-identity. . . . It's an important experience in which one invents, for as long as one wants, pleasures which one fabricates together [with others].[9]

It is necessary to highlight here the emphasis Foucault places on the *political* importance of desubjection and subjectivation. Echoing the previously quoted passage in which Foucault asserts the primacy of the self-to-self relation for politics, Foucault offers here a concrete relational strategy for the cultivation of the self—a strategy that might in turn lead to the formation of non-normative, anti-identititarian communities. Anonymous sex—in the case of our letter, anonymous voyeurism—allows subjects to free themselves from the shackles of identity and relate to one another in ways that run counter to the modern demand for self-knowledge. The bonds emerging from such encounters might be best designated impersonal friendships: relationships that urge the mutual cultivation of other pleasures, other selves. Guibert's invisibility and the watched man's facelessness in this letter become emblematic of a larger political project fostering anti-intersubjective forms of relationality and resistance through anonymity, impersonality, and creative cooperation.[10]

Impersonality likewise plays an important role in Foucault's understanding of the self-to-self relation. The self to whom one becomes a friend in ancient ascetics, for example, is a thoroughly impersonal essence. It is neither an authentic self that must be discovered nor the locus of individualized uniqueness, but an unknown self with which one maintains a rapport of distance and respect while in the process of molding it. David Halperin best summarizes the conception of self in ancient ascetics as follows:

[T]he "self" which is to be cultivated by means of an "art of life" (whether in the ancient world or in the modern) is not a personal *identity* so much as it is a *relation of reflexivity*. Hence, to cultivate oneself—and the "self" referred to here, both in ancient texts and Foucault's French text, is nothing but the bare reflexive pronoun—is not to explore or experience some given self, conceived as a determinate, private realm, a

space of personal interiority, but instead to use one's relation
to oneself as a potential resource with which to construct new
modalities of subjective agency and new styles of personal life
that may enable one to resist or even to escape one's social
and psychological determinations. (*Saint Foucault* 76–77)

Like a sculptor who takes a step back from his work to remind himself
of the formal rules of his art, contemplating the material's shape and
style in relation to such rules, the relationship with the self could be one
of detached and disciplined concern—not seeking its secret truth, but
bringing it into existence according to aesthetic and ethical guidelines.[11]
Halperin also characterizes Foucault's self as a site of "radical alterity,"
a "not-self," the cultivation of which requires "*se déprendre de soi-même*,
to fall out of love with oneself, to get free of oneself, and to reconstitute
oneself in a calculated encounter with otherness" (77). In this rendering
of subjectivity, one does not relate intersubjectively to the stranger within:
The self is ontologically multiple, different from itself, radically variegated.

Cultivating an impersonal self requires impersonal encounters
with other selves—both within and without. Foucault's writings on
sadomasochism (S&M) and monosexual cultures, however justly
criticized for their idealism,[12] here become relevant. In his estimation, the
de-genitalization of pleasure in S&M scenarios—shifting attention from
the genitals and the teleological goal of orgasm to the anus, the nipples,
the entire body as a playground of pleasure—enacts a desexualization,
a decentering of the self. In other words, fist-fucking and master–slave
performances, to use two of Foucault's favorite examples, pressure the
link between sexuality and identity, desire and truth. Comparing S&M sex
games to chess, in which players are inserted into roles for which there is
a set of rules yet nonetheless a certain freedom of play,[13] Foucault sees the
relations developing in and out of such games as processes of invention
that might extend beyond the walls of the dungeon or the backroom. These
inventive relationships develop in part as a result of the impersonal, if not
anonymous, nature of the event. Roles and types allow players to "get free
of the self," to shed socially determined identities, so as to experiment
with others and other selves. Such play could open onto understandings
of the self as infinitely variegated; such relational encounters might
encourage an anti-intersubjective receptivity to difference. In this respect,
gay male "clone" cultures are likewise of interest to Foucault as sites of
depersonalization and invention. He notes: "[T]he relations between these
men are filled with tenderness, with communitarian practices of life and
sexuality. Beneath the sign and under the shelter of masculine theatrical
displays, the sexual relations that take place reveal themselves to be of a

masochist sort.”[14] Wearing the mask of masculinity, performing Marlboro Man or Bad Lieutenant, clones potentially, perhaps counterintuitively, defect from identity by becoming variations, or, calculatedly imperfect replications, of the same fantasized ideal. In so doing, they prompt a rethinking of sameness: not as a fascist assimilation of difference into identity, but as an internally differentiated ontological oneness.[15] Read in the context of his other work on impersonality, then, Foucault's letter to Guibert hints at the type of communal forms that can emerge from depersonalization: an ethics of impersonality in friendship encourages an anti-identitarian politics.

Estrangement

In sharing voyeuristic reflections with his anonymous friend, at least two Foucaults emerge: a writer taking pleasure in the world outside and a seemingly lonely man removed from actual human contact. Concerning the latter, Foucault's ostensible obsession with sleep and fatigue in his descriptions of the watched man beg a closer look. The man across the way appears almost somnambulant, even zombified:

> [O]ne can see that he is draping himself again in the night; and if he comes to the edge of his balcony it is not to cast light on the last shadows where he is caught, it is to show to everyone, to no one (since it is only me who is watching him) that there is no day that can overthrow the gentle obstinacy that remains with him and sovereignly masters him. He shows to the face of daytime the tender power of sleep.

Sleep is ever present, all powerful, and yet gentle enough in its reign that the man chooses to "drape" himself in it, to accept it. It is hard to resist connecting these myriad references to sleep, counterposed to daylight, mobility, and consciousness, with the "big sleep," that is, death. This character is poised on the cusp of consciousness and unconsciousness, between dreaming and waking. Although described as a young man (*garçon*), his arthritic movements and gestures betray old age; is he perhaps ill, forced to give himself over to death at a young age? If so, what do we make of the moment when he "straightens up, he sits down at a table where he might read? Write? Type?" Does sleep/death's presence, or, perhaps walking the tightrope between life and death, prompt such activity? Indeed, why does Foucault repeatedly note that the boy is caught between two states (e.g., "it is not that he is resting or trying to wake up.")? As in Guibert's "*L'ami*," the moment of the "in-between" is apparently quite important here. In focusing on it, Foucault subtly invokes and dramatizes Nietzsche's conception of the movement from negation to production: *pars destruens, pars construens*.[16] For Nietzsche, the in-between is the zero hour between acts of absolute destruction and unfettered creation. Deleuze and Guattari likewise describe such a moment in their introduction to *What is Philosophy?* It is only in this instant that they are able to ask their sobering titular question, which comes to them at midnight, a suspended minute of "quiet restlessness" in the interstices of today and tomorrow.

> There are times when old age produces not eternal youth but a sovereign freedom, a pure necessity in which one enjoys a moment of grace between life and death, and in which all the parts of the machine come together to send into the future a feature that cuts across all ages: Titian, Turner, Monet. (Deleuze and Guattari, *What is Philosophy?* 1–2)

The in-between is filled paradoxically with anxiety and peace, urgency and calm, between two states of mind and two activities. It prompts Foucault's boy to begin whatever creative task, it perhaps inspires Foucault himself to bring this character into existence. Confronted by "the tender power of sleep," both Foucault and his boy "read, write, type," as if their lives depend on it.

So what exactly happens in the in-between? In Deleuze and Guattari's account, events occur. Such events are irreducible to any one or one hundred causes, they belie a logic of plotting cause and effect altogether. Events are the result of a radical break from their constituent conditions, and share a conceptual kinship with Nietzsche's theory of the untimely and his practice of active forgetting.[17] Although a confluence of forces and relations, the event is always more than the sum of its parts: The event of love, for example, is never reducible to one or the other lover but exists rather as a third term emanating from the encounter. Thus, the "feature that cuts across all time" emerging in the "moment of grace" is pure becoming: what Walter Benjamin saw in the angel of history, what Deleuze and Guattari understand as the virtual shooting through actual diachronic time, what Foucault calls power in its productivity, and what we see in the creation of the concept of shared estrangement.

I argue in Chapter 4 that AIDS ushers in this "moment of grace" with a vengeance. In so doing it engenders new forms of subjectivity, new forms of friendship, a new politics. Foucault's characterization of a man at the brink of life and death offers a sneak preview of what is to come:

As a radically destructive yet absolutely immanent force, AIDS forces an acknowledgment of life's precariousness and of death's immanence to life. Facing such destruction produces suffering, despair, alienation, and estrangement from others and the world. And yet in embracing this estrangement, in abandoning oneself to finitude and making necessary those contingent, historically determined aspects of existence, new relational, ethical, and political possibilities emerge. In actively willing the past, in embracing the brute force of absolute negation, a path is cleared for pure creation, for an absolute affirmation of life. I understand the inventive politics of ACT UP to have emerged from such a movement—from destruction to creation, from death to life.

Having broached the subject of AIDS, we must now focus greater attention on Foucault's cherished boy. Might he be a stand-in for Foucault himself in the throes of AIDS? If so, given the biographical accounts of the philosopher's last days, suffering from a hacking cough and debilitating headaches yet determined to complete his works in progress, it is no surprise that Foucault writes this exhausted character as suddenly eager to read, write, or type.[18] Enveloped in death, he does so out of pure necessity. One must question at this point if the *garçon* ever existed, whether he is an actual historical figure. Although the letter reads like an observational, day-in-the-life piece, its protagonist may be a mere product of the author's imagination. In this respect, the spectral character could be understood as Foucault's "invented self," a figure through which the author speaks of his own state of being. Eleven months from death, his body betraying him, Foucault is creating this character in his own moment of the "in-between," taking a snapshot of his *modus vivendi* with one foot on death's doorstep. In this sense, the friend across the way might in fact be the unknowable stranger within—finitude. By welcoming finitude into his living room, Foucault contemplates death's immanence to life and arguably cultivates a relationship with death adversative to biopolitical dictates.[19] Even more, our *garçon* may be prompting Foucault to chronicle the moment of immanent salvation so important to his Ancients; such an achievement requires being at peace with finitude, befriending it. Historical figure, finitude, and/or immanent salvation: the man on the balcony is many men, many things. He is Foucault's double, the two tangled up in blue, the color of the boy's towel and underwear resonating with the author's stationery (a mutual depression, a mutual funk). He is a screen onto which Foucault projects his own thoughts, feelings, physicality—his despair, his fatigue, his powerful dreams, his inability to escape the dark shadows of sleep/death. The man's nonappearance on this day, then, signals both the boy's and the author's final absence. Reflecting on his own death, Foucault offers Guibert this letter—this gift, as Guibert describes it. The

cutting final line now once again reads differently: Is Foucault writing to
Guibert in order to be left alone with his own mortality? Is the parting
gesture an attempt to push Guibert away once and for all? To abandon
himself to finitude?

The dreams Foucault's character finds in the fold of his arms are
a result of death's presence: He sleeps to dream, he allows death in,
cohabits with it, so that new "words or drawings" might be born. Once
again, Foucault's metaphor of the chrysalis is significant. A rebirth, a new
life in a completely different form, requires a certain type of death, or,
at the very least allowing a certain part of oneself to die. The chrysalis
not only appears in word in the penultimate sentence of the letter, but
arguably in form, in another sentence's grammatical structure. At the
bleakest point in the writing the descriptive flow is interrupted: "he then
takes up his initial position, tucking his face back in his elbow to look
there for strong, intense, and powerful dreams, which leave him in a great
(darn, [I need] more blue paper) depression." The parentheses inserted
between "great depression" bespeak an immediacy: a frustrated author
in need of the very material required to continue his work. A form itself
almost cocoon-like, "( )," the contents of these parentheses communicate
an urgent desire for further production. As such they are a chrysalis in
their own right, a vehicle through which despair becomes creativity. The
depressive blue that saturates the earlier descriptions, uniting Foucault
and the man in despair, now takes on a different hue. Not unlike the
use of the color as a polyvalent metaphor in Derek Jarman's 1993 film
Blue or the aquamarine monochromes of painter Yves Klein, blue here
is simultaneously deadening and creative, constricting and rife with
potential.[20] The metamorphic quality of blue in this letter reflects the
metamorphic processes of the AIDS body. Dying little deaths each day,
experiencing depression, loss, estrangement opens onto new forms of
becoming—not simply "the blues," but the boundlessness of the sky,
the ocean, in Jarman's words, "infinite possibility" (*Blue*). Flanked and
surrounded by a great depression, the chrysalis/parentheses in which this
new blue appears signify a refusal to let death's forbiddance dampen a
passion for invention, for a "new self" both across the way and at home.
In his will to persist, to continue to produce, Foucault's Nietzschean roots
are again manifest. In "The Thought of Death," an aphorism from *The Gay
Science*, Nietzsche marvels at people's simultaneous incognizance of and
perseverance to live within death's ubiquity:

> How strange it is that this sole certainty and common element
> makes almost no impression on people, and that nothing is
> further from their minds than the feeling that they form a

brotherhood of death. It makes me happy that men do not want at all to think the thought of death! I should like very much to do something that would make the thought of life even a hundred times more appealing to them. (225)

In a time of AIDS, a time in which the death of friends is inescapable, an acceptance of death's immanence to life becomes unavoidable. Life becomes "perhaps a hundred times more appealing" when death is omnipresent and yet a clear separation between the two realms becomes a fantasy no longer sustainable. The demise of this fantasy renders friendship a relation of shared estrangement.

Chapter 2

An Ethics of Discomfort

Foucault's Friend

The problem is not to discover in oneself the truth of one's sex, but, rather, to use one's sexuality henceforth to arrive at a multiplicity of relationships. And, no doubt, that's the real reason why homosexuality is not a form of desire but something desirable. Therefore, we have to become homosexuals and not be obstinate in recognizing that we are. The development towards which the problem of homosexuality tends is the one of friendship.

—*Foucault ("Friendship as Way of Life,"*
Essential, V1: Ethics 135–36)

In his account of reverse discourse, Foucault argues that nineteenth-century homosexual emancipationists strategically inverted the subject–object positions assigned by medical discourses, and in so doing performed a significant act of political resistance within the discursive frameworks that constituted their "invention." Gay liberation, while an important and necessary stage in what Foucault calls "becoming homosexual," was never for him an end in itself. The dialectical reversal of subject–object only paves the way for future becomings—a beyond sexuality, a postliberationist politics—which may preeminently take the form of friendship as a way of life, yielding a culture, an ethics, and as yet unseen forms of relation. Although such friendships might well emerge out of same-sex sexual practices, the acts and desires that may or may not occur within those relations are not for Foucault of primary importance. His interest lies instead in the "tying together of unforeseen lines of force and the subsequent formation of new alliances" (136). In a culture that construes sexuality as a knowable and manageable truth of a subject, homosexual practices are not necessarily radical in and of themselves. The bonds that might result from these practices, however, may go some way in forging new modes of life and political forms. Foucault makes clear in "Friendship as a Way of Life" that the intergenerational, interclassed, and interracial friendships developing in gay communities are worthy of exploration.

In the interview, which appears in the queer magazine *Gai Pied*, Foucault reveals that friendship could play a part in the delinking of sexuality from truth. Although critiqued time and again for failing to delineate concrete solutions and specific sites of resistance,[1] he offers here a direct strategy for homosexuality's "development." What is it about friendship that prompted Foucault to remove his philosopher's mask and speak so frankly? For a thinker who detested polemics—"Has anyone ever seen a new idea come out of a polemic?"[2]—Foucault is quite insistent on the value of friendship for the gay community's political future. However vague his formulation of friendship, however scant the references, questions remain as to why he spoke of it at all, and, when he did, in a tone that resembled what Paul Rabinow has termed "a quasi manifesto" ("Introduction," in Foucault, *Essential, V1: Ethics* xxxviII.

Foucault's thoughts on friendship and, importantly, the tone through which these thoughts are articulated, must first of all be read as strategic. If, following David Halperin, we understand Foucault as a philosopher of strategy *par excellence* (*Saint Foucault* 30–31), his direct yet simultaneously vague statements about friendship must themselves imply a politics. And although I argue that when speaking of friendship Foucault speaks uncharacteristically, the politics that suffuse this aberrant tone are nonetheless consistent with his earlier activist interventions. Specifically, Foucault's approach to prison reform with the GIP (*le Groupe d'Information sur les Prisons*) is similar to what I understand as his approach to a queer politics of friendship. The GIP strategy involved not *giving* voice to prisoners, but letting them speak for themselves, in their own voices, about their needs and their desires. The GIP aided the prisoner's "reverse discourse" by channeling the thoughts and words of these objects-turned-subjects to the French public. The group's goal, as stated in one of its early pamphlets, was to "disseminate as quickly and widely as possible the revelations that the prisoners themselves make—the sole means of unifying what is inside and outside the prison, the political battle and the legal battle, into one and the same struggle."[3] In "Friendship as a Way of Life," Foucault deploys a similar strategy: He refuses to tell his gay audience what to do with friendship nor does he tell them exactly what it is or means. Instead, he encourages the audience of *Gai Pied* to take seriously something too often taken for granted—to ponder, perhaps, how to implement friendship as a tool in a local struggle.[4]

Foucault describes a queer friendship between two men as "the sum of everything that moves between one and the other, everything that gives them pleasure," as a relation "without form" that must be "invented from A to Z," and, most interestingly, as "a desire, an uneasiness, a desire-in-uneasiness, that exists in a lot of people" (216). Although designated a specific becoming of homosexuality, Foucault's vague definition of friendship in this essay makes the relation seem utterly amorphous, a relation that might be and become just about anything. In this sense, Foucault acts not as a spokesperson plotting the political future of gay rights and culture. Instead, he makes manifest some things that gay-liberationists already know well: Friendship is a vital facet of queer politics; friendship and sex are not diametrically opposed; the ties that bind this diverse community might be best designated as bonds of friendship. Foucault thus calls attention to an already extant politics of queer friendship; his gay audience surely understands the importance of friendship for queer life as they are themselves the "inventors" about whom he speaks.

And yet "Friendship as a Way of Life" hardly parrots gay folk wisdom. In the context of his earlier work, Foucault's thoughts on friendship in this essay pressure the in–out, repressed–liberated mentality of gay rights struggles. Are gays "prisoners" themselves within the truth-telling game of out-politics? Are they perhaps most enslaved to the historical construct of sexuality which in its deployment severely impoverishes the very sexual/relational life for which they struggle? Foucault offers friendship as an exodus from sexuality and the relational models that accompany it. Although a politics of friendship suffuses new social movements from civil rights to feminism, gay and lesbian communities—in part because they have been historically denied access to legal forms of relation—have a unique claim on friendship. If marital bliss was never an option, friendship in all of its messy malleability was. While proposing an alternative to marriage, Foucault resists defining the parameters of friendship so as to let others take hold of it, reflect on it, form it, work on it. That is to say, Foucault's friendship, understood as the becoming of homosexual relationality, entails the construction of a new ethics.

Which leads me back to that strategically vague formulation of friendship as a "desire-in-uneasiness." In the friendship interview, Foucault follows this formulation with an example concerning intergenerational gay male relationships:

> Between a man and a younger woman, the marriage institution makes it easier: she accepts it and makes it work. But two men of noticeably different ages—what code would allow them to communicate? They face each other without terms

> or convenient words, with nothing to assure them about the
> meaning of the movement that carries them toward each
> other. They have to invent, from A to Z, a relationship that is
> still formless, which is friendship: that is to say, the sum of
> everything through which they can give each other pleasure.
> (136)

What's most unsettling in this description is not Foucault's familiar
emphasis on invention, experimentation, and pleasure, but rather his
mention of the dearth of cultural and institutional codes through which
two men of "notably different ages" can relate. Is Foucault conveniently
overlooking the relational structures that form the very backbone of
patriarchal homosociality, namely the Oedipal father–son and mentor–
student models? Is he forgetting that intergenerational same-sex relations
in Antiquity ultimately determined a young man's usefulness for patriarchal
society? Are modern gay intergenerational friendships any different?
Indeed, is Foucault unwittingly championing very conservative, "boys'
club" patriarchal structures?

On closer inspection of the "the movement" that draws Foucault's
friends together, these questions become more complicated. Foucault's
friendship model is neither the "pure sexual encounter" nor the "lovers'
fusion of identities," referred to as "the two ready made formulas' of
homosexuality" (137). These formulas offer no threat to established
relational norms: The former "responds to a reassuring canon of beauty,
and it cancels everything out that can be troubling in affection, tenderness"
(136); the latter bolsters Romantic myths of monogamous love crucial
to the institution of marriage, which serves merely to "reproduce the
interplay of relations and maintain the law that governs them."[5] Although
institutional sites (the family, the university, the army, the office) and
likewise institutional relational models for male–male intimacy (father–
son, mentor–student) may be the conditions of possibility for Foucault's
friendship, what differentiates it from patriarchal bonding is its potential
to surpass institutional utility, to spin farther and farther away from that
which gave it birth. Foucault thus recognizes the importance of male–male
friendship for the perpetuation of patriarchal institutions, yet calls our
attention to the non-homosocial potentialities immanent to this bond:

> The institution is caught in a contradiction; affective intensities
> traverse it which at one and the same time keep it going and
> shake it up. Look at the army, where love between men is
> ceaselessly provoked [*appellé*] and shamed. Institutional codes

can't validate these relations with multiple intensities, variable colors, imperceptible movements and changing forms. These relations short-circuit it and introduce love where there's supposed to be only law, rule, or habit. (137)

Provocation and disavowal, obligatory camaraderie coupled with the threat of homophobic blackmail—such is the logic of institutionalized homosociality.[6] But what is it like, Foucault asks, to be "naked" among men, outside of traditionally masculine relational norms? "It's a desire, an uneasiness, a desire-in-uneasiness that exists in a lot of people." It is therefore this desire, this discomfort, that moves men toward each other and potentially beyond the boundaries of traditional, patriarchal friendship.

An earlier essay by Foucault titled "For an Ethic of Discomfort" sheds some light on this troubling desire-in-uneasiness. Although the essay is at face value a review of *L'Ere des Ruptures* [*The Age of Ruptures*], a book concerning the history and vicissitudes of the post-war French Left by *Le Nouvel Observateur* founder, Jean Daniel, Foucault emphasizes here the importance of an intellectual restlessness, a ceaseless discomfort with one's own presumptions. Praising Daniel's history as "a quest for those subtler, more secret, and more decisive moments when things begin to lose their self-evidence" (*Essential, V3: Power* 447), Foucault remarks on the kinship between the book's method and the philosophy of one his mentors, Merleau-Ponty:

> Impossible, as one turns these pages, not to think of Maurice Merleau-Ponty's teaching and of what was for him the essential philosophical task: never to consent to being completely comfortable with one's own presuppositions. Never to let them fall peacefully asleep, but also never to believe that a new fact will suffice to overturn them; never to imagine that one can change them like arbitrary axioms, remembering that in order to give them the necessary mobility one must have a distant view, but also look at what is nearby and all around oneself. To be very mindful that everything one perceives is evident only against a familiar and little-known horizon, that every certainty is sure only through the support of a ground that is always unexplored. The most fragile instant has its roots. In that lesson, there is a whole ethic of sleepless evidence that does not rule out, far from it, a rigorous economy of the True and the False; but that is not the whole story. (448)

The "sleepless evidence" that highlights the contingency of meaning and truth gives way to an ethic of unremitting interrogation: an incessant discomfort even with that which one takes most for granted. If this ethic of discomfort is Foucault's model for intellectual pursuits, it likewise influences his conception of friendship. When he calls our attention to its unfulfilled potential for gay male communities, we see a similar intellectual skepticism in the established truths of the relation. Although commonsensically understood as a site of mutual comfort, compatibility, and affirmation—indeed, the sexless, nonthreatening cradle of commonality, the relation in which one's self is most accurately mirrored in another, the union of desires and interests, reflected and shared as one—friendship in Foucault's hands becomes something quite opposed to such philosophically traditional and commercially profitable renderings. The desire-in-uneasiness at the root of Foucaultian friendship finds its expression in an ethic of discomfort whose origins he locates in ancient Greece. The transposition of such an ethic onto modern gay male relations is what Foucault is at pains to suggest.

In his late work Foucault makes specific connections between Antiquity and the post-Stonewall era. In both periods, the moral codes determining the positive or negative values of actions are quite weak. The modern gay community might, then, take advantage of this weakness so as to revivify an untimely relational ethic unencumbered by the "truth" of sexuality. Foucault writes in "On the Genealogy of Ethics":

> Well, I wonder if our problem nowadays is not, in a way, similar to this one [i.e., fourth century, B.C.], since most of us no longer believe that ethics is founded in religion, nor do we want a legal system to intervene in our moral, personal, private life. Recent liberation movements suffer from the fact that they cannot find any principle on which to base the elaboration of a new ethics. They need an ethics, but they cannot find any other ethics than an ethics founded in a so-called scientific knowledge of what the self is, and so on. I am struck by this similarity of problems. (*Essential, V1: Ethics* 255–56)

It is necessary to emphasize here that Foucault is not seeking a *return* to the Greeks—perhaps with Heidegger in mind Foucault declares "I do not feel homesick"[7]—but instead highlights the ethical similarities of the historical periods, noting the alternatives available within our own (Western) history. If Foucault locates the ontological immanence of the subject in Hellenistic practices of the care of self, as I noted in Chapter 1, he likewise discovers in ancient friendships a relational ethics divergent from those attending modern sexual formations. Rather than returning to the *ars erotica* of Eastern cultures to offer a point of contrast to the modern Western regime of sexuality (arguably the weakest, most orientalist section of *The History of Sexuality, Volume One*), Foucault unearths a different Antiquity in his own culture's history and ponders how its ethical principles (regarding pleasure, regarding the cultivation of an aesthetic self) might be of some use today. The similarity he finds between the two eras is thus a historical *opportunity*: a chance to elaborate a modern ethics of sexuality unconcerned with identity. Foucault looks back to a time when moral life was not completely governed by Christian confessional imperatives in order to envision from the past a future beyond sexuality. Because the free men of ancient Greece invented ethical principles that never quite cohered into prescriptive laws, their ethics inspire in Foucault a modern challenge: Can gay liberationists invent a sexual ethics based neither on (pseudo)scientific knowledge of the self nor New Age spirituality? Without returning to the social conditions of Antiquity, which involved the subjugation of women and slaves, can we learn from ancient practices of the self how to live and love in a different form of freedom?

Foucault's classical studies concern "the games of truth in the relationship of the self with the self and the forming of oneself as a subject" (*HoS, V2* 6). In these games, sexual desire did not reveal the truth of being. Rather, each man was encouraged to develop and nurture a thoroughly singularized relation to the self through social practices that could transform an individual life into a work of art. David Halperin describes ancient ascetics as follows:

> Ancient self-cultivation aimed accordingly not at realizing a personal self but at actualizing or instantiating an impersonal essence. . . . The ancient practice of self-cultivation, highly individualistic as it was, did not constitute a technology for producing unique individuals; rather it took the form of an ascetic art, a spiritual exercise designed to *empty* the self of precisely those passions and attachments that make the self, according to the modern view, something individual, personal, unique. (*Saint Foucault* 74–75)

With this notion of self-as-alterity in mind, I explore here two practices discussed in *History of Sexuality, Volume II* that highlight the cultivation of an immanent impersonality: namely, techniques toward a self-mastery and the problematization of the love of boys.

In Antiquity, bodily desires, pleasures, and sexual acts were conceived as at once natural and indissoluble, linked ontologically by a conception of force. Although natural, sexual desire and the use of pleasure—understood through the category of *aphrodisia*, "the acts, gestures, and contacts that produce a certain form of pleasure" (*HoS, V2* 40)—were considered excessive in their very nature. The problem was to understand the dynamics of desire, pleasure, and sex acts in order to control the excess inherent in the force that binds them. The project of self-mastery became an individual project of modulating, folding, or bending such force. Freedom was practiced in restraint: Through exercises in self-discipline and self-transformation, (i.e., ascetics), *aphrodisia*'s excess could be moderated. In contrast to later Christian formulations of the "self-versus-self" battle, the sexual force was not an alien entity. Instead, the Other within was natural, immanent, ontologically equi-primordial. Foucault writes:

> [T]he thing to remember in trying to define the general style of this ascetics is that the adversary that was to be fought . . . did not represent a different, ontologically alien power. The conceptual link between the movement of concupiscence, in its most insidious and secret forms, and the presence of the Other, with its ruses and power of illusions, was to be one of the essential traits of the Christian ethics of the flesh. In the ethics of *aphrodisia*, the inevitability and difficulty of the combat derived, on the contrary, from the fact that it unfolded as a solo contest: to struggle against "the desires and pleasures" was to cross swords with oneself. (57–58)

Rather than an external Other generating a self or an abject exclusion constituting Being—that is, what we now understand as a Hegelian dialectical ontology[8]—Foucault sees in Antiquity a radical self-constitution: The Self–Other dialectic is displaced by an immanent self-modulation of an extra-discursive force simultaneously within and without the subject.[9] The regimen by which free men achieved such self-mastery included considered practices of dietetics, economics, and erotics and was suited to individual needs and adaptations rather than to the dictates of a prescriptive code. "A regimen was not good if it only permitted one to live in one place, with one type of food, and if it did not allow one to be open to change. The usefulness of a regimen lay precisely in the possibility it gave to individuals to face different situations" (105). The quest for self-mastery was especially laborious in the practice of erotics. The love of boys, specifically, posed a difficult ethical dilemma.

To be clear, the primary category that structures Greek *aphrodisia* is not gender but power. *Aphrodisia* is not what we know today as sexuality, a hermeneutic of desire that gives way to the truth of Being. The extra-discursive force that binds the three tenets of *aphrodisia* is not in and of itself gendered. Gendered differentials of power, of course, did exist in Antiquity: As noted earlier, the very idea of freedom was founded on the subjection of women and slaves. The binary of masculine–feminine is not inoperative here, but its dynamism pales in comparison to the structuring social principle of activity–passivity. Only in the service of the paradigmatic active–passive binary does masculinity–femininity come to mean. Through this lens, self-mastery is conceived as an active freedom that structures the category of virility. Those men not sufficiently in control of their pleasures are passive–effeminate, and have no business in public and political affairs. In order to take part in the ruling of others, men must master themselves.[10] Contrasting modern psychoanalytic and Greek understandings of effeminacy and sexual immoderation, Foucault writes:

> In the experience of sexuality such as ours, where a basic scansion maintains an opposition between masculine and feminine, the femininity of men is perceived in the actual or virtual transgression of his sexual role. No one would be tempted to label as effeminate a man whose love for women leads to immoderation on his part; that is, short of doing a whole job of decipherment that would uncover the "latent homosexuality" that secretly inhabits his unstable and promiscuous relation to them. In contrast, for the Greeks it was the opposition between activity and passivity that was essential, pervading the domain of sexual behaviors and that of moral attitudes as well; thus, it was not hard to see how a man might prefer males without anyone even suspecting him of effeminacy, provided he was active in the sexual relation and active in the moral mastering of himself. (85)

Regarding the love of boys, the ethical problem for free men is not homosexuality. It is rather a question of how to preserve and nurture a boy's nascent manhood while at the same time asking him to compromise it by playing the passive–effeminate beloved. A precarious exchange, pubescent boys "become men" in their subservience yet must never identify with the dishonorable role of desired object. The ethical problem thus revolves not around the *subjects* of pleasure (the free men), but around the objects (the boys). The way the boys deal with their object-ness (submitting too easily, playing too hard to get) has consequences for their adult social status. Significantly, in this awkward relationship are to be found the roots of Foucault's definition of friendship as a desire-in-uneasiness. But what might an analysis of ancient friendships do for a modern gay community that "cannot find any other ethics than an ethics founded in a so-called scientific knowledge of what the self is?" What can be gleaned from this very retrograde ethics of sex in which sexual positions are linked to one's social worth, and in which the desire for sexual passivity reveals a moral weakness?

First of all, we have a strategic blurring of relational boundaries— between sex and friendship, between teacher and student, between generations. Furthermore, we see in these intergenerational mentorships what might be called a love without transcendence: a friendship operating neither as a fusion of two souls nor a mutual affirmation, nor a repetition of that which is common to both. Rather, this relation is shot through with an unrest that pushes each individual to experiment, to transform the "known" self. Foucault is clearly referencing the dynamics of this ancient relation when he writes in the friendship interview: "But two men of noticeably different ages—what code would allow them to communicate? They face each other without terms or convenient words, with nothing to assure them about the meaning of the movement that carries them toward each other." And just as Foucault sees excessive affective intensities traversing the patriarchal institutions of the present, so in the past a relational excess exists in these homosocialized, rite-of-passage mentorships. This excess comes in the form of potentiality: the free men of Antiquity did not love boys per se but the burgeoning manhood that lay within them. Although all men were "naturally sensitive" (213) toward youthful male bodies, it was the striving toward manhood with its attendant compromises and adjustments that was deemed beautiful. Like Sweeney Todd but devoid of murderous intention, the elder wished to halt the boy's movement toward manhood—to freeze a moment of potentiality—knowing all the while that this passage is not only insuspendable but necessary.

Failure and finitude were thus built into the system: The impossibility of capturing a budding manhood presages the end of the mentorship. This love, then, without transcendence, without future, accepts mutual estrangement as its bedrock. Rather than limiting the terms of the friendship, however, such an acceptance allows for new freedoms. As in Guibert's "L'ami," the emphasis here falls on the suspended moment, the in-between, when the friend could do-whatever, become-whatever, when friends grow to be the potential of one another. The frustrating and problematic mentorship, saturated with power differentials, dissymmetries, and compromising positions, ideally resolves in an equal friendship among social elites. "The love of boys could not be morally honorable unless it comprised . . . the elements that would form the basis of a transformation of this love into a definitive and socially valuable tie, that of *philia*" (225). *Philia* develops, then, in the student–mentor relation only to envelop the love therein; it folds the love relation into itself in a manner similar to the modulating of force in the self-to-self relation. Although the bedrock of patriarchal homosociality, a "brotherly love," *philia* is constituted in the awkwardness of vulnerable masculinity, in a moment when the desired self expected to emerge out of this compromise—the adult citizen in control of himself and others—is still fledgling, unpredictable. Foucault calls attention to the ethical implications of this transition: Is it possible to keep a moment of potentiality in its potentiality, to tarry within a means without a predetermined end? What type of ethical system would this encourage? When Plato shifts the ethical analytic from the object of love to its subject in the *Phaedrus* and the *Symposium* this ethical concern is displaced by a turn toward introspection that ultimately anticipates sexuality.[11] Before this shift, however, Foucault makes note of a very different form of friendship: one that begins and remains in a mutual discomfort and allows for individual and collaborative experimentation, one that nurtures singular and collective potentiality, and one in which the role of sexuality is neither that of truth-teller nor the fulcrum that ultimately distinguishes and divides friend from lover. Thinking through such a friendship specifically in a time of AIDS we can begin to contemplate the strategic radicality of this relation for queer political movements.

Guibert's Friend

Hervé Guibert's 1990 novel *To the Friend Who Did Not Save My Life* must be understood, in the context of—indeed, as an extension and a reconceptualization of—Foucault's writings on friendship and postliberation politics. I read this book not only as a quasi-diary that documents in painstaking detail the horrors of living with AIDS, but also as a philosophical treatise, oftentimes joyous and buoyant in its creativity, that grapples with the very meaning of friendship in the age of AIDS. Three questions will henceforth occupy this chapter: Who is the friend referred to in the title of Guibert's book?; What type of friend, or rather, what theory of friendship is offered in this text?; and, Why does the AIDS pandemic demand us to revisit friendship: In other words, how has AIDS rendered untrustworthy conceptions of friendship as transcendent fusion and site of mutual commonality and comfort? This necessarily entails an engagement with four thinkers—four friends—whose work has influenced my reading of Guibert's text: Foucault, Maurice Blanchot, Gilles Deleuze, and Félix Guattari.

A fictionalized memoir, *To the Friend Who Did Not Save My Life* interrogates the status of truth in its very form. Just as Foucault calls into question the modern notion that sexual desire bespeaks the truth of subjectivity, Guibert plays with the recently popular genre of the truth-revealing literary memoir. Predicated on a notion of confessional authorial authenticity, the memoir becomes for Guibert a medium through which this authenticity is given lie. Hence, the confessions emanating from this book should never be trusted as such. Although a self-identified gay man, Guibert resists the truth-telling imperatives of out-politics. In both form and content, *To the Friend* expresses a desire not to tell its author's truth, a desire to be anonymous, interior-less, opaque. The title itself—which is in fact not a title at all but rather an address—attests to this desire; it resists entitlement, deflects the modern compulsion to identify oneself and others, and displaces the proper name with a dedication. Like Foucault's letter to Guibert, which lacks a personal greeting, this text skips the formalities of names and titles in favor of a vague inscription. Hence, the crucial questions: Who is the friend who deserves such a dedication?; and for that matter, whose life is not saved?

Judging from the first-person narrative voice written from the perspective of the character "Hervé Guibert," the life not saved is most obviously his, and the friend who did not save it is the unreliable Bill, an American who wields power over Guibert by promising, yet never delivering, AIDS treatment. So far so good. But is the title, then, merely a reactive expression full of spite, bitterness, and *ressentiment*? If Bill is the only friend to which the title refers, why, then, after not saving the narrator's life, is he still considered a friend? The protagonist relates to other characters above all *as* a friend (rather than as a husband, a son, a boyfriend, or a worker); thus, is there more than one friend, and more than one conception of friendship at work in the title? Guibert the protagonist certainly spews bile at his companions throughout the hundred chapters of the novel, and it might even be argued that these expressions of hate frame the narrative itself. Toward the beginning of chapter 3: "me—a man who has just discovered that he doesn't like his fellow man, no, I definitely don't like them, I rather hate them instead" (4), and then finally in the last chapter: "Just how deep do you want me to sink? Fuck you, Bill!" (246) At the same time, Guibert devotes the majority of the book's pages to loving descriptions, portraits and stories of friends. In this rendering of friendship, love and hate are not mutually exclusive and, more interestingly, the traditional boundaries between self–Other, life–death, singular–multiple, and sexual–nonsexual relations are blurred if not demolished.

Such categorical nebulousness raises questions concerning the "my life" of the title/dedication: Is it only Hervé-the-protagonist's life not saved? How are we to understand "life" and the possessive pronoun "my"? As the plot progresses—disjunctively, disruptively—Hervé becomes doubled, multiplied. Concerning his lover-friend Jules (with whom he shares a birthday): "I now had the feeling that we were part of one and the same being" (153); concerning Jules' family (the Club of Five): "the HIV virus had allowed me to become part of their blood" (194); concerning Rainieri, his blood-work accomplice: "So we advanced side by side, like shadows of each other, going at the same speed in the same direction" (218); concerning an episode of mistaken identity at the lab: "we decided that a certain Margherita had provided the contents of Hervé Guibert's test tubes" (222); and, finally, concerning Guibert's last meeting with Bill: "I kept splitting into two people during the dinner" (242). Furthermore, this "self" becomes increasingly phantasmal: a ghost rather than a stable, autonomous ego; a self shot through with both memories of friends who have died and encounters with the living whose deaths are imminent; a presence whose absence becomes increasingly visible in the daily confrontation with death. In Guibert's rendering of friendship, a shared spectral self thus effaces individual identity: The possessive pronoun "my" becomes multiple, the life not saved plural. In the face of AIDS, Guibert is forced to reconceptualize the friend and the self. What ultimately motivates this rethinking is HIV: The haunting other within becomes a collective finitude without. The singular Guibert mutates into a host of different characters as a radically common virus courses through his veins. As evidenced in the passages quoted at the outset of this paragraph, this character can no longer distinguish his personhood from others'; his self dissolves into the multitude that shares a similar fate.

Yet each friend, including Guibert, is left to die a singular death. "As soon as he'd gone I felt better: I was my own best nurse, for I was the only person able to cope with my suffering" (154). Although the friends in the novel often merge to the point of indistinguishibility, a recognition of each other's final absence—a fate that can never be shared—becomes the common ground of their relationships. But how can one build a relation on that which is unrelatable? How can one share the unsharable? Such questions form the backbone of Guibert's ethics of friendship. The desire-in-uneasiness and the ethics of discomfort that unite and guide Foucault's friends take on a new meaning when, in the time of AIDS, the finitude of friendship becomes so baldly unavoidable. The love without transcendence we glimpse in the Greeks becomes literalized in friendships ending in AIDS deaths; the cultivation of an immanent alterity in the self becomes an exercise in befriending finitude. Guibert's ethical imperative involves transforming the shared estrangement between self and self and between self and other into a friendship productive of new powers and pleasures. When finitude becomes the constituent ground of friendship, when a relationship is built on the impossibility of finding oneself in the other, and when the futility of owning or sharing an absolutely unknowable alterity is acknowledged at the outset, only then might a genuine community emerge: One not based on identitarian difference or property relations, one Maurice Blanchot calls "the ultimate form of communitarian experience."[12]

Immersed in death's ubiquity, then, Guibert-the-protagonist becomes a philosopher of new relational and communal forms. Not surprisingly, this transformation occurs most intensely through the death of Muzil, the Foucault-like character likely named after the Austrian writer Robert Musil whose novel *The Man without Qualities* resonates in both Foucault's and Guibert's texts.[13] "I understood for the first time . . . that Muzil was going to die and very soon; a certainty that disfigured me in the eyes of passersby, for my face disintegrated, washed away by my tears and shattered into fragments by my cries" (92). Guibert sees his disappearance, his own becoming-man-without-qualities, in the death of Muzil. In the recognition of the friend's death, Guibert is exposed: that which he believed to be most his, his finitude, is multiplied and shared. At the same time, Guibert's death, by nature unsharable, remains his alone: Only his body will suffer that singular death. That which unites Guibert with his friends, then, is precisely what tears them apart. We saw this simultaneous merger and severance of selves in Guibert's photograph "*L'ami*"; now, however, a "common thanatological destiny" is the force that binds and separates. As Guibert and his friends disappear into an anonymous "we" of AIDS-related death statistics, the absolute singularity of each life becomes all the more pronounced. With finitude as its constituent ground, friendship emerges at the point where relating with the Other is impossible. This is a difficult, if not disturbing, relation to imagine. Maurice Blanchot's eulogy for Georges Bataille entitled "Friendship" resonates with Guibert's conception and perhaps helps clarify what Guibert is trying to define. Blanchot writes:

> We must give up trying to know those to whom we are linked by something essential; by this I mean we must greet them in the relation with the unknown in which they greet us as well, in our estrangement. Friendship, this relation without dependence, without episode, yet into which all the simplicity of life enters, passes by way of the recognition of the common strangeness that does not allow us to speak of our friends but only to speak to them, not to make of them a topic of conversations (or essays), but the movement of understanding in which, speaking to us, they reserve, even on the most familiar terms,

an infinite distance, the fundamental separation on the basis
of which what separates becomes relation. (*Friendship* 291)

The finitude that Guibert recognizes in himself and others, as Blanchot
reminds us, can never be shared. Upon the recognition of the infinite
distance between singular lives, however, new relational possibilities
emerge. On the status of gay bathhouses amidst the pandemic, Muzil
remarks: "The baths have never been so popular and now they're
fantastic. This danger lurking everywhere has created new complicities,
new tenderness, new solidarities. Before no one ever said a word; now
we talk to one another" (22). AIDS merely magnifies the impermanence
of the self and the friend, and in so doing pushes both to think and to
relate differently.

Indeed, building friendships on a "fundamental separation" leads to
new conceptions of community and politics: In short, a way through the
quagmire of identity, and communities founded on commonalities. For a
double-bind exists within the very conception of identity as manifested in,
for example, gay rights movements. On the one hand, the construction of
a political bloc based on social, physical, and psychic identifications—what
we can call strategic essentialism, the founding of a community based on
notions of belonging (e.g., "I belong to x group . . . ,") and commonality
(e.g., "We in this group have x in common . . . ,")—has been a necessary
and demonstrably self-empowering strategy. On the other hand, such
identifications, precisely because they must function within prevailing,
normally binary, sociodiscursive structures (women vs. men, black
vs. white, gay vs. straight, sick vs. healthy, etc.) and because they are
organized around a fixed, stable, and permanent conception of identity
tend to foreclose ways of envisioning a form of sociality based not on
divisions and property but rather on impermanence and contingency.
To the Friend Who Did Not Save My Life, then, is not an idyllic or elegiac
ode to romanticized friendship. Rather, it is a recognition of the friend
as simultaneously indissociable and irrevocably separated from the self,
a recognition of the absolute singularity of each life and the common
yet unsharable finitude in-between. This is to say, in friendships among
People With AIDS (PWAs) Guibert recognizes a radical, ontological being-
in-common.[14]

So, I ask again, finally, who is "the friend who did not save my life?"
For Guibert, HIV is:

a disease that gave death time to live and its victims time
to die, time to discover time, and in the end to discover life,
so in a way those green monkeys of Africa provided us with

a brilliant modern invention. . . . If life was nothing but the presentiment of death and the constant torture of wondering when the axe would fall, then AIDS, by setting an official limit to our life span . . . made us men who were fully conscious of our lives, and freed us from our ignorance. (164)

If AIDS is a "brilliant modern invention" that shortens a life span yet allows Guibert to live more fully and more consciously, is the virus his friend? Or, if the friend is one who acknowledges the finitude in another and relates with this other precisely at the point of unrelatability—and thus never truly possesses the power to save the other's life—is the friend not Bill, but perhaps Muzil? If so, this entire book could be Guibert's response to the letter from his "Cher Michel,'" his contribution to the joint production of a discourse of impersonal friendship.

In a related collaboration, Deleuze and Guattari consider the importance of friendship for thought itself in *What is Philosophy?* Although their analysis of classical friendship is quite different from Foucault's, having more to do with the ways in which friendship informs philosophy (e.g., providing the conceptual persona of thought for the Ancients), Deleuze and Guattari nevertheless offer a definition of "Greek" friendship: "The basic point about friendship is that the two friends are like claimant and rival (but who could tell them apart?)" (4). If we understand friendship in this sense, as an agonistic contest between equals involving "competitive distrust" as well as "an amorous striving towards the object of desire" (4) then Bill in the novel is certainly this type of friend.

AIDS has allowed Bill to take the role of master of ceremonies in our little group of friends, which he manipulates as though it were a scientific experiment. . . . To "save" my life, I've had to be transparent to Bill for eighteen months: to be prepared to report at any moment on one's plunging T4 count is worse than having to show what's in one's pants. (Guibert, *To the Friend* 228)

If the cure is the object of desire and Guibert and Bill are in competition for it, Guibert realizes by the end of the novel that he must drop out of this race. "When I tried to extricate myself from this game by denouncing it, Bill must have felt exposed, and feared losing his place as ringmaster in this circle of friendships he's craftily built up. . . . Bill was able to manipulate by enticing them with the fictitious power of salvation" (228–29). In this statement, salvation takes on an air of impotency, reactivity, and *ressentiment*: the cure becomes a transcendent, just-out-of-reach savior, a telos that regulates life. Dangling this cure before the noses of those who need it most, Bill harnesses power reactively. And when death is construed as the opposite of life, saving, preserving, and hoarding it is of utmost importance. But if death is understood as immanent to life, what does it mean to be saved? Foucault's ancients had one answer: Immanent salvation in old age occurred when the subject united true knowledge (philosophy) with true action (spirituality). Guibert and company, however, do not have the luxury of old age. Their salvation comes only in the realization that refusing to "save life" is not necessarily a plea for death, that it might take the form of understanding the two realms as immanent to one another. Perhaps not saving life but living it as if each moment were one's last, pushing the materiality of the body and its capacity to relate to the limit, is, in a sense, the prize Guibert receives for dropping out of Bill's game. The book, then, is dedicated to the friends that helped Guibert understand life and death in such a way. In this case, the friend who did not save my life is a very different friend: not a rival to be distrusted, but a friend who helps us understand living as something that should *not* be saved but spent, a friend who helps us abandon life to its finitude so as to live all the more intensely and passionately.

The community of friends in the novel emphasizes that which cannot be shared and is founded on estrangement in regard to the unknown. And although these friends seem in one way or another united through their marginalized sexual identities and practices (i.e., organized in some ways like a traditional community) the importance of the sex act is diminished in relation to the bonds that develop out of it. The status of the sexual act in Guibert's book echoes the Foucault passage quoted earlier in this chapter: "The problem is not to discover in oneself the truth of sex but rather use sexuality henceforth to arrive at a multiplicity of relationships." Because sexuality, according to Foucault, has been transformed from an object of knowledge into a cumulative effect of power, sex practices and the resulting relations are incessantly reined in—granted rights and representation in governmental procedures—so that the state may regulate and contain the uses of the body that threaten the reproduction of sovereign power.

If sexuality is merely a means by which the state deploys its power over life, is friendship a difficult relation to administer? If we are referring to male claimant/rival friendships, sexless relations of emotional attachment and competition, the answer is a resounding No. These friendships are the nuts and bolts of the homosocial boy's club networks comprising most contemporary governmental and corporate hierarchies, and are hence crucial for the functioning of the state and capital.[15] But what about Guibert's friendships? Ones that blur the lines between the sexual and the nonsexual?; friendships that begin where most others end, that is to say, in a recognition of another's finitude?; friendships that forge new alliances between members of different generations, classes, and races? Are these friendships valuable to the state and capital? Deleuze and Guattari again are helpful here. Writing obliquely about their own prolific collaboration, the authors assert in *What is Philosophy?* that friendship is "a condition for the exercise of thought," that is to say, immanent to philosophical thought itself. I quote here a longer portion of the passage that begins the Introduction:

> The philosopher is the concept's friend; he is potentiality of the concept. That is, philosophy is not a simple art of forming, inventing, or fabricating concepts, because concepts are not necessarily forms, discoveries, or products. More rigorously, philosophy is the discipline that involves creating concepts. Does this mean that the friend is the friend of his own creations? Or is the actuality of the concept due to the potential of the friend, in the unity of the creator and his double? (5)

The philosopher, the friend of knowledge, the one who seeks wisdom yet does not formally possess it, needs the friend to practice his or her work, to create concepts. The friend lies at both the etymological and the practical roots of Greek philosophy and is in this sense the original conceptual persona of thought in the West. Yet the friend embedded within philosophy is not necessarily an external persona: Thought needs the thinker-as-friend to actualize the concept. Thought, in its process of actualization, is divided: Thought and thinker become claimant and rival and vice versa, reversible and indistinguishable from each other. The problem for philosophy in modernity, according to Deleuze and Guattari, is that the classical claimant/rival conception of friendship can no longer be the conceptual persona of thought, for two reasons: First, powerful rivals have emerged in the forces of advertising and marketing—the new "idea men" of our time—transforming friendship's relation to thought and putting philosophy to work in the service of capital; second, after the "inexpressible catastrophe" of modernity (in historical terms, the atrocities committed under totalitarianism, the Holocaust, Stalinism; in philosophical terms, the Heideggerian mistake of confusing the Nazis for the Greeks), the friend as conceptual persona of philosophy has changed irrevocably. Homosocialized, commodified, and rendered fascistic, classical conceptions of friendship have become disgraceful and untrustworthy.[16] The relationship of friendship to thought is now one of shame. In order to be viable again, friendship must undergo a metamorphosis:

Unless we are led back to the "Friend," but after an ordeal that is too powerful, an inexpressible catastrophe, and so in yet another new sense, in a mutual distress, a mutual weariness that forms a new right of thought (Socrates becomes Jewish). Not two friends who communicate and recall the past together but, on the contrary, who suffer an amnesia or aphasia capable of splitting thought, of dividing it in itself. (*What is Philosophy?* 71)

Where Deleuze and Guattari leave off, Guibert begins. In *To the Friend Who Did Not Save My Life*, he grapples with the classical understanding of thought as friend and ultimately attempts to conceptualize a new friendship in the face of AIDS. Deleuze and Guattari's vague summoning of an "inexpressible catastrophe" which prompts a rethinking of the relation between friendship and thought is realized in the mathematically sublime number of AIDS corpses. In the midst of this, Guibert becomes the friend of a concept of friendship that could breathe new life into the relation. At the outset of the text, he claims that the book he is writing, the thought he is actualizing on the page, is his friend: "I'm beginning a new book to have a companion, someone with whom I can talk, eat, sleep, at whose side I can dream and have nightmares, the only friend whose company I can bear at present" (4). But this friend eventually becomes a rival and can no longer be trusted. Caught in a race to save his life in a contest similar to his rivalry with Bill—another figure who promised salvation—Guibert the thinker competes with Thought in an attempt to ward off death. In the end, his book, the friend that was once trusted, the classically conceived friend at once claimant and rival, turns on Guibert. "My book is closing in on me. I am in deep shit" (246). Both Bill and Thought, as friends in the claimant/rival sense, have failed him: The friends who did not save his life, the friends who withheld the prize of salvation, are multiple. Yet the friends who did not save his life in a *creative and positive* sense—Muzil, Rainieri, even the virus—the friends who helped transform his conception of life and death, the friends who have helped him abandon his life and his self to finitude, also are multiple. The friend that did not save my life, in this sense, then, is simultaneously at least two types of friend at once. As a philosopher grappling with the status of friendship in the face of a catastrophe, Guibert leaves behind a classical notion of friendship in order to invent a new one. No longer besmirched by shame, the new conceptual persona of thought is still a friend: but this one greets the other only in the acknowledgment of a mutual estrangement that can never be shared.

Chapter 3

Ontology Matters

"Lesbians are not women."

—Monique Wittig[1]

In Chapter 1, I noted that Foucault's interest in immanentist conceptions of subjectivity is coincident with his exploration of friendship. This parallel development in Foucault's late work likewise has profound implications for his theories of sexuality and power. Indeed, only with a clear understanding of this shift in focus can we adequately address the ethics and politics of Foucaultian friendship. For this reason, I explore more carefully in this chapter Foucault's relation to dialectical and nondialectical ontological traditions. I stage an encounter between the "immanentist Foucault" and two queer theorists whose interpretations of Foucault have had remarkable purchase in the American academy, namely, Judith Butler and David Halperin. Using these thinkers' work as a point of departure, I come to two main conclusions:

1. Just as Wittig's "lesbian" emerges in the aftermath of the always-already patriarchal category "woman," Foucault's friend only comes to be when the sexological category of "homosexual" is overcome. In other words, Foucault requires a Nietzschean conception of radical negation so that his friendship can be an autonomous creation.

2. Halperin's and Butler's theories of subjectivity and resistance fail to take into account Foucault's final turn from Hegelian conceptions of being. This is not, of course, the result of "bad reading"; Foucault's immanentist turn becomes most apparent in the late *Collège de France* seminars and lectures published well after Halperin's and Butler's seminal work in queer theory.

In light of Foucault's recent publications, the time is ripe to reassess some queer theoretical axioms. This final chapter on the philosophical genealogy of Foucault's friendship begins, then, with an exploration of the philosopher's fraught relationship with Hegelian dialectics, moves on to a re-evaluation of key Foucaultian concepts (power, becoming, biopower, resistance, etc.) bearing in mind his late immanentist turn, and closes with a sketch of Foucault's "new" political vision, which features friendship as a form of biopolitical resistance.

Subjects of Resistance

According to Michael Hardt's overview of 1960s French intellectual culture, *les salles de classe de philosophie* were steeped in a generalized Hegelianism.[2] Althusser and Deleuze, to name just two, weary of this "foul-smelling" air, sought refuge in alternative immanentist philosophical traditions (Spinoza, Nietzsche) so as to work around and away from the ever-powerful dialectic. Foucault, on the other hand, a student of Jean Hyppolite, one of France's most prominent Hegel scholars, approached the Hegelian tradition with a bit more reserve. In his 1971 inaugural address to the *Collège de France,* "The Discourse on Language," he expresses at once frustration with Hegelianism and skepticism for anti-Hegelians:

> But truly to escape Hegel involves an exact appreciation of the price we have to pay to detach ourselves from him. It assumes that we are aware of the extent to which Hegel, insidiously perhaps, is close to us; it implies a knowledge, in that which permits us to think against Hegel, of that which remains Hegelian. We have to determine the extent to which our anti-Hegelianism is possibly one of his tricks directed against us, at the end of which he stands, motionless, waiting for us. (235)

Given the productive role that negation and opposition play in Hegel's method, turning away from the dialectic *re*turns us to its very heart. For, in Hegelian terms, opposition is to be subsumed and superseded; opposition constitutes; opposition is generative. The bind for Foucault, then, is clear: An escape route from the Hegelian dialectic might U-turn directly back to Hegel; it cannot be forged through opposing such a totalizing system (or, as Foucault later called it, a "totalitarian theory,"[3]) but, rather, by beginning from a different ontological site and moving elsewhere. Whereas Deleuze throughout his career explicitly seeks out a non-Hegelian philosophical method, a search that leads him counterhistorically from Bergson to

Nietzsche to Spinoza,[4] Foucault contemplates a break with the Hegelian tradition with a certain amount of ambivalence.

As I have been arguing, however, Foucault finds an alternative to that tradition in his studies of Antiquity and in his interrogation of friendship—the entry of a reworked subject and a reconceptualization of power in his late work reflect this shift. Although in 1971 Foucault sees Hegel at the end of the road, by 1983 he seems to have found a viable detour. The very vocabulary of "Friendship as a Way of Life," for example, betrays Foucault's investment in an immanentist philosophical tradition. "Homosexuality is the historic occasion to reopen *affective* and relational *virtualities*, not so much through the intrinsic qualities of the homosexual but because of the 'slantwise' position of the latter, as it were, the *diagonal lines* he can lay out in the social fabric allow these virtualities to come to light" ("Friendship" 138, emphasis mine). Affect? Virtualities? Diagonal lines (essentially, "of flight")? The author of this passage could easily be mistaken for Deleuze. Foucault's writings on friendship thus reflect his immanentist leanings; along with his final investigations into power and ancient ascetics, friendship allows him to escape Hegel and move toward new becomings in thought and politics.

Judith Butler, however, holds steady in her claim that resistance to Hegel is futile. In *Subjects of Desire*, a book concerning the reception of Hegel in twentieth-century French philosophical thought, she writes: "References to a 'break' with Hegel are almost always impossible, if only because Hegel has made the very notion of 'breaking with' a central tenet of his dialectic" (184). Comprehending the conundrum of anti-Hegelians and suggesting that their efforts amount to a lost cause, Butler stakes her tent in the Hegelian camp, forcing the dialectic—blasphemous from Hegel's point of view—into the service of a defiantly anti-heteronormative subject. Although inspired by Foucault, Butler's subject differs from his in significant ways.

At the risk of being reductive, I refer to the different ontological strains in Butler's and the late Foucault's concepts of subjectivity as dialectical and nondialectical, respectively. My investigation into these divergent philosophical traditions lays the groundwork for the remaining two chapters: Only with an understanding of Foucault's immanentist turn can we appreciate the political thrust of his friendship model. The questions motivating this analysis include the following:

1. Is there such a thing as a radical break?

2. Can a subject leave something behind absolutely, or are all departures subject to the Law?

Answers to these questions require a discussion of three key terms: *negation, becoming,* and *power.*

Negation

In *The Phenomenology of Spirit,* Hegel conceives of negation as that which "supersedes in such a way as to preserve and maintain what is superseded, and consequently survives its own supersession" (188). In this dialectical ontology, the operative binaries are Self–Other and identity–difference. Hegel posits an undifferentiated, pure being that actively negates its opposite (i.e., nothingness) and incorporates the Other in order to become determinate. Negation in this scenario thus plays a key role in the constitution of the subject. Valorized to the extent that it is always in some way a part of determinate being, negation is the motor of change and production. Never absolute (in the sense of negating completely; an understanding of negation which, for Hegel, signifies pure death and nihilism), negation is always pointed toward a resurrection of sorts, a teleological end point containing the promise of supersession. For Hegel, in short, negation constitutes being.[5]

This understanding of negation finds its contemporary incarnation in Butler's work, but with a twist. Siding with the undervalorized terms that are always sublated in Hegel's dialectic (Other, difference), Butler appropriates, or rather resignifies, Hegel's ontology so as to explore the bind of a subjectivity that is always-already gendered and sexed. In *Bodies That Matter,* she writes: "The forming of a subject requires an identification with the normative phantasm of 'sex,' and this identification takes place through a repudiation which produces a domain of abjection, a repudiation without which the subject cannot emerge" (3). The heterosexual–sexist matrix (that "normative phantasm of 'sex'") is always exclusionary: In negating its abject (e.g., homosexuality, woman), it constitutes itself and the subjects emerging through it. Yet the repudiation of the abject is never fully "forgotten" or left behind: The abject bedevils the subject in its development, forcing a repeated appeal to, a citation and reiteration of, the normative Law that enables its emergence. The Law, however, comes to be authoritative only through these repeated citations: Having no authentic origins, reiterations of the Law constitute and legitimate its edicts. The promise of resignification, then, is contained in this paradigm of subjectivity, and this becomes Butler's subversive strategy. Resignification involves a repetition of the ever-unstable "origin" only to displace that origin as *the* origin. Citations repeat the constitutive exclusions of the Law, yet, because these reiterations can only but approximate the normative ideal of the phantasmatic matrix, the hope or the possibility of repeating the normative *differently* over time becomes a potential site of resistance. She writes in *Bodies*:

> To the extent that the "I" is secured by its sexed position, this "I" and its "position" can be secured only by being *repeatedly* assumed, whereby "assumption" is not a singular act or event, but, rather, an iterable practice. . . . And a citation will be at once an interpretation of the norm and an occasion to expose the norm itself as a privileged interpretation. . . . Since the law must be repeated to remain an authoritative law, the law perpetually reinstitutes the possibility of its own failure. (108)

Butler's connection to Hegel's dialectical ontology should be clear: Although filtered through a Derridean deconstructive reading and Lacanian psychoanalytics, Hegel's understanding of negation remains, now morphed into the "excluded abject," which continues to haunt the subject in its development. In contradistinction to Hegel, however, Butler sides with the negated abject, and posits a subject with the potential to subvert the (heteronormative) Law over time through resignification. Like Hegel's tightly sealed system, however, Butler's inverted schematic—as productive and important as it has been for feminist and queer theory—comes with its own exclusions and negations. Although a resignification, Butler's ontology repeats the necessary exclusions that enable the Hegelian system to operate. Thinking dialectically for a moment, then, the abject of the Hegelian tradition—the very exclusion necessary to its functioning—lies in a repudiated nondialectical conception of negation.

"Nondialectical difference, despite its various forms, is the labor of the negative which has lost its magic" (184), so writes Butler in *Subjects of Desire*. But what is the "magic" lost in this conception of negation? In Hegelian thought, the potential for rebirth, movement, self-consciousness. And yet, is this really negation? What if negation holds no futural promise, if it is in no way generative, only unremittingly destructive? In Hegelian thought, this is nihilism, absolute death. On this point, Nietzsche, self-proclaimed arch nemesis of Hegel, concurs, but finds use for such a form of negation: he recognizes in it a pure, active power. In Nietzsche's estimation, Hegel's productive negation is only partial: It is a force turned back against itself, ultimately reactive. Hegel valorizes this reactive, partial negation especially in his account of the master–slave narrative. It is helpful to look briefly at this often evoked drama as it crystallizes the competing conceptions of power and negation in Hegel and Nietzsche (and, by extension, Butler and Foucault). If, following Michael Hardt, we understand master and slave in this schematic not as personal entities but as impersonal forces, it becomes clear that the master's power is unrestrained, a "force inseparable from its manifestation" (*Gilles Deleuze* 42). Slave power in this reading is, then, a force turned back on itself. Two types of negation are simultaneously at work: absolute (the master seeking to consume/kill) and partial (the slave seeking to live/work). In the unfolding of the relationship, slave power confronts master power and productively negates it: Through a confrontation with a harbinger of death, the slave comes to affirm his life. The slave transforms this negativity into an interiority, an identity—the force of negation is turned inward resulting in an independent self-consciousness for the slave—a realization of his essential nature.

The partial negation that affords the slave an understanding of his essence runs counter to Nietzsche's interest in a transvaluation of values. For what Hegel affirms in his emphasis on interiority is an acceptance of the moral status quo: the slave, however enlightened, affirms the system of values that defines him as such. Because negation is partial, the essential nature of the slave remains. In heralding "the death of man," however, Nietzsche is ultimately calling for a moratorium on interiority altogether. This occurs only through an act of total destruction: The liberation of a force that is not obstructed and turned inward but expressed fully. In actualizing a force that negates completely, the slave eradicates both his essential nature *and* the value system that affirms it. Clearing the playing field in such a way thus allows for autonomous invention: *pars destruens, pars construens*.[6] (40–44)

Nietzsche's critique of the weakness of Hegelian negation has a direct bearing on Foucault's interest in overcoming the identity of "homosexual." Foucault's account of reverse discourse is arguably an updated version of the master–slave narrative told from a Nietzschean perspective. It is worth recounting his genealogy of the "homosexual" to advance the argument that Foucault *requires* a Nietzschean conception of negation to posit friendship as the becoming of homosexuality. Put another way, Foucault's homosexual is Hegel's slave from a Nietzschean standpoint. As Foucault's story goes, eighteenth-century medical and psychiatric discourses of non-normative sexualities enacted a stricter regime of control, a more subtle yet more effective regulation of bodies and pleasures than heretofore seen in Western civilization. When "perversions" such as male same-sex sodomy became an object of study within the human sciences, deviant sex acts were transformed from a category of forbidden pleasure to "a personage, a past, a case history, . . . a species" known as the homosexual (*HoS, VI* 43). With a name, an identity, and a body on which the truth of the individual was writ, the homosexual became a permanent, recognizable reality in Western society—fixed, essentialized and, because of the overweening heteronormativity of the *scientia sexualis*, systematically categorized into a knowable pathology. The homosexual consequently began to "speak in its own behalf . . . [and] demand that its legitimacy or 'naturality' be acknowledged" (101). As deviants claiming their right to love one another, gay liberationists strategically reversed the subject-object positions assigned by medicalizing discourses and performed a significant act of political resistance within the discursive frameworks that constituted their invention. However, as I noted in Chapter 2, for Foucault this resistance is only a stepping stone, a means to an end that is always postponed and never predetermined. While the (Hegelian) resignification of homosexual is subversive, its (Nietzschean) destruction—in the form of devalorization—is required for autonomous becoming. Foucault says as much in "The Social Triumph of the Sexual Will":

> Rather than saying what we said at one time: "Let's try to re-introduce homosexuality into the general norm of social relations," let's say the reverse: "No! Let's escape as much as possible from the type of relations which society proposes for us and try to create an empty space where we are new relational possibilities." The gay movement has a future which goes beyond gays themselves. . . . [I]t may include the possibility of a culture in the large sense, a culture which invents ways of relating, types of existence, types of values, types of exchanges between individuals that are really new and are neither the same as, nor superimposed on, existing cultural forms. (*Essential, V1: Ethics* 160)

Coupled with previously quoted passages concerning Foucault's affirmation of the anti-sex grumbling in Guibert's work and his wish to topple the "monarchy of sex," Foucault's plea to escape here is a call for exodus: a turning away from the identities dispensed by various biopolitical institutions, a turning away from established relational norms. Foucault's indebtedness to Nietzsche becomes clear: the creation of an "empty space" for future relational forms begins with the divestiture of a homosexual interiority.[7] "Types of values" that are "really new" come only as a consequence of an absolute negation. Interiority, the product of a force turned inward in the master–slave drama, has no place in a transvaluation of values. If friendship is "the development towards which the problem of homosexuality tends," a relationship that must be "invented from A to Z," then such friendship only comes into being when homosexuality as a sexological concept is annihilated.

Foucault's desire to discredit the notion of sexuality as interiority, furthermore, has all the earmarks of a Nietzschean total critique. As the "essential nature" resulting from a similarly dialectical master–slave struggle, gay identity is smeared with the blood of the "master's" hands and serves to validate the system of values that undergirds sovereign power. A total critique involves not simply championing the negated abject, but attacking with full force the system that devalues such "monsters" by destroying the essence that results from the intermingling of master–slave. From this perspective, Butler's strategy of resignification and, as we shall see, Halperin's concept of queer resistance pale in comparison to Foucault's radical gesture. Their partial critiques—relying on an understanding of negation in which force is not internal to its manifestation, but turned in on itself and made productive—spare the "essential nature" of the homosexual. In Butler and Halperin's strategies of resistance, the empty space Foucault requires to build anew is thus filled with the detritus of a dialectical negation.

A parallel example helps illustrate what I see as a new politics emerging in Foucault's late work. In *Gilles Deleuze*, Michael Hardt explicates Nietzsche's concept of total critique in invoking the principles of Marxist Autonomism. "If the worker is to reach a point of genuine affirmation, of self-valorization, the attack has to be directed at the 'essence,' at the values that define the worker as such—against servitude, against work" (44). In refusing the established value of work, the worker destroys his proletarian essence, the very self afforded him through the employee–employer relation. This refusal is not an attack on labor as such, but an attack on capitalist exploitation and the devaluing of creative labor. The worker's self-annihilation is thus a radical negation of the system of values that valorizes his essence: In order to create new forms of life, in order to allow the force of creative labor to reach its potential, new selves are needed. Thus, the workers must overcome themselves *essentially*: a movement that resonates with Nietzsche's concept of the *Übermensch*— and with Foucault's theory of friendship.

Becoming

What then comes after this moment of destruction? How does being move from negation to affirmation? In the midnight hour, between destruction and creation, contingency must first be affirmed. For there is no foreseeable order, no determinate form to the becoming of being. An art of life, an ethical aesthetics, is needed to guide being toward an active affirmation, and Nietzsche finds such an ethics in the eternal return. Although never mentioned by name in Foucault's theorizations of subjectivity, this concept suffuses his analyses of ancient ascetic practices. Explaining this connection requires a bit of back-pedaling, specifically a look into Nietzschean concepts of difference, power, and ethics.

Just as there are two different forms of negation in dialectical and nondialectical ontologies, there are likewise two concepts of difference. Nietzsche's will to power, the substance of being, is internally differentiated. Difference is primary and being is self-productive, self-caused, not reliant on external relations or environments to motivate its perpetual movement. In contrast to Hegel's ontology, Nietzschean being does not develop along a teleological path—there exists no transcendence and no salvation to theorize. As a third term of sorts that rests at the point of contiguity between the poles of Self–Other and One–Multiple in dialectical thought, Nietzsche's always-becoming being is not tied to a substantial entity but rather to contingency itself. What is at stake in subject development, as Althusser has pointed out,[8] is the becoming *necessary* of contingency.

Although Hegel and Nietzsche agree that power is the essence of being, their understandings of force and movement diverge. Hardt writes: "Both [Hegel and Nietzsche] seek to locate essence in the movement of being, but Hegel discovers a force reflected back into itself (self-consciousness or interiority), and Nietzsche proposes a force that emerges unhaltingly outside itself (the will to power or exteriority)" (*Gilles Deleuze* 42). Nietzsche's will to power is the substance of being and yet being itself must be willed in order for it to be an original creation. The eternal return for Nietzsche constitutes both the affirmation of contingency and the active willing—the creation—of being. In this schematic, a force inherent to a mode of being can be evaluated according to its principle of activity. Given Nietzsche's definition of power and his critique of Hegel's, an ethical horizon can now be delimited. If a force goes to the limit of what it can do, if its intensity is neither turned back on itself nor blocked, it is active, or, "good." If a force is separated from its power to act, if it is stunted or denied its might, it is reactive, or, "bad." For Nietzsche, ethics and ontology thus overlap, or, rather, his ethics implies an ontology: the ethical will to power—the will whose force is inseparable from its manifestation, and hence good—must will being repeatedly. The eternal return is then an ethical-ontological principle: "Always do what you will" spake Zarathustra, implying a selective process, an affirmation of the ethical will and a constitution of an active mode of being (Nietzsche, *Zarathustra* 191). Pure being—a goal akin to the Hellenistic conversion to self—results from the lifelong selection and affirmation of practices that promote an active will. Because Nietzsche's is a being of perpetual becoming, pure being is not a telos but an ongoing process. Kathi Weeks, in *Constituting Feminist*

Subjects, follows Nietzsche in developing the concept of the eternal return into an ethics for feminist practice. She writes:

> What Nietzsche invites us to affirm is not the eternal return of *the*
> *identical*, but the eternal return as a *principle of selection.* . . . This
> selection is not an act of "free will" or "self-determination," as if
> there were a will or a self that were radically free to determine a
> will to be. Moreover, this selection is the work not of reflection
> but of practice; that is, we do not just think what to be, we
> enact it in word and deed. This process of selection must be
> conceived—as the process of subjectivization was conceived in
> Butler's account—as an ongoing process, an enactment, rather
> than as the product of a single decision or declaration. To build
> on the Nietzschean model, this selection is a process that is
> simultaneously *deconstitutive* and *constitutive*; specifically, we
> selectively will that which is active over that which is reactive,
> that which enables us to do and be more over that which would
> limit or separate us from what we can do or be, that which
> augments our power over that which detracts from it. (137)

Weeks understands the eternal return as the ethical framework that emerges from Nietzsche's conception of an internally differentiated, ontological will to power. She finds in this concept the normative criteria for judging action as well as a model for an alternative subjectivity. The first moment of the eternal return, she explains in a strikingly Sartrean formulation, involves facing the self as a sum of past experiences and accidental determinants: the race, gender, class, sexuality, into which we are born, for example. A fatalistic evaluation of such determinants—"I am only the sum of my parts; My self is utterly determined by contingent historical factors"—must be overcome in the second moment when we will all that we are, when we make the contingent factors of our personal history the necessary elements for our futural becoming. "To will the past is to affirm what we have become as an ongoing achievement and a basis for action as opposed to a permanent fact and a source of resignation" (41). Importantly, this moment lasts a lifetime: Like the lifelong practices of the self in Foucault's analyses of the ancient ascetics, the active willing of being is an art of life, an aesthetics of existence.

The pure being sought in Nietzsche's ethics mirrors the salvational self-conversion that occurs in ancient practices of *parrhesia*. For Hellenist philosophers, the half-hearted prescription to "know thyself" only finds completion in self-transformation: the *parrhesiastes* finds his moment of pure being when he comes to embody in act and in speech the truth he has spent his life seeking. In selecting and living practices that produce active modes of being, practices that enable the subject to have access to truth, Foucault's *parrhesiastes* arguably develops along a similar ethical path as the one laid out in Nietzsche's eternal return. The aesthetics of existence needed to create an original form of life come into play only after a certain self-destruction—an overcoming of the known self, the given self—which allows for the creation of a new self in the selection of affirmative life practices. This is not to say that Foucault merely discovers Nietzsche in the Ancients. Rather, it is to point out the Nietzschean—as opposed to Hegelian—inflections in Foucault's reworked subject and the politics this ethico-ontological schematic implies.

Although the eternal return as an ethical principle resonates with Foucault's account of the ethical practices in ancient ascetics, Foucault takes care to distance himself from his forebear. Concerning Nietzsche's understanding of asceticism in the cultivation of the self, he writes: "I think he [Nietzsche] was entirely mistaken on the subject of asceticism. . . . I do not think that Nietzsche can be read in any way as a reappearance or a reactivation of the culture of the self." ("19 April 1983" 10). Again provocatively vague, Foucault adds nothing further to this needling comment. Is Foucault himself attempting to reactivate the culture of the self? If so, what does he offer that Nietzsche did not, or could not? According to Kathi Weeks, nothing. In her reading, Foucault provides less than Nietzsche in the way of mapping out strategies of affirmation. Weeks argues that Foucault's work enacts only half of the Nietzschean total critique: Foucault's genealogy of subjectivity and truth is ultimately destructive as it fails to offer a positive political project. "In Foucault we find no criterion of evaluation, no eternal return; that is, no sustained discussion of how historical subjects are also constituting agents, no affirmation of an alternative model of subjectivity" (Weeks, 45). Not taking seriously enough Foucault's theories of power and friendship, Weeks overlooks the Foucault beyond Nietzsche. With friendship, Foucault does indeed offer a positive political project—the overcoming of "homosexuality"—and in reconceptualizing power, he establishes an ethical framework for a politics of friendship. Moreover, Foucault's analyses of ancient practices of the self, as has been shown, provide him with an alternative model of subjectivity as radical self-constitution: The subject emerges at the interstices of subjection and subjectivation as the result of an immanent modulation of an extra-discursive force simultaneously within and without. A closer look at Foucault's concept of power reveals that he offers much more than Weeks—and Butler—imagine.

Power

In summary, the late Foucault resists the Hegelian conception of the constitutive outside and the productive negation. Being does not progress as a result of the dialectical struggle between self and other, between being and nothingness, but rather through an emanation of difference that is primary and constitutive of the self. The essence of being is force—an unwavering force inseparable from its manifestation. Negation is thus total and creation autonomous. Forces of negation and creation do not mix in a dialectical fashion, and, consequently, the Hegelian moment of resurrection and synthesis is lost. But an absolute negation can engender new forms of being and relation not answerable to that which constituted them. In this ontological schematic, the past *can* be left behind. Although subjects might emerge in the most oppressive and constrictive of contexts, in actively willing one's past, in making the contingent conditions of life a necessity of becoming, they can create anew and become other. Rather than being forever wed to the Law, practices of nondialectical negation are necessary for breaking with the (familial, heteronormative, etc.) ties that bind. "My way of being no longer the same," Foucault writes in "For an Ethic of Discomfort," "is, by definition, the most singular part of what I am" (*Essential, V3: Power* 444).

In understanding the singularity of being as "being no longer the same," Foucault reveals that difference and multiplicity are primary to his ontology. While in Butler's schematic many powerfully resistant, abject "monsters" (e.g., the phallicized dyke, the feminized fag and vice versa) come to be through the exclusionary operations of the heterosexual matrix, the "magic" of the negation that gives life to these creatures is only so much hocus-pocus next to a nondialectical negation that can make even the most securely moored of forms disappear. Because difference is *secondary* in the Hegelian ontology—coming only and always after pure and simple being—the laws of this matrix are never escapable, only resignifiable. Even such seemingly subversive practices as drag, to appropriate one of Butler's favorite examples, cannot break free. For Butler, drag is at best "the allegorization of heterosexuality and its constitutive melancholia" (*Bodies* 237). But what if, in addition to resignifying familial forms and revealing the imitative structure of gender, drag practices also *create* autonomous modes of collectivity and new ways of being in the world? What if drag families, as seen in the film *Paris is Burning*, for example, actually leave behind the heteronormative matrix that constitutes them and come to operate under rules of their own? What if such families are the creative result of the absolute negation of masculinity and femininity, hetero- and homosexualities?[9]

Such questions invite an understanding of Foucault's friendship as queer becoming, as the open-ended and malleable relation invented in the wake of homosexuality. Immanent to queer cultures yet exceeding the identities resulting from the gay liberationist/sexological dialectical struggle, friendship, as a "post-homosexual" practice, requires an ethics of becoming. Weeks finds an ethical framework for feminist practices in Nietzsche's eternal return. Foucault's analysis of ancient practices of self-cultivation likewise offers a model—however outmoded and in need of renovation. These two models are compatible: Nietzsche's subject, whose "self" must be continually affirmed and created anew in the lifelong selection of practices that affirm the ethical will stands in close proximity to Foucault's *parrhesiastes* who emerges at the end of a lifetime of ascetic practices as one who not only speaks but embodies the truth. Nietzsche's model of force also shares a kinship with Foucault's late conception of power. However, in historicizing Nietzsche's concept of the will to power, Foucault devises a politics beyond Nietzsche.

In reconceptualizing power as the extra-discursive plane of force relations (made manifest, of course, through discursive forms), Foucault is able to refigure a previously deterministic theory of subjectivity. The result is an ontology of antagonism in which the self comes into being between and through experiences of subjection and practices of subjectivation—a subject shot through with force relations that fold into an "interiority" of a sort radically different from Hegel's slave. Though Foucault's subject exists always-already within the discursive realm of power/knowledge, the concept of power as extra-discursivity frees his subject from an utterly determined existence.

For Foucault, power is at least two things at once. He distinguishes between "Power" with a capital "P" (constituted, potentially repressive) and "power" with a lower-case "p" (immanent and constituting). Building on Nietzsche's distinction between active and reactive forces, Foucault's distinction likewise offers an evaluative criterion for action—an ethics that implies an ontology that implies a politics. He writes:

> [I]t [lower-case "p" power] is the moving substrate of force relations which, by virtue of their inequality, constantly engender states of power [what he later refers to as "states of domination," capital "P" Power], but the latter are always local and unstable. . . . Power is everywhere; not because it embraces everything, but because it comes from everywhere. And "Power" insofar as it is permanent, repetitious, inert, and self-reproducing, is simply the overall effect that emerges from all these mobilities, the concatenation that

rests on each of them and seeks to arrest their movement.
(*HoS, V1* 93)

The internal differentiation in Foucault's concept of power here involves
a distinction between productive/mobile and self-reproductive/stagnant.
The former refers to power in its productivity, its infinite variation, its
becoming; the latter, power in its sheer repetition of the same, in its
concretization of difference. Metaphorically, Foucault's concept of power
could be understood as static electricity, a force likewise ubiquitous yet
felt only in its effects. The point of resistance, the shock, is the event that
materializes power into the world of things; resistance is thus necessary
to transform the ever-present force into a concrete form. The residue of
this event, the conjunction of power and resistance, is comparable to
a juridico-discursive form of power, which potentially becomes a state
of domination. The difference between these two moments of power is
crucial to any understanding of Foucault's late work: The event finds
power in its productivity, its coming into the world; the residue that
remains is a sedimentation of that event, often only powerful in its ability
to repeat the juridico-discursive order. Putting a material face on this
concept, one could argue that oppressive institutions and even classes
thrive on exploiting the power/productivity that is at work within them.
In and of themselves they are dead: Only in usurping the power of the
exploited do they live and reproduce the conditions of oppression. For
this reason, these concatenations of power are unstable: Although they
seek to arrest the movement of power's productivity, there is always, and
always will be, movement. The key to fighting exploitation, then, lies in the
harnessing of this productive power, in acknowledging and actualizing a
common substance between radically different forms. A site of domination
expropriates, hoards, and privatizes a collective power held in common
between singularities for whom "being is no longer the same." If such power
were organized toward the active becoming of dissimilar singularities, as
opposed to the reproduction of a system of order that makes difference
identical, power would then be valorized in its life-affirming creativity.[10]
And yet, these singularities do not necessarily "possess" such power but
are shot through with asubjective power relations informed by historical
circumstances and conditions. Foucault's concept of extra-discursivity
consequently historicizes Nietzsche's will to power: The substrate of
force relations is not a universalist will but instead is shaped by history.
In *Foucault*, Deleuze designates that which organizes the intentionality
of force relations in a given historical moment the diagram.

The machinic assemblage of power that organizes force relations
in a certain manner—the diagram—shifts over time and both affects

and is affected by historical developments. The diagram is a formless, abstract function immanent in force relations that has an effect on discourse and knowledge. Knowledge, in Deleuze's reading of Foucault, is a relation that occurs between forms that are themselves of radically different natures—words and things, the articulable and the seeable, the discursive and the nondiscursive. Knowledge overlaps with force relations (power) but never quite enters into or onto this plane of relations. Because the ontological ground in this schematic is one of multiplicity and difference, a ground that functions through a proliferation of difference rather than a homogenization, as in Hegel's ontology, the relation between knowledge and power, and also between life-forms, is a relation of difference, a relation of nonrelation between things that are absolutely exterior to each other (Deleuze, *Foucault* 70–73; Foucault, *This is Not a Pipe* 19–31). The distinction between the extra-discursive and the discursive is important as it informs Foucault's conceptualization of subjectivity: To reiterate, Foucault's subject is not utterly determined in its subjection to the (discursive) force of power/knowledge but also has at its disposal the means of undoing and putting to work differently the very force relations that solidify into repressive forms. Foucault's concept of subjectivation reveals an alternative way of organizing a given historical period's force relations, one that would valorize power in its activity, that would offer the opportunity to become other. The political project lies, then, in (a) understanding the diagram in a given era, and henceforth; (b) developing self and communal practices between and among singularities that mobilize the common substance—the capacity for creativity and invention—toward a different diagram. Because diagrams and the moral codes they instantiate shift over time, there is always a potential beyond the present order. A past diagram, in fact, might re-emerge in a different form, in a different era—hence the links Foucault draws between Antiquity and the present, hence his return to Antiquity so as to understand the present. Although similar in some ways, a key difference between these historical moments lies in the diagram itself. In the modern era, the diagram is biopower.

Biopower and Resistance

Foucault begins his historical account of biopower in the seventeenth century when a "power over life" emerges as a tendency alongside an earlier, overtly repressive, penal form of power that disciplined subjects through juridical systems. In contrast to a negative form of freedom predicated on "thou shalt not," which found its logical conclusion in public spectacles of death, biopower encourages an art of living: Thou shalt live a good life as devised by state-informed expert knowledge; thou shalt do what is best for you, which conveniently coincides with what is best for biopolitical administration. The family, medicine, psychiatry, education, and employers cooperate with state apparatuses to ensure a uniform standard of living, to produce subjectivities and forms of life that benefit the authorizing officiates. A docile subject is produced when procedures of totalization combine with techniques of individualization, or, in Foucault's vocabulary, when the anatomo-politics of the body and the biopolitics of the population become two poles in the art of governance. These poles correspond chronologically to different historical moments: the anatomo-politics of the body, "the first to be formed it seems . . . centered on the body as a machine: its disciplining, the optimization of its capabilities, the extortion of its forces," while the biopolitics of the population, "formed somewhat later, focused on the species body, the body imbued with the mechanics of life and serving as the basis of the biological processes" (*HoS, V1* 139). The anatomo-politics of the body and the biopolitics of the population play two roles in the operation of biopower: the former, analytical, concerning the individual; the latter, quantitative, concerning the population. In an essay entitled "The Subject and Power" we learn that biopower derives from a form of power implemented in archaic Christian institutions—what Foucault designates pastoral power.[11] Christian pastoral power promised individuals salvation in the afterworld while anchoring one's earthly life in a community of believers. Its efficacy lay in its ability to govern a population both as individuals and as a mass. Now secularized, techniques of pastoral power function under biopower to ensure a worldly salvation of health, security, sufficient wealth, and citizenship (334–35).

On Foucault's view, sexuality is the central *dispositif* deployed by the modern state and capital to manage life directly, the site at which biopower's individuating and totalizing techniques converge. In the psychiatrization and medicalization of sexuality the individual becomes legible, recordable, disciplined: Sexuality is mobilized as a hermeneutic of desire to reveal the truth of the subject and to fasten it to an identity. At the same time this marker of individuality becomes useful in administering a social totality. Techniques of the state such as the population census, fertility rates, and life-expectancy statistics appeal to this hermeneutic to organize individual subjects into a manageable whole. The discursive link between sexual desire and self-identity (i.e., "sexuality") is thus implemented as a means of social control, deterring movements of collective revolt and imprisoning bodies and pleasures. Because sexuality has been transformed from an object of knowledge into a cumulative effect of power, sex practices and the resulting relations are harnessed so that the state may have purchase in bodily practices that might operate outside the sociopolitical frameworks of biopower. Such control, however formidable, is not total; because Foucault conceives power and subjectivity in an immanentist fashion, he is able to note: "It is not that life has been totally integrated into techniques that govern and administer it; it constantly escapes them" (*HoS, V1* 143).

So, what then is to come of these lives that escape? What exactly do they do in their flight? Because ontology so pervades political strategy, Foucault and Butler answer these questions quite differently. That is to say, the subjects that emerge in Foucault's and Butler's work practice different politics of resistance. So much so that perhaps "resistance" is not an adequate designator of what Foucault's subjects "do." If, as the *OED* defines it, resistance is "a force that tends to oppose or retard motion" (*New Shorter Oxford* 2562), then this signifier surely does not belong to Foucault's subject whose "opposition" lies in practices of leaving behind and creating anew, of turning away and becoming other. If resistance is opposition only in the dialectical sense, Foucault's politics are not properly resistant. If resistance requires the arrest of subjectivation and the formation of an immovable identity, Foucault's subject is not resistant. For if resistance occurs only after interpellation—even when this hailing is resignified into a self-empowering marker of identity—then such resistance begins only after the being of becoming freezes. In their understanding of resistance, then, Butler and Foucault come to a crossroads and part ways.

Foucault, however, does not neglect actual states of domination and the anti-authority struggles that oppose them. In "The Subject and Power," for example, he delineates the commonalities between diverse forms of opposition (". . . of men over women, of parents over children, of psychiatry over the mentally ill, of medicine over the population, of administration over the ways people live" [*Essential, V3: Power* 329]) and concludes that these struggles do not oppose power itself but the power effects of a biopolitical order. Again, the distinction between capital "P" juridico-discursive Power and lower-case 'p' power as productivity allows Foucault to distinguish states of domination from force relations. Articulating such a distinction, he writes in "The Ethics of the Concern for the Self as a Practice of Freedom":

> The analyses I am trying to make bear essentially on relations of power. By this I mean something different from states of domination. . . . The analysis of power relations is an extremely complex area; one sometimes encounters what may be called situations or states of domination in which the power relations,

> instead of being mobile, allowing the various participants to adopt strategies modifying them, remain blocked, frozen. . . . In such a state, it is certain that practices of freedom do not exist or exist only unilaterally or are extremely constrained and limited. (*Essential, V1: Ethics* 283)

In disengaging juridico-discursive power from the realm of force relations, Foucault bestows upon his subject mobility: the chance to engage in creative "practices of freedom" outside of states of domination and beyond resistance. Butler collapses the distinction between the two modalities of power and argues that juridico-discursive power subsumes force relations: "There is no power that acts, but only a reiterated acting that is power in its persistence and instability" (*Bodies* 9). But for Foucault, there *is* a power that acts, an outside to discourse that is not a constitutive outside but an absolute exteriority. What Butler understands as power is actually the repetition of particular power effects, of a certain configuration of power relations stabilizing itself. Because of this, she remains in the realm of the discursive, bound to the signifier, and her strategies of resistance against the heterosexual matrix are always and only resignifications.

Reading Foucault from the vantage point of the discursive—disregarding any account of extra-discursivity—Butler critiques Foucault for failing to offer more tangible forms of resistance. In *The Psychic Life of Power*, she writes:

> [I]n Foucault the possibility of subversion or resistance appears (a) in the course of a subjectivation that exceeds the normalizing aims by which it is mobilized, for example, in "reverse discourse," or (b) through convergence with other discursive regimes, whereby inadvertently produced discursive complexity undermines the teleological aims of normalization. Thus resistance appears as the effect of power, as part of power, its self-subversion. (92–93)

Here, Butler seems to be perceiving only half the picture. Although power might only be seen or felt in its effects, there is more to power in Foucault's account than Butler suggests. In collapsing two concepts of power into one, Butler offers a resistance that will be subsumed by the power effects it opposes. At best this resistance holds the promise of a futural salvation. In searching for a subject perhaps beyond resistance, however, Foucault introduces us to a friend whose self and social practices foster new communal forms, and, indeed, a new politics.

A New Politics

So, what's wrong with reading Foucault as a dialectician? Why revisit and critique work fifteen-plus years old by seminal queer theorists? For starters, given their importance to the history and development of American queer theory, Butler and Halperin's ideas simply deserve another look. Moreover, I find it necessary for the further development of queer theory to reveal how their understanding of Foucault as a Hegelian-dialectical thinker at best distorts his political vision and at worst neutralizes his philosophical and political radicality. In this section I take a look at David Halperin's *Saint Foucault* to tease out what he has in mind when speaking of Foucaultian queer political strategy and to offer an alternative interpretation.

In his preface to the French edition of *Saint Foucault*, written five years after the book's original publication, David Halperin points to ACT UP meetings to exemplify what he understands as the "new politics" inspired by Foucault's vision. He writes:

> *Foucault lui-même était queer avant la lettre, à la fois par sa sympathie qu'il avait éprouvée envers les fous, les malades, les délinquants et les pervers, et par sa compréhension nietzschéenne de l'homosexualité comme vecteur de transmutation de valeurs sociales. Et c'est pour cette raison que tant d'intellectuels de la gauche traditionelle n'ont cessé d'accuser Foucault de rendre la politique impossible. C'est précisément ce que Foucault voulait faire: rendre impossible la politique pour rendre possible une nouvelle politique, une politique jusque-là impensable et qui engloberait ceux dont l'exclusion avait fondé la définition de la politique sur laquelle vivait la gauche traditionelle. Ce modèle foucauldien de la politique se trouvait mis en ouvre dans chaque réunion d'ACT UP à laquelle j'ai assisté, où ceux que étaient normalement les objets du discours de l'expertise, à savoir les homosexuel(le)s, les séropos et les malades du sida, renversaient le dispositif du pouvoir/savoir et se donnaient les moyens de résister avec l'autorité aux discours autorisé des médecins et des responsables politiques. (15–16)*

[Foucault himself was queer *avant la lettre*, both for the sympathy he had shown toward the insane, the sick, delinquents and perverts, and for his Nietzschean understanding of homosexuality as a means to the transvaluation of social values. It is for this reason that so many intellectuals of the traditional left have not ceased to accuse Foucault of rendering politics impossible. And this is precisely what Foucault set out to do: to render impossible politics as we know it in order to make possible a new politics heretofore unthinkable, one that would encompass those whose exclusion forms the definition of politics upon which the traditional left rests. This Foucaultian political model could be seen in action at each ACT UP meeting that I attended, where those who were normally objects of expert's discourse—the homosexuals, the seropositive, PWAs— reversed the power knowledge *dispositif* and gave themselves the means to powerfully resist the authorized discourses of doctors and politicians. (translation mine)]

I quote this somewhat obscure passage from Halperin's book for three reasons:

1. It encapsulates a key argument from *Saint Foucault* concerning the importance of Foucault's work for ACT UP and queer activism in general;

2. It allows us to continue our discussion of "resistance"—that overused yet undertheorized buzzword of Foucaultian-based queer theory in the 1990s; and

3. It offers, however fleetingly, a glimpse of what Halperin understands to be Foucault's "new politics."

Halperin begins his study of Foucault with the assertion that even though *The History of Sexuality, Volume One* offered no particular agenda for queer politics, it had a profound influence on its political strategies. Instead of sermonizing, Foucault analyzed closely a problematization: how sexuality became a problem of truth, how sexuality developed into a hermeneutic through which we discover ourselves. This historicization of sexuality coupled with a retheorization of power illuminated for activists possible ways to maneuver within a seemingly stalemated political situation. According to Halperin, ACT UP used Foucault's analysis of the deployment of sexuality to combat heteronormativity and AIDS phobia in its various discursive manifestations: the medical/scientific front, the criminological/juridical front, the mass-mediated representational/informational front, and the religious/moral front.

Although Halperin's rendering of ACT UP's history might unduly and exaggeratedly canonize Foucault the organization's patron saint, his insistence on linking Foucault's work with ACT UP strategy is itself politically strategic: if *Saint Foucault* is anything it is an exercise in positive political myth-making.[12] Pitched at a skeptical American Left as well as the first generation of undergraduate queer theorists, *Saint Foucault* is at pains to make Foucault's work accessible and to prove its political efficacy. Halperin nominates *The History of Sexuality, Volume One* the bible of AIDS activism and resistant queer practices in order to persuade nonbelievers and to encourage frustrated Foucault readers. The notion that one book, a heady and difficult one at that, is "the single most important intellectual source of political inspiration for contemporary AIDS activists" (15) certainly simplifies a complex history of conscious and unconscious intentions, motivations, and reactive formations. Culled from an "admittedly unsystematic survey" of ACT UP members whom the author "happened to know," the claim is consistent with Halperin's investment in nominating Foucault as the "founding spirit of a new militant form of popular resistance" (16). The results of Halperin's survey are used effectively, however, as a rhetorical gambit: on the one hand to prove wrong those "traditional leftists" (whom he defines as humanists, Hegelian Marxists, those resistant to continental philosophy, and those who have not been to a demonstration in twenty years [*Edition française*, 12-13]); on the other, to inspire a younger generation of queer activists and academics to revisit both the work of Foucault and the innovative activism of ACT UP. If it takes a little mystification to bridge the gap between present and future queer academics and activists and to prove that Foucault's work is politically efficacious beyond the redoubts of the academy, so be it.

It is not, then, Halperin's mythical Foucault with whom I am taking umbrage. Rather, it is his political Foucault, his presentation of Foucault as visionary of a "new politics." Although this move is consistent with a rhetoric of myth-making, it requires a bit of summarization and oversimplification in order to maintain its urgency and accessibility. Halperin is cognizant of this fact and addresses the problem of reductivism in his introduction to the American edition. He writes:

> I am well aware that my treatment of his [Foucault's] thought is often crude, reductive, overly general, abstracted from its contexts, and signally lacking in the subtlety which Foucault himself never ceased to display. I am also aware that by concentrating on Foucault's importance to lesbian/gay culture, I shall seem to be trivializing his work or, at the very least, to be privileging a single aspect of his intellectual contribution at the expense of what many may be pleased to consider its "general significance," "wider relevance," or "broader appeal." But my

> intention is not to present Foucault's overall achievement or
> to account for his attractiveness to non-gay people. (14)

Reductivism for the sake of legibility and myth-making is forgivable to a
point: When it begins to distort that which it is simplifying, which I believe
Halperin's rendering of Foucaultian resistance indeed does, it becomes
misleading. Judging from the very positive references I have already made
to *Saint Foucault* (e.g., my reliance earlier on Halperin's definition of the
concept of self involved in ancient ascetics), my critique of the book is
born of my intimacy with it—to paraphrase one cliché or another, we
only hurt the ones we love. That said, such love gives way to a tripartite
critique, concerning: (a) Halperin's quite un-Foucaultian tone; (b) the
author's overemphasis on reversal as Foucaultian political strategy, and
(c) above all, Halperin's, like Butler's, reliance on Hegelian dialectics to
explicate Foucault's theories of power, subjectivity, and resistance. These
aspects of *Saint Foucault* ultimately serve to make palatable Foucault's
work for the critics against whom Halperin is writing. In glossing the
unsavory, immanentist implications of Foucault's work, however, Halperin
blunts the radical edge of Foucault's political vision.

Tone

The tone through which Halperin makes his claims is above all defensive. In
the passage quoted earlier, for example, Halperin renders reductivism moot
by preempting the critique with an admission of his own shortcomings.
Proving to the "nonbelievers" Foucault's political efficacy begins as an
exercise in confessional storytelling. Halperin reveals that his defense of
Foucault is a product of the disqualification he experienced as a queer
scholar. In an impassioned and sometimes hilarious account of how he
came to "worship" Foucault, he narrates two life tales concerning the
double-bind of partisanship and discredit he encountered as an out gay
intellectual. About the first experience, an episode of profound writer's
block while attempting to critique James Miller's *The Passion of Michel
Foucault*, he writes:

> The problem for me was this: Could I specify what I found
> politically odious about Miller's personalizing strategy
> without at the same time convicting myself of narrow-minded
> partisanship in the eyes of *Salmagundi*'s readership? Would
> not the overall effect of my political defense of Foucault and
> my political critique of Miller be to discredit myself through a

kind of guilty association with the former and an insufficient generosity toward the latter? (10)

Halperin's second tale likewise deals with the issue of "the permanent crisis of authority faced by an intellectual in our society who is also gay" (10), this time concerning a vicious gay-baiting episode at his former place of employment. Both these biographical vignettes make clear the deeply ingrained homophobia at the heart of even the more liberal-minded institutions in the United States. Both reveal the obstacles facing gay-identified academics, whose very *raison d'être*—their thoughts and words—risks instant disqualification in a heteronormative discursive game of authorization and accreditation. And yet, Halperin never quite leaves the realm of interpellation that this game requires: *Saint Foucault* seems the product of negation—a negation of previous negations of Foucault's work, a negation of experienced gay-baiting—that traffics in counterattacks and confessions. The "personalizing strategy" for which Halperin critiques Miller is turned inward: Instead of psychoanalyzing Foucault as Miller does, Halperin lays bare his soul and reveals that *Saint Foucault* is the result of a classic reactive formation. In short, contrary to Foucault's own investment in an anticonfessional discourse, Halperin's book begins with a guilty declaration that colors the entire project.

Reversal

Although there is indeed something charming about Halperin's opening storytelling gambit, why would a thinker so enamored with Foucault place himself "on the couch" and perform the role of confessor? In so doing, Halperin situates the reader in a priestly position, leaving us either to absolve his sins of reductivism and defensiveness, or to refuse to read further until he repents. That is to say, Halperin's confessional storytelling resets the very epistemological trap of out-politics that the author so skillfully critiques in ensuing pages. In "coming out" as a guiltily reductive yet worshipful Foucaultian, he perhaps unconsciously re-enacts the naiveté he critiques himself for having had when coming out as a gay man:

> The point of coming out, I had thought, was precisely to deprive other people of their privileged knowingness about me and my sexuality; . . . a means of claiming back from them a certain interpretive authority over the meaning of my words and actions. As I discovered to my cost, however, it turns out that

if you are known to be lesbian or gay your very openness, far
from preempting malicious gossip about your sexuality, simply
exposes you to the possibility that, no matter what you actually
do, people can say absolutely whatever they like about you
in the well-grounded confidence that it will be credited. (13)

For a thinker so savvy about Foucault's work on the confession and so
critical of the double binds enacted by coming-out scripts, Halperin
nonetheless supplicates himself to the "privileged knowingness" of others.
In his attempt to reclaim an "interpretive authority" over Foucault's
posthumous critical demonization, he seems to lose sight of whose game
he is playing. Put another way, Halperin's apology for Foucault does not
move beyond the discursive parameters of the very negative critique that
spawned it.

Foucault himself strategically avoided this trap in his late interviews.
In, for example, "Sex, Power, and the Politics of Identity" and "Sexual
Choice, Sexual Act,"[13] he refuses to be interpellated by his critics and
opts instead to revise and re-elucidate points from his books. Although
he gives credence to complaints and misreadings, Foucault is hardly
apologetic: He responds to critique by building on and expanding previous
ideas. This mode of response is important as it exemplifies aspects of
Foucault's philosophical standpoint and political engagement which I
believe Halperin overlooks. Rather than remaining locked within the
discursive rules of Socratic dialogue, Foucault strategically disengages from
dialectical exchange and steers the conversation toward new developments,
new thought. One can see in these late interviews the outline of a larger
political project beyond "reverse discourse," beyond dialectics—a strategy
that couples exodus with invention, defection with creation. Halperin,
however, heavily relies on a strategy of discursive reversal both in his
attempt to reclaim Foucault for queer politics and in his elaboration of
Foucault's concept of resistance.

Although Halperin claims the book will not "account for Foucault's
attractiveness to non-gay people" (14), it is ironic that he devotes a great
amount of energy to legitimating Foucault in the eyes of the presumably
heterosexual left. Unwilling to disengage from Foucault's critics, he implies
that these "non-gay-identified" detractors misunderstand Foucault's
politics seemingly because of their sexual preference. For example, in the
first essay, "The Queer Politics of Michel Foucault," Halperin explores why
Foucault's concept of power rattled and confused the intelligentsia of the
American Left. He argues that a misinterpretation arose from Foucault's
"*reversal* of the standard liberal critique of totalitarianism," and that these
critics were reacting to Foucault's claim that liberal power "normalizes,

'responsibilizes,' and disciplines" (*Saint Foucault* 18). But might Foucault's claim that "power is everywhere" hit a more painful nerve for leftist critics? Isn't Foucault's reconceptualization of power encapsulated in this catchphrase much more radical than a reversal of terms, having more to do with *ontological* reconceptualization than mere inversion?

Halperin amplifies his remarks on Foucaultian power with more summarizations that raise yet ultimately skirt the issue of the ontological radicality of Foucault's concept: "Power is thus a dynamic situation, whether personal, social, or institutional: it is not a quantum of force, but a strategic, unstable relation. . . . Freedom is a potentiality internal to power, even an effect of power" (17). He notes the scandal—"especially, it would seem, to non-gay-identified academic left-wing men" (21)—caused by such ideas, and yet fails to engage substantively those critics who resist and critique Foucault on ontological grounds. Edward Said's savvy reference to Foucault's power as a "Spinozist conception"[14] and Peter Dews's Habermasian reading of the concept as a "ubiquitous, metaphysical principle" that cannot "provide a substitute for the normative foundations of political critique,"[15] are counterposed against Halperin's claim that Foucault's redefinition of power aided and abetted political activism. Said's and Dews' inquiries into ontological aspects of Foucault's concept become Halperin's rhetorical straw men: They misunderstand Foucault—because of their encrypted, engrained, and essential heterosexuality?—and claim that his theory of power results in nothing but political impotency. Halperin moves in for the kill. The queers on the front lines, unlike the heterosexual intellectuals in their ivory towers, *really got* Foucault: "[I]f 'political quietism' actually was the covert message of Foucault's inquiries into the nature of power, as Said implies, that message was certainly lost on the AIDS Coalition to Unleash Power, or ACT UP" (22). Halperin thus makes good on his earlier claims concerning the connections between Foucault's new politics and ACT UP strategy, and details thereafter the myriad ways Foucault's ideas were implemented in AIDS activism.

Dialectics

Although in some ways I appreciate Halperin's rendering of Foucault's concept of power in terms of "It's a gay thing, you wouldn't understand," his reluctance to engage Foucault's critics coupled with his failure to offer his own more profound investigation into this concept is disappointing.[16] Instead of taking Said's and Dews's claims seriously and interrogating why, perhaps, a "Spinozist" conception of power is seemingly so threatening to Hegelian dialectical thinkers—to the point where Said not only has to disavow Foucault's immanentist leanings, but also all adherents to a nondialectical philosophical tradition who "wish to go beyond Left optimism and Right pessimism so as to justify political quietism with sophisticated intellectualism"[17]—Halperin resorts to name-calling: "non-gay," above all. Had he explored how an immanentist conception of power as productivity undercuts the bedrock of most New Left formulations of resistance indebted to dialectical Marxist and/or psychoanalytic traditions, perhaps the true radicality of Foucaultian politics would rear its head. Instead, we see another instance of discursive reversal exemplified in a vengeful game of "hetero-baiting." In repeatedly designating Foucault's detractors as "non-gay" (yet another example, "Foucault has often been attacked for his politics by non-gay-identified liberal critics" [14]) Halperin seems to be inversely re-enacting the personal "gay-baiting" he himself experienced.

The *ressentiment* that suffuses such a gesture is anything but subtle. And although such a form of revenge is satisfying in a reactive sense, does Halperin move beyond it? Does he display an understanding of Foucaultian resistance as activity and creativity? Yes and no. Following Foucault, Halperin spends a good amount of space revealing the political and epistemological pitfalls of liberationist politics. After nicely summarizing the Freudo-Marxist (Marcusian) theory of sexual repression/liberation (i.e., modern society represses spontaneous drives and thus true sexual liberation can only come to be through the overthrow of capitalism), Halperin comments on Foucault's intervention in this debate concerning the deployment of sexuality, as follows:

> On Foucault's view, the modern political movements for sexual liberation have been complicitous with—indeed they have been a part of—the modern regime of sexuality; the sexual revolution has merely strengthened the political powers it has purported to overthrow. . . . To paraphrase the Sex Pistols [*sic*], the modern regime of sexuality takes away our freedom in the name of liberty—or, to be more precise, it takes away our freedom by imposing on us its own brand of liberty, by requiring us to be "free" according to its own definitions of freedom, and by constructing freedom as a "privilege" that we must, on pain of forfeiting it, use responsibly and never abuse.[18] (20)

The effect of sexual liberation is that it has *required* us to speak of our sexuality, consequently enslaving us to the discursive construction of our "truth," imprisoning bodies and pleasures, and tying us ever more tightly to the normative "monarchy" of sexuality so necessary to biopolitical administration. Gay liberation discourses participate in the regulation of sex in constructing freedom as a normative ideal of responsible and self-respecting human conduct. Oppositional politics, according to Halperin, thus begins with resistance to regimes of the normal, in embodying and embracing a marginal positionality. In his explanation of such queer resistance, however, Halperin relies heavily on Derrida's—not Foucault's—methodology. His definition of queer identity, for example, reads like a textbook example of deconstruction:

> To shift the position of "the homosexual" from that of object to subject is therefore to make available to lesbians and gay men a new kind of sexual identity, one characterized by its lack of a clear definitional content. The homosexual subject can now claim an identity without an essence. To do so is to reverse the logic of the supplement and to make use of the vacancy left by the evacuation of the contradictory and incoherent definitional content of "the homosexual" in order to take up instead a position that is (and has always been) defined wholly relationally, by its distance to and difference from the normative. (61)

Emphasizing reversal, contradiction, and ultimately supersession, Halperin understands queer identity as the result of a dialectical *frisson*. As I have been arguing, Foucault's theory of subjectivity simply does not work like this—he learned from the Ancients otherwise. The self as a relation of reflexivity—between subjection and subjectivation, between sociohistorical determinants and virtual becomings—is not clearly a product, for Foucault, of constitutive outsides, sublations, and magical negations. Regarding his relationship to the Hegelian tradition, Foucault is ambivalent at best; as I pointed out in the previous section, he devoted the last part of his life to unearthing ancient theories of subjectivity that do not conform to a dialectical ontology. Although Halperin does an admirable job of discussing many aspects of Foucault's work (e.g., the ruse of gay liberation, the deployment of sexuality), he seems to overlook the immanentist implications of the theory of subjectivity that Foucault derives from his analyses of ancient ascetics. In positing his Foucault-inspired queer identity, Halperin adopts the language and methodology of a dialectician. The theory of resistance that follows this formulation is similarly indebted to an understanding of Foucault himself as a dialectician.

　　Once again, Halperin's preface to the French edition is helpful in understanding his concept of queer resistance. He reiterates that, in hindsight, he wrote *Saint Foucault* against American intellectuals of the "traditional left" who, although anti-Reaganist, were reluctant to embrace "the new politics of gender, of race, of ethnicity, of sexuality, and of subjectivity" (*Edition française* 13), inspired by the anti-humanism of French thinkers such as Lacan, Foucault, Barthes, and Derrida.[19] He emphasizes in the passage quoted at the outset that Foucault's "new politics," though unthinkable now, will come to be when politics as we know it is rendered obsolete. Halperin not only displays here an understanding of Nietzsche's double movement of radical destruction and absolute creation, but also its influence on Foucault's ideas concerning history and same-sex political-discursive formations. Coupled with his reference to Foucault's "Nietzschean comprehension of homosexuality," Halperin seems to be leading us in this passage toward an exciting and enlightening explanation of Foucault's vision of a future queer politics. Disappointingly, however, he conflates "unthinkable" politics with actual ACT UP strategy sessions: "This Foucaultian political model could be seen in action at each ACT UP meeting that I attended, where those who were normally objects of expert's discourse—the homosexuals, the seropositive, PWAs—reversed the power-knowledge *dispositif* and gave themselves the means to resist powerfully the authorized discourses of doctors and politicians." ACT UP is thus exemplary of reverse discourse: objects turned subjects who not only challenge their institutional oppressors but also American leftist politics itself, in the sense that the exclusions of ACT UP members "forms the definition of politics upon which the traditional left rests." But isn't this account of ACT UP wholly compatible with such a politics? Is ACT UP's acceptance by the left contingent upon rendering their politics identical to the New Social Movements of the 1960s and 1970s?

At pains to fortify the link between ACT UP and Foucault, at pains to legitimate ACT UP and Foucault in the eyes of their respective detractors, Halperin appeals to the traditional leftists against whom he is writing by making both Foucault and ACT UP "resistant" according to "traditional leftist" standards. Halperin's "will to oppose" becomes a will to please and ultimately enmeshes him more deeply into his adversary's discursive web. Foucault, also writing in response to the traditional left in *The History of Sexuality Volume One*, was arguably more successful in escaping this sort of entrapment in acknowledging yet ultimately leaving behind dialectical notions of power as repression/liberation. Had Halperin heeded Foucault's gesture of turning his back on previous leftist understandings of resistance as dialectical struggle—as opposed to taking the time to prove to "his primary target" (*Edition française* 13) that Foucault in word and ACT UP in deed embodied such a form of resistance—we might have seen a more complex explication of Foucault's political vision. As is, Foucault's "new politics" is rendered with all the earmarks of dialectical magic (productive negations, constituent exclusions), and seems, once again, more Derridean than Foucaultian, more Hegelian than Nietzschean. Halperin's own "reverse discourse" against Foucault's critics, his over-emphasis on the power of inversion, and his insistence on oppositional resistance add up to a Foucault that is all too familiar to a "traditional left" schooled in dialectical materialism and Freudian psychoanalysis.

A New Economy of Power Relations

So, beyond dialectical reversal, what does Foucault's "new politics" entail? An adequate answer to this question requires a more thorough investigation into a concept that has been in recent years so thoroughly investigated, appropriated, and transformed that it bears little resemblance to its original self. This concept, of course, is biopower. In this final section I take a look at Foucault's "The Subject and Power," an essay written and first published in English in 1982—significantly, three years after his "Birth of Biopolitics" seminar at the *Collège de France*—in order to locate the key features of biopower and to outline Foucault's strategy for undoing it. Unlike the more nuanced biopolitics seminar, which essentially traces the origins and Western adoption of neoliberal economic theory, "The Subject and Power" reads almost as an American primer in Foucaultian power studies (with section titles including "Why Study Power?"; "How is Power Exercised?"; "How is One to Analyze the Power Relationship?," etc.). Moreover, perhaps because it was written in his second tongue, the essay offers an unusually straightforward and direct summary of his theories of power. Even after the revelatory publication of the biopolitics seminar, then, I find it worth revisiting this essay because it reads as Foucault's final word not only on the subject *and* power but on the subject *of* power. Moreover, it is in this essay, I argue, that Foucault reveals the basic characteristics of biopower through an analysis of the commonalities uniting movements struggling against it. In so doing, he traces the rise of a global multitude seeking forms of life incommensurate with biopolitical standards. In contrast to more recent accounts of this same history (specifically, as discussed in the next chapter, the work of Michael Hardt and Antonio Negri), Foucault in "The Subject and Power" locates the origins of what we now call the *altermondialistes* in the biopolitical struggles against sexuality.

At the outset of the essay, Foucault argues against analyzing power in its internal rationality, favoring instead a study of political movements that resist certain forms of power. An analysis of "power relations through the antagonism of strategies" (329) via an investigation of specific power struggles shifts the focus from a totalizing theory of political power to an understanding of "power rationalities," or, the logic behind specific manifestations of power. To readers of Foucault, an emphasis on positionality and locality is nothing new—examples from his earlier work include studies of madness that seek to historicize sanity and analyses of criminality conducted to understand legality.[20] In this essay, however, Foucault's task is to locate the commonalities between disparate political movements fighting what at first glance seem very different forms of power. In his quest for such a common ground, Foucault, as I have suggested, paves the way for what Hardt and Negri later designate a politics of the multitude. But who is Foucault's "multitude" and what exactly is it up against?

Foucault lists six shared qualities of anti-authority struggles that have developed "over the last few years," specifically, "opposition to the power of men over women, of parents over children, of psychiatry over the mentally ill, of medicine over the population, of administration over the ways people live" (329). It is worth pondering here Foucault's choice of struggles and the order in which he presents them. The first two resist what Foucault, in *The History of Sexuality, Volume One*, designates two key nexuses of power/knowledge useful for disciplining sexuality beginning in the eighteenth century: the hysterization of women's bodies and the pedagogization of children's sex (103–104). Although in "The Subject and Power" Foucault discusses social movements of his time (here, we can surmise, second-wave feminism and, generally speaking, anti-child abuse), it is remarkable that he begins his survey of the contemporary political landscape by highlighting the very same struggles that opposed two centuries-old power/knowledge strangleholds that played a part in molding a new form of rule. Why is this remarkable? Six years after the publication of his seminal *History*, three years after a seminar on the birth of biopolitics, Foucault continues to locate the origins of biopower in the invention and policing of sexual identity. If the rise of biopower and the invention of sexuality are, in fact, coincident, inextricable, then attempts to move beyond this administration of life must involve in some form or another the overcoming of sexuality itself. Although at first glance, Foucault's decision to exemplify recent social movements with women's and children's rights seems somewhat bizarre (especially the latter—why not, instead, the more "popular" civil rights struggles or, closer to home, gay liberation?), read in the context of his earlier work concerning the origins of biopower this decision seems strategic. He is calling our attention here to key components of biopolitical production and the common points of interest between movements that resist the administration of life: first and foremost, sexual identity. The list then moves centrifugally from identity politics (women's rights, children's rights) to health care (mental and physical) to what can be designated a global politics of the *altermondialistes* (resistance to "administration over the ways people live"). Foucault's sequencing, too, is remarkable: The development from identity politics to a more generalized, globalized politics of social justice—that is to say, a struggle over the practices and care of the self—is emblematic of Foucault's political vision. Just as his politics of friendship begins with—only to eradicate—the "homosexual," so this "multitude" overcomes disparate identities in the recognition of a common project that maintains and valorizes internal differences and seemingly incompatible forms of life.

Having established that Foucault's anti-authority struggles are united in their resistance to biopolitical administration, their shared traits reveal the key features of biopower as such. Foucault notes that these struggles are "transversal," transnational, "not confined to a particular political or economic form of government" (329–30). They target power effects, as opposed to particular political or economic forms, and are "immediate" in the sense that they "criticize instances of power that are closest to them, those which exercise their action on individuals" (330). From within a revolutionary program or from the vantage point of political theory, the struggles appear anarchistic—neither tied to a hidebound rationale, a totalizing theory of action, nor awaiting futural solutions or resolutions. They are "struggles against the 'government of individualization,' " which is not to say that they are necessarily for or against individualism, but that they "question the status of the individual" (330). The stakes of this predicament concern a dialectic of conformity and alienation. On the one hand, these struggles assert the right to individual difference: They withstand total identification with a community, with a demographic, with specific sociopsychological determinants; on the other, they simultaneously resist the separation of the individual from the community and oppose forces that break social ties and that alienate the individual in her or his own difference. Although Foucault is claiming here to describe simply what he sees around him, this particular feature of his movements gives pause. Is Foucault not merely describing the forms of contemporary political struggle but surreptitiously positing a new theory of community? Is he transposing the terms of, say, his friendship with Guibert—what I have been calling a relation of impersonal intimacy and shared estrangement—onto larger community forms? Is this type of community, this type of politics, even possible? The final two characteristics move us closer to an answer.

Next, Foucault points out that these struggles are in opposition to "the way in which knowledge circulates and functions, its relations to power. In short, the regime of knowledge" (331). As mentioned earlier, Foucault begins his list with two struggles that oppose two particular nexuses of power/knowledge concerning sexuality that gave biopower its nascent forms. All of these movements, then, are critical of the collusion of expert knowledges and state administration and question the institution of state-sanctioned knowledges in the social management of life. Finally, referencing Kant's "What is Enlightenment?," Foucault argues that these struggles begin with and turn on Kant's primary question in that essay: Who are we? In a fight for self-definition, these groups refuse the abstractions "of economic and ideological state violence" that ignore individual difference and defy the findings of scientific and governmental knowledges that dictate to constituents who or what they are (331).

If my hypothesis holds—that we can learn the key features of biopower by understanding the commonalities that Foucault argues unite the movements that resist it—it follows from Foucault's initial observation that biopower itself is likewise "transversal," not bound by the nation-state, and not exclusive to a particular national, political, or economic form of government. There is thus no center to biopower: It is globally distributed in form and composed, like these struggles, of dispersed networks. Furthermore, biopower's tendency is *globalizing*, or, totalizing in its ability to insinuate itself across not only state institutional sites but the entire social body. "The family, medicine, psychiatry, education, and employers," as Foucault points out, cooperate with state apparatuses to ensure a certain standard of living, to produce subjectivities and forms of life that benefit the officiates of this global power. Procedures of totalization thus combine with techniques of individualization in biopower and resistance to these heretofore strange bedfellows takes place in the realms of subjection (institutionalized forms of power that oppress and exploit individuals) and subjectivation (the struggle to escape the self brought into being via biopolitical production). In Foucault's estimation, the latter struggle, subjectivation, takes a front seat in recent social movements:

> The form of power that applies itself to immediate everyday life categorizes the individual, marks him by his own individuality, attaches him to his own identity, imposes a law of truth on him that he must recognize and others must recognize in him. It is a form of power that makes individuals subjects. . . . And nowadays, the struggle against the forms of subjection— against the submission of subjectivity—is becoming more and more important, even though the struggles against forms of domination and exploitation have not disappeared. (331)

A struggle against "the submission of subjectivity" is a struggle for new forms of being, or, in a word, subjectivation. Sexuality is, of course, according to Foucault, the "law of truth" to which we moderns readily subject ourselves—it is that which ties us to our identity, promises self-revelation, and invites us to entertain notions of futural salvation. Sexuality thus serves as the lynchpin between the individualizing and totalizing techniques of biopower. For Foucault, then, overcoming or turning away from sexuality is paramount to modern practices of subjectivation because toppling the "monarchy of sex" (i.e., delinking sexuality from truth) involves freeing oneself from a biopolitically administered identity. Foucault observes this exodus in sexual subcultures and forms of relation that call into question the truth of sexual identity. Friendship "as a way of life," for example, becomes a practice of freedom that forges a line of flight from the regime of sexuality. As I have been arguing, the friend comes into the spotlight only when sexuality as truth-telling soothsayer leaves the stage. Especially for, although not exclusive to, queer resistance movements, friendship plays a crucial role in subjectivating practices and politics. Foucault's model of friendship—involving critical distance, a deflection of commonality, and a refusal of transcendence—becomes a micro-model for alternative communal and political forms. In the next chapter, I attempt to bring queer theory up to speed with debates regarding biopolitics via a critique of Hardt and Negri's "multitude" and a discussion of the conceptual affinity between Foucault's friendship model and the AIDS buddy system.

Chapter 4

Labors of Love

Biopower, AIDS, and the Buddy System

Since its initial appearance in *The History of Sexuality, Volume One* Foucault's concept of biopower has indeed taken on a *bios* of its own. Ubiquitous in recent academic analyses of the contemporary sociopolitical landscape, the concept and its kin (biopolitics, governmentality) find their most productive—although, as I hope to show, somewhat misguided— articulation in the collaborative work of Michael Hardt and Antonio Negri (*The Labor of Dionysus* and the *Empire* trilogy).[1] Shifting Foucault's focus from population and social management to labor, globalization, and sovereignty, these authors conceive of biopolitics in economic terms, detailing the consequences of the transition from Fordist to post-Fordist labor practices. Significantly, whereas Foucault designates sexuality the principal apparatus in the functioning of biopower, Hardt and Negri argue that sexuality in the post-Fordist era is no longer the privileged site of biopolitical control: when human affect, language, and cooperation are subsumed into the productive processes of capital, the gestures, expressions, and movements—indeed, the very flesh—of the social body become commodities. Their thesis raises a number of pressing questions that bear on the future of sexuality studies: Has sexuality itself been totally subsumed into the productive processes of postmodern capital? Is Foucault's "deployment of sexuality" too blunt an analytical tool to understand biopower in post-Fordism? Indeed, is sexuality any longer a productive category for social analysis at all?

Although such questions are not the primary focus of this chapter (my aim here is far more modest), they take on quite different meanings in the face of AIDS, a subject that receives no serious discussion in Hardt and Negri's work. If, as I argue, AIDS is understood as a primary locus of biopolitical struggle, sexuality simply cannot be ignored or subsumed into a generalized concept of *bios*. Even a cursory glance at the focus and scope of recent HIV-prevention research reveals that the "life" valorized in biopower continues to turn on that most stubborn of discursive constructions, the homosexual–heterosexual binary. A 2006 study by the U.S. National Institutes of Health (NIH) concerning male circumcision as an HIV preventative for men engaging in "heterosexual intercourse," for example, appears more invested in naturalizing the homo–hetero binary than in disseminating accurate and practical HIV-prevention information.[2] Although AIDS education campaigns have attempted for decades to distinguish high-risk behavior from high-risk groups and identity-specific sexual behavior from corporeal acts (not "gay sex," but vaginal, anal, oral sex, etc.), the use of the phrases such as "heterosexual intercourse" in the NIH press release reveals the persistence of heteronormative assumptions and objectives in contemporary AIDS research and funding.

The scientific research that proved definitively that HIV does not discriminate based on sexual orientation, then, ironically serves to perpetuate discrimination against sexual minorities. In the early 1980s, AIDS Service Organizations (ASOs) responded to such discrimination by emphasizing the *human* devastation wrought by AIDS and by delinking HIV from sexual identity. Specifically, the AIDS buddy system strategically shifted the discursive terms of AIDS politics from sexuality to friendship. Guided by an ethics of discomfort, this support network, I argue, sets the stage for a politics of friendship as shared estrangement in later AIDS activism.[3] As a collaborative project that communized caregiving, the buddy system engenders a biopower "from below," providing an alternative to the often prejudiced health care of AIDS-phobic medical institutions and fostering new forms of cooperation between the sick and the healthy, between the gay-identified and straight-identified, between lesbian separatists and gay male liberationists.[4] By situating the buddy system on a larger historical-theoretical grid concerning biopolitics, AIDS, and affective labor, I understand it as a modern project of subjectivation—a defection from the biopolitical administration of life—consistent with a Foucaultian project of toppling "the monarchy of sex."

The Life of Biopower

In Chapter 3, I placed emphasis on the fact that Foucault's (early and late) articulations of biopower stress the centrality of sexuality. In order to resist the biopolitical administration of life, according to Foucault, the link between sex and truth must be broken. In elaborating and ostensibly updating Foucault's concept, however, Michael Hardt and Antonio Negri desexualize it by asserting that biopower no longer employs sexuality as the principal apparatus in the social management of life. Whereas, according to the authors, Foucault limits his analysis to the state's across-the-board use of biopower, Hardt and Negri argue above all in *Empire* that the reach of biopower extends beyond the nation-state, which comes to play second fiddle in the supranational march of capital. They analyze in *Empire* the multiple processes of globalization—the worldwide saturation of capital, the steady "bourgeoisification" of the globe, the withering of the nation-state, the post-imperialist political landscape—and argue that the new sovereign, the new order of the globalized world, is a decentered and deterritorializing apparatus of rule they designate (capital 'E') Empire. Empire is neither a metaphor nor a term by which other historical empires can be characterized. Rather, distinguished by a lack of boundaries and a suspension of history, Empire is an extreme form—or the logical conclusion—of Foucaultian biopower. Although accorded a privileged status in the logic of Empire, neither the United States nor any other single nation-state is the superpower Svengali pulling the strings behind the scenes.[5] Gliding on a smooth, unstriated plane of fluid boundaries and hybrid identities, Empire operates beyond the nation-state, beyond imperialism, unlimited and unbound by any geographical region—a topography at once liberating and daunting for any progressive political project. In a historical moment, "when language and communication, . . . when immaterial labor and cooperation, become the dominant productive force" (*Empire*, 385) a moment in which the material effects of global capitalism are mystified perhaps more than ever due to—not in spite of—the explosion of information technologies, exploitation proliferates in increasingly protean forms. As Hardt and Negri traverse this postmodern terrain of exploitation, they discern an emerging multitude seeking an alternative global society and examine political sites and phenomena in which the immanent workings of biopower are not so much countered as comprehended and redirected toward alternative ends (e.g., demonstrations against immigration policies as a move toward global citizenship; the generality of biopolitical production prompting a demand for a new social wage, etc.). In doing so, the authors affirm and nurture the potentialities of a new constituent power in the form of a multitude.[6]

Conceptually, multitude is Hardt and Negri's attempt to think beyond the limits of political models founded on either identity or difference. These authors locate an organizational form for their multitude in the network, a configuration that emerges at the point of contiguity between identity and difference. As they write in *Multitude*:

> The two dominant models posed a clear choice: either united struggle under the central identity or separate struggles that affirm our differences. The new network model of the

multitude displaces both of these options—or, rather, it does not so much negate the old forms as give them new life in a different form. . . . In conceptual terms, the multitude replaces the contradictory couple identity-difference with the complementary couple commonality-singularity. In practice the multitude provides a model whereby expressions of singularity are not reduced or diminished in our communication and collaboration with others in struggle, with our forming ever greater common habits, practices, conduct, desires—with, in short, the global mobilization and extension of the common. (217–18)

The commonality–singularity dyad cuts a transversal line through the dialectic of identity-difference. The network form, characterized by decentralized leadership and horizontal linkages between autonomous nodes, is most effective in the struggle for (and, conversely, the dismantling of) democracy in a biopolitical world. Resistance movements organized as networks are distributed, open, and thus mimic, or, at times, take advantage of, the dispersed structure of biopower. These struggles come into view on the political horizon in an era when life-forms previously held in common—affect, language, indigenous knowledges; what Marx in the *Grundrisse* designated "the general intellect"[7]—become increasingly privatized and commodified. Although biopower promotes a standard of life and a form of individuality in the service of realizing the capitalist dream of a "global village" of consumers, it likewise brings into being new forms of community, new power structures, and new avenues for creative cooperation. Progressive networks use the tools of biopolitical production to work toward an alternative form of globalization. Counterpoised by the G20 and the World Trade Organization (WTO), the multitude is formed "from below" through communicative networks that collaborate to actualize common goals. The small-scale Creative Commons project (software engineers who exchange ideas over the internet to create the best possible version of a free computer application) as well as the large-scale convergence movement (composed of diverse progressive groups protesting together, most famously in the anti-WTO demonstrations in Seattle, 1999) implement biopolitical strategy (*biopotenza*)[8] to reclaim the common and to resist the inhumane, profit-making imperatives of the market.

The multitude in Hardt and Negri's estimation is thus a thoroughly positive concept: It is the political model through which the dream of democracy—the rule of all by all—can be realized. By contrast, the network form appears in many guises and can be used by organizations with contradictory objectives. Anti-democratic, terrorist organizations, counterinsurgency military operations, and progressive political movements all have adopted the network form to achieve their ends (*Multitude* 54–56). Formally, then, the network is ambivalent and malleable: It can be seen in protest movements that vanish from one part of the globe only to rematerialize in another, as well as in thoroughly local insurgencies that disintegrate after achieving their goals. Because of their nomadic, often swarm-like activity, movements structured as networks often sneak under the radar of traditionally organized political blocs, appearing from the latter's vantage point as monstrous and ill-conceived. Significantly, however, the network is the organizational model the modern state and capital have implemented and mastered in the age of Empire. As used by the multitude in the pursuit of an alternative model of globalization, it is most effective, according to Hardt and Negri, in actualizing absolute democracy.

One such progressive use of the network form, mentioned in brief earlier, emerges in the convergence movement for global justice, as exemplified in the 1999 WTO protests. Here Hardt and Negri find the most palpable manifestation of the multitude—a site in which the political potentialities of an immanentist ontology are realized.[9] Characterized by the coordination of self-governing groups toward common goals, the convergence movement becomes for them the social expression of Spinozan anatomy. If "the human body is composed of many individuals of different natures, each of which is highly composite" (*Multitude* 190), the convergence movement follows the body's lead in respecting difference at an ontological level and allowing its constituent parts to collaborate without sacrificing their autonomy. In doing so, this body grows ever more powerful as singular habits and practices in their repetition become increasingly common.

What's striking, however, both in the demographics of the actual convergence movement and in Hardt and Negri's theoretical assessment of its constitution, is the glaring absence of those who likewise formed a political movement in heeding the call of the body—that is, queers. Although the direct-action tactics and street theatrics of queer vanguard groups such as ACT UP, The Lesbian Avengers, and SexPanic! often are cited as the inspiration for convergence movement political strategy, those groups' founding principle for action—generally speaking, that the discursive construction of sexuality ties into larger issues of social power, privilege and access—falls by the wayside. In the words of convergence movement participant and critic, Liz Highleyman:

> Progressive thinking has evolved with regard to racism and sexism, and most now agree that the issues of people of color and women are integral to the larger project of achieving

> social justice. . . . But when it comes to queers, the issues of
> sexuality and gender are still downplayed. There remains a
> sense among some on the left that issues of sex, sexuality,
> desire, and gender are frivolous, a luxury of the privileged or
> a waste of time. They are seen as private rather than public,
> and are associated with leisure rather then work. ("Radical
> Queers or Queer Radicals?," *From ACT UP* 116)

Even though the much-lauded, creative forms of protest invented by queer
radicals of the 1980s and 1990s are arguably the result of queer sexual
practice and sensibility, as I argue in Chapter 5, sex and sexuality, from
the standpoint of many a convergence movement activist, are identity
issues that belong to a bygone political era. While there is something quite
appealing in understanding the convergence movement as beyond identity
politics, the exclusion of sexuality from its purview smacks of the same
scorn heaped on gender and sex activists in various twentieth-century
Marxist movements (Highleyman, 117–18). Put differently, based on the
experiential and theoretical accounts of queers involved in the convergence
movement, it appears that our multitude has not necessarily toppled the
monarchy of sex (i.e., has not extracted sexuality from a regime of truth),
but instead appears to be repeating past mistakes and reopening old
wounds that have had all too brief a time to heal.

Hence, although much can be gleaned from Hardt and Negri's
analysis, questions remain concerning the status of sexuality in the age of
Empire. In a published conversation between Antonio Negri and Cesare
Casarino entitled "It's a Powerful Life," Casarino raises such questions.
Concerning Foucault's theorization of sexuality in relation to politics, Negri
notes: "[R]ather than disregarding or neglecting Foucault's elaboration
of biopolitics in the context of the deployment of sexuality, I assumed
such an elaboration and expanded it so as to account for the overall
construction of the body in the indistinguishable realms of production and
reproduction, that is, the realm of immaterial labor" (167). Building on a
crucial insight of standpoint feminism (i.e., that labor power reproduces
itself through sexuality) Negri argues that when immaterial labor is the
primary productive force, production and reproduction collapse into one,
and corporeality itself—including but not limited to sexuality—becomes
the link between individualizing and totalizing techniques of biopower. In
a succinct formulation of this crucial shift in production, Sylvère Lotringer
explains in his foreword to Paolo Virno's *A Grammar of the Multitude*:

> In the post-Fordist economy, surplus value is no longer
> extracted from labor materialized in a product, it resides in

the discrepancy between paid and unpaid work—the idle time of the mind that keeps enriching, unacknowledged, the fruits of immaterial labor. . . . Workers used to work in servile conditions, leaving them just enough time to replenish. Now their entire life is live labor, an invisible and indivisible commodity.[10]

By extension, when thoughts, affect, and human cooperation are for sale, when life itself is the chief agent of production, biopower "from above" [*biopotere*], according to Negri, no longer needs to deploy sexuality *qua* sexuality to achieve its ends.

Our multitude theorists, however, can de-emphasize the importance of sexuality for biopower only because the politics of AIDS figures so marginally in their analyses. When it comes to AIDS funding and research, sexuality remains without question a determining factor in the distribution of resources. A 2006 NIH HIV-prevention study, to cite just one minor example, calls attention to the continued relevance of sexuality for biopower.[11] The study, conducted in Kenya and Uganda with 7,780 heterosexually identified, HIV-negative men divided into circumcised and uncircumcised groups, tested the effectiveness of male circumcision in the prevention of HIV transmission from a woman to a man. Its press release concludes that "medically performed circumcision significantly reduces a man's risk of acquiring HIV through heterosexual intercourse." Tellingly, however, "the amount of benefit provided by circumcision is unknown" for men who have sex with men, among whom, at least in the United States, most new HIV infections occur.[12]

The rationale for the study rests squarely on heteronormative assumptions and its findings obscure rather than illuminate the basic facts of HIV transmission. Its focus on "heterosexual intercourse," as opposed to identity-less sexual behavior, for example, is vague to a fault. "Heterosexual" in the study's wording qualifies an act, "intercourse." Although the presumed behavior here is penile–vaginal intercourse, this is in no way clarified or specified. "Heterosexual intercourse" can be taken to mean, willfully or unconsciously, oral, anal, and/or vaginal penetrative sex between men and women—even though these behaviors carry radically different levels of risk and are understood in proper safer-sex education as unique and discrete acts. Such imprecise language is also misleading and dangerous because it grants circumcised heterosexually identified men a permission of sorts to practice less-safe sex—be it anal, oral, or vaginal sex, such heterosexuals apparently are taking fewer risks than homosexually or bisexually identified men (who may in fact be practicing exactly the same, or even less risky, types of sex). Finally, as we learned in the early days of AIDS panic, the use of sexual-identity terminology in HIV prevention has done more to demonize sexual minorities than to prevent the virus's spread. In failing to use more precise language (penile–vaginal intercourse) and the less discriminatory, more scientifically accurate term *risk behavior*, this study, at worst, insinuates that risky *types of people* transmit HIV: Sexually specific "risk groups" become the infectious agents, not the ordinary, average citizens who do risky things when having sex. The effect of this casual slippage is that entire social groups are blamed for the transmission of a virus that cares little about the sexual or national identity of its transmitter. As Jan Zita Grover pointed out almost twenty-five years ago, the medical term *risk group*, when taken out of its epidemiological context, "has been used to stereotype and stigmatize people already seen as outside the moral and economic parameters of 'the general population.' . . . [It is used] to isolate and condemn people rather than to contact and protect them."[13] Although reliable HIV-prevention campaigns discuss high-risk behavior instead of high-risk groups and corporeal acts instead of identity-specific "homo" or "hetero" sex, this study does more to naturalize the homo–hetero binary than to disseminate scientifically sound health information.

Indeed, quite disturbing questions follow from the study's conclusions: Is anal or oral sex between a man and a woman "heterosexual intercourse?" Or, are these activities by default "homosexual intercourse?" Is penetrative vaginal sex—apparently, the sole focus of the study—more important or more prevalent than these other acts? Do these findings intimate that unprotected vaginal sex is now safer sex for circumcised men? What about the women? What is unspoken here speaks volumes. Do the categories "homosexual" and "heterosexual" hold the same meaning in Africa as they do in the United States?[14] Are women in general, or, perhaps even female sexuality itself—historically associated with insatiability and contamination—held symbolically responsible for the spread of sexually transmitted disease? Would such an experiment—in which certain subjects are given a hypothetical advantage over others in protecting themselves from HIV—be conducted in the United States? Bearing in mind the potential harm to the trial's subjects, is an African life less valuable than an American one?

To add insult to injury, in *The New York Times* report on the study risk groups expand exponentially into "risk countries" and "heterosexual intercourse" becomes the vaguer—and even more misleading— "heterosexual sex."[15] The result is a confusing jumble of heteronormative disinformation and Western cultural bias: Unprotected heterosexual sex is 48 percent safer with male circumcision; heterosexual sex is in general safer than homosexual sex, which remains unexplored. Kenya and Uganda are perilous and potentially contagious in their very existence as nations; Africa, by extension, remains—no surprise here—"The Dark Continent," the dangerous, libidinal underbelly of the rational and enlightened West.

It is clear, then, that the rationale of the NIH study and the reportage surrounding it betray a patriarchal, heterosexist, and colonialist bias. Moreover, the conception of sexuality on which this study rests and which it indisputably affirms is precisely the one Foucault understood as crucial to the functioning of biopower. Practicing two completely different types of sex, according to this study, heterosexuals and homosexuals become distinct species. Sexual behavior is assumed to be naturally linked to personal identity and the lives of the social groups associated with these sexual identities—one, heterosexual: comprehensible and worthy of study; the other, homosexual: "unknown" and mysterious—are valued hierarchically and treated unequally. It is thus clear that in the distribution of AIDS treatment and funding, sexuality has *not*, contrary to Negri's claim, been completely assimilated into a generalized concept of "life."

Although in their first collaboration, *The Labor of Dionysus*, Hardt and Negri praise AIDS activists for calling into being a new form of subjectivity "that has not only developed the affective capacities necessary to live with the disease and nurture others, but also incorporated the advanced scientific capacities within its figure" (13), in *Empire* and *Multitude* such praise is by and large directed toward the organizational innovations of contemporary labor movements. The shift of focus raises further questions: What has become of these AIDS-activist subjectivities? Is their work only relevant for its influence on the new, supposedly "post-sexual" multitude? Does the absence of AIDS from these discussions speak to the same historicidal will-to-forget that motivates the ideological relegation of the syndrome to the Third World, the same will that fostered the false sense of security in the West after the discovery of antiretroviral therapy? In *Empire* and *Multitude* AIDS, when it is mentioned, is appropriated as a useful metaphor for the boundlessness of global capital, the fear of HIV's spread becoming the symbolic crystallization of postcolonial anxiety surrounding "the new dangers of global contagion" (*Empire* 136). Such a rendering, to put it mildly, is somewhat cavalier: Lest we forget, from its very inception AIDS was and continues to be a matter of life and death. And the new forms of life invented in AIDS activism still inhabit—and irrevocably alter—the global biopolitical landscape. Especially in regards to AIDS research, then, sexuality remains a vital factor in determining the value of life (and hence the time and money it should be allocated) and thus must be included in any and all discussion of biopolitics. In contradistinction to Hardt and Negri, then, I take seriously Foucault's claim that sexuality is a linchpin between the individualizing and totalizing techniques of biopower and find in early forms of AIDS caregiving strategies for delinking sexuality from truth.

Labors of Love

The elision of AIDS in Hardt and Negri's analysis of the biopolitical turn thus mirrors and perpetuates the silencing of sexuality in twentieth-century labor movements and recent convergence activism. When AIDS is taken seriously as a site of biopolitical struggle, sexuality, as I have been arguing, does not disappear in *bios*. Initially appropriated in the United States as a means of reinforcing a normative "Us vs. Them," namely, homo- versus heterosexual, binary, AIDS only became meaningful through, and ultimately overdetermined by, discourses of sexuality. As the reality of the disease changed (epidemic became pandemic), heteronormative binary oppositions became increasingly difficult and finally impossible to sustain—at least on a conscious, rational level. A rigid, politically charged representation gave way to a variety of countervailing perspectives concerning exactly what AIDS is and how it should be understood. Yet through its ideological demonization ("AIDS is God's punishment to fags") and the opposition to that demonization ("AIDS does not discriminate"), AIDS, as glimpsed in the NIH study, remains servile to King Sexuality. My purpose here is not to offer a close analysis of representations of AIDS nor to detail the intersections between discursive constructions of AIDS and the policing of sexuality—this has already been done so admirably by Simon Watney, Cindy Patton, and Elizabeth Waldby, to name just a few.[16] Rather, my aim is to point out that our multitude theorists can de-emphasize the importance of sexuality only because AIDS figures so marginally in their analysis of biopolitics. Foucault's understanding of sexuality as a tool deployed to encourage a navel-gazing self-discipline that thereby ensures the smooth functioning of *biopotere* becomes meaningful again when considering the specific strategies of ASOs and AIDS activists.

From struggles with multinational pharmaceutical giants to genericize AIDS drugs to the almost visible north–south divide demarcating the top-heavy distribution of both global capital and antiretrovirals, AIDS has become a key locus of biopolitical exploitation, resistance, and creativity. Foucault's observation, analyzed in Chapter 3, that anti-authoritarian struggles in the biopolitical era are struggles "against the submission of subjectivity" and for the valorization of new forms of life becomes relevant here. Like those struggles (women's rights, children's rights, etc.), AIDS activism arguably begins in identity politics and expands centrifugally to a larger project of social justice. Although AIDS has been given many identities by mainstream media—the gay male with Kaposis Sarcoma lesions, the emaciated IV drug user, the poverty-stricken African mother, the Indian prostitute—it exceeds all of them. As the pandemic spreads, social categories blur and ossified boundaries between ethnicities and nationalities become less distinct. And yet in the distribution of treatment and funding, hard geographical, racial, and class lines are drawn. AIDS thus crystallizes the paradoxes of both biopolitical production and global capitalism in the age of Empire: However radically indiscriminate, it continues to be associated with particular social groups, regions, cultural "Others," and minoritarian politics.[17] By calling into question the validity of the identity categories assigned to it, AIDS in turn questions the efficacy of a politics founded on such categories. In early AIDS caregiving and activism, then, I find the seeds of a post-identitarian politics—the overcoming of biopolitically administered identities and the creation of new forms of being in the recognition of a common project. This is to say, in revealing the instability of national, cultural, and ethnic identities, AIDS gives rise to a multitude of its own making.

With AIDS now situated at the heart of biopolitical struggle, Hardt and Negri's discussions concerning the revolutionary potential of affective labor and love become useful. In "Twenty Theses on Marx," Negri begins this discussion by interpreting Marx's conception of living labor as immanent production. Whereas the early, humanistic Marx, according to Negri, understood revolution as a dialectical return—the de-alienation of labor and hence the reunification of the individual with his species-being—the later Marx can be shown to understand it differently. The capitalist system for Marx becomes a mere concretization of the force relations immanent to the social field: It is dead, objectified labor. Living labor, by contrast, is power in its productivity and creativity; in its infinite movement living labor by definition tries to free itself from the constrictive grip of capital. Negri writes:

> Up until now we have excavated in the system of dead labor, of capital, of Power, and we have seen how, wedged into that system, there was a clandestine, subterranean, hidden motor pulsing with life—and with such efficiency! We have, in a manner of speaking, rediscovered the Marxian affirmation of living labor in today's world, when living labor is already completely separated, autonomous and positioned against every naturalistic rigidification of being. (170–71)

With a Spinozan twist, Marx's living labor becomes ontological potentiality. Capitalism flourishes only to the extent to which it can usurp a force that always threatens to overflow its containment and seep through the (metaphorical and literal) factory walls. Hardt and Negri argue that these walls begin to crumble as postmodern capital tends toward immaterial production. In this process of dilapidation, the possibilities of redirecting living labor toward more democratic ends become ever more palpable.

The project in *Empire*, then, is to theorize a historical passage in social forms—from Fordism to post-Fordism, from disciplinary society to control society—to tease out the democratic possibilities of living labor. "[T]he entire first phase of capitalist accumulation (in Europe and elsewhere)," the authors write, "was conducted under this [disciplinary] paradigm of power" (23). Disciplinary power functions through the organization of sites of confinement (the prison, the school, the factory, the asylum) that "produce and regulate customs, habits, and productive practices," that determine normal and deviant behavior, and that enforce obedience through fear of social exclusion (23). In control societies, by contrast, biopower is the rule: They are characterized by fluctuating networks, variable flows, and modulative mechanisms of command. Deleuze, from whom Hardt and Negri borrow this historical schematic, describes the difference between the two societies in his essay "Postscript on Control Societies":

> Money, perhaps, best expresses the difference between the two kinds of society, since discipline was always related to molded currencies, containing gold as a numerical standard, whereas control is based on floating exchange rates, modulations depending on a code setting sample percentages for various currencies. . . . [C]apitalism in its present form is no longer directed toward production . . . it's directed toward meta-production. . . . What it seeks to sell is services, and what it seeks to buy is activities. It's a capitalism no longer directed toward production, but toward products, that is, towards sales or markets. (*Negotiations* 180–81)

This passage hints at a decisive shift in capitalism critical to Hardt and Negri's analysis: the passage from the formal subsumption to the real subsumption of labor. The authors build on Marx's thesis in the *Grundrisse* that abstract knowledge becomes the principal productive force in capitalism's development. This "general intellect"—common knowledges, habits, and affects that for a time were of little interest to production— becomes objectified into fixed capital. Labor in turn is increasingly immaterial and the proletariat as a class becomes dispersed, if not residual (*Grundrisse* 704–707). "What it seeks to sell is services": services of the communication- and information-technological variety (cellular/wireless technologies, news services, etc.); knowledge-based services (computer help-lines, consultants); and problem-solving services (brokering, financial advising, etc.). In the post-Fordist era, in a control society in which the immaterial is increasingly put to work, the production and manipulation of affect is essential. As the life force of living labor, however, affect can likewise be harnessed for anti-capitalist, democratic projects.

Historically, women and queers have been the primary participants in affective labor practices: from childrearing to social work to nursing, affective labor in earlier phases of capitalist production denoted femininity (or effeminacy) and was thereby relegated to the margins. In the shift from disciplinary to control societies and the real subsumption of labor under capital, however, affective labor becomes more generalized and diffuse. Immaterial yet corporeal, affective labor produces not a product but an intangibility: feelings of ease, comfort, love. Hardt and Negri describe it as follows in *Empire*:

> Affective labor is better understood by beginning from what feminist analyses of "women's work" have called "labor in the bodily mode." Caring labor is certainly immersed in the corporeal, the somatic, but the affects it produces are nonetheless immaterial. What affective labor produces are social networks, forms of community, biopower. (293)

Deborah B. Gould, following Brian Massumi, marks a distinction between affect and emotion that helps clarify Hardt and Negri's investment in affective labor.[18] Whereas affect refers to the "nonconscious, and unnamed, but nevertheless registered, experiences of bodily energy and intensity that arise in response to stimuli impinging on the body," emotions are "what [part] of affect—what of the potential of bodily intensities—gets actualized or concretized in the flow of living" (*Moving Politics*, 19–20). Although affects and emotions can occur simultaneously, the former always exceed the latter: emotion is only an approximate representation of affect and is subject to the rules of semiotic systems (language, culture, bodily gesture and expression, etc.—all historically determined). Affect, by contrast, is unrepresentable: In the remainder not captured in social life lies the potential for articulating, gesticulating, and communicating in ways incomprehensible to extant semiotic systems. Moreover, whereas emotions are attributable to a subjective interiority, affects shoot through the subject, unfolding its interiority. No individual or corporation can thus own affects: They are common property, radically social. It is the immanence and ambivalence of affect, then, its nonpredetermination, its unruly, communal nature, that entices Hardt and Negri as they chart capitalism's increasing reliance on affective labor.

Although affective labor in post-Fordism is a primary source of surplus value, it at the same time "provides the potential for a kind of spontaneous and elementary communism" (*Empire*, 294). The cooperative interactivity endemic to affective labor can extend beyond the confines of the workplace. A radical "elementary communism" emerges when communities fostered in such labor practices put their cooperative interactivity to use in a different arena. Like living labor, then, affect exceeds its usefulness for the market. In control societies, capitalism thus becomes, unwittingly or not, communistic: Biopower, which involves the integration and exploitation of affect, creates new forms of association and cooperation that hold the potential to engender other, more authentically democratic, biopolitical worlds.

In addition to being highly effective emergency-response networks, then, the ASOs developed in the early 1980s and continuing today, must be understood as an innovative response to postmodern capital's affective turn.[19] Indeed, such support systems reclaim affect from its commodification and put it to work in the service of a grassroots biopolitical project. Because the care of the self falls under the auspices of the state in biopower, fostering dependence rather than self-transformation, ASOs furthermore instantiate a modern project of subjectivation: Like the Hellenist philosophers of yore, discussed in Chapters 1 and 2, ASOs work with the community both to achieve self-autonomy and to reconnect exercises of self-transformation with self-knowledge. Dissatisfied with biased and inadequate health information from medical and governmental authorities, ASOs modify and/or invent caregiving and health regimens that give rise to powerful subjective and relational forms. Consequently, the affects produced and the ethical practices encouraged in AIDS caregiving pave the way for a resistant politics; it took five brutal years of nursing, loving, and grieving to usher ACT UP into existence. However exploited in the post-Fordist workplace, the affective labor of grassroots ASOs ultimately found outlet in a rageful activism.[20] Such activism, I argue, is informed by the politicization of friendship as shared estrangement in the AIDS buddy network, an early AIDS support system whose work involved the delinking of sexuality from truth, relationships of entrustment, and an ethics of discomfort.

A volunteer program to assist people with AIDS, the AIDS buddy system was developed by New York's Gay Men's Health Crisis in the early 1980s and became *de rigueur* in international AIDS caregiving soon thereafter. One of many early efforts to come to terms with an illness initially believed to affect only gay men (hence AIDS' early medical acronym GRID [Gay-Related Immuno Deficiency], or, the more derogatory and illusorily encompassing "gay plague"), the buddy system changed the direction of a public discourse seeking to scapegoat the gay community for its purportedly irresponsible sexual "lifestyle." Modeled after buddy systems used in the military, the Boy Scouts of America, and even scuba diving, the AIDS buddy system can be understood as an attempt to humanize PWAs and to promote a social acceptance of homosexuality.[21] In a political climate rife with AIDS-related discrimination and denialism, in a society divided by the Reagan White House—in decidedly genocidal fashion—into the "general" (natural, lawful) heterosexual population and (monstrous, dangerous) risk groups,[22] the AIDS buddy system borrowed the organizational form of respected institutions to draw attention to the human dimension of AIDS, to distance itself from mass media and medical prejudices regarding homosexuality, and to seek community aid and funding for a health crisis by and large neglected by federal institutions. However, in addition to lobbying for the social legitimacy of homosexuality and the social tolerance of PWAs, the buddy system at the same time strategically shifted the AIDS debate from a politics of sexuality to a politics of friendship. If AIDS became meaningful, political, through discourses of sexuality, the turn toward friendship—traditionally understood as a relation free from sexuality—short-circuited discursive links between AIDS and sexual identity. Given Foucault's presentiment that the future of homosexuality lies in friendship, it is significant that one of the gay community's first steps in AIDS caregiving was the desexualization of AIDS via the quasi-institutionalization of friendship. Beyond a bid for social respectability, such strategy is consonant with a Foucaultian project of friendship invested in both emptying sex of its truth content and in reclaiming a privatized relation for a communal politics. As I have argued, for Foucault the overcoming or turning away from sexuality as a truth-revealing hermeneutic is paramount to modern biopolitical struggles. The AIDS buddy system, then, can be interpreted as a step toward toppling the monarchy of sex: that is, as a movement of subjectivation that works toward freeing the "homosexual self" from the straitjacket of sexual identity.

The buddy's role is to offer a PWA functional support in her or his everyday life; the volunteer is more or less a caregiver, a home health aid, an errand runner, a friend to sit and chat with indoors, a friend to go on a walk with outdoors. In *RePlacing Citizenship*, Michael P. Brown notes the open-endedness of the relationship: "The open-ended definition of support stems from the variegated and diverse needs any particular person living with AIDS might have at any given stage of the illness's progression. That open-endedness also denotes the widespread failures of both state and family structures to provide adequate support immediately during the years of the crisis" (125). Buddies are matched according to the volunteer's availability and the client's needs. The absence of a shared history, according to Brown, is precisely what makes the relationship successful. With a freedom from a common past and a foundational acknowledgment of finitude, the unencumbered buddy can do things that family or life friends often cannot—giving the client "permission to die," for example (147–48). The buddy friendship, then, has no foundation other than the experience through which it is forged; it is a malleable relation that not only has the potential to transform individuals on a personal level but one that also offers a window onto a heterogeneous conception of community. Differences of wealth, race, gender, class, age, and sexual orientation between buddies are not ignored. The organization provides a framework encouraging certain intimacies, but clearly marked rights and duties for each buddy prevent power disparities arising from social differences from developing into exploitative relationships.

This relational structure corresponds with the "entrusted" friendships in the Milan Women's Bookstore Collective, an Italian feminist group also active in the 1980s.[23] Entrustment secures each women's distinct role in the collaborative effort of inventing a new social identity for women. Difference becomes the very ground on which the friendship is built: Disparities with respect to social and economic privilege are not conveniently swept under the rug but instead become a productive tension that propels the relationship. Teresa de Lauretis describes entrustment as follows:

> Briefly, the relationship of entrustment is one in which one woman gives her trust or entrusts herself symbolically to another woman, who thus becomes her guide, mentor, or point of reference—in short, the figure of symbolic mediation between her and the world. Both women engage in the relationship . . . not in spite, but rather because and in full recognition of the disparity that may exist between them in class or social position, age, level of education, professional status, income, etc. That is to say, the function of female symbolic mediation that one woman performs for the other is achieved, not in spite but rather because of the power differential between them, contrary to the egalitarian feminist belief that women's mutual trust is incompatible with unequal power. ("Essence" 14–15)

Buddy friendships are a similar experiment in difference. Their goal is not to eliminate social/economic/health dissymmetries from the relationship but to maintain them precisely as a productive tension. The "desire-in-uneasiness" that marks Foucault's friendship thus binds the buddy relation; indeed, an ethics of discomfort becomes its practical guide. Power differentials form the backbone of the friendship and individual autonomy is not fused into an identity but maintained in the pursuit of a common objective. To paraphrase de Lauretis, buddying reveals that mutual trust is not incompatible with unequal power. Instead, thanks to, not in spite of, such disparity these friendships begin and remain in a mutual discomfort that nurtures singular and collective potentiality. In practice, buddying is a functional, sometimes instrumental form of friendship—a way to ease the burden of another in need. Formally and philosophically, however, it offers an ethical model capable of provoking radically democratic subjective and social formations.

The relational terms of the buddy relationship, then, encourage an ethics of discomfort akin to the sort glimpsed in the problematic friendships of Antiquity. Like those, a "desire-in-uneasiness" forms its bedrock. The buddy system emerged as a response to the social and sexual stigma—often including familial rejection—which accompanied an HIV-positive diagnosis. As more customary social support systems faltered, friendship bonds were no doubt invested with an urgent intensity. And yet, traditional philosophical models of friendship in the face of AIDS ring hollow and unreliable. Montaigne's "soul-fusion" in which selves merge and endure beyond the grave; Aristotle's complete friendship as the non-threatening cradle of common virtue; Plato's teleological ideal, which begins in lack and culminates in an otherworldly Good; reified, sentimental representations offered by the culture industry—all of these friendships are impotent when death is ubiquitous, imposing, impending.[24] In its capacity for radical destruction, in its absolute immanence, AIDS gives lie to dreams of transcendence. To its credit, the AIDS buddy relation incorporates this fact into its very form: it refuses to soften death's blow, let alone triumph over it via the various clichés of friendship's salvationist promises. Founded on the bald fact of each friend's finitude—that "unspeakable" which must remain most private in biopolitical regimes[25]—buddying begins at the point where "normal" friendships end. Given the disparities in health, social status, and station between many participants, given the fact that death overshadows each meeting of these strangers, buddying is an uncomfortable, awkward, often contentious, and always difficult relationship.

In this sense, I see in these friendships traces of ancient intergenerational *philia*, discussed in Chapter 2. The ethics encouraged in those relationships demanded a simultaneous respect for the alterity of the other and a cultivation of the unknown in the self. What sets the buddy relationship apart from its predecessor, however, is that the metaphorical death immanent to the ancient friendship, that is, the friendship's transformation into institutionalized patriarchal homosociality, is here literalized. In the buddy relation, there is no "afterlife," no hope of ruling the *polis* together, no becoming equal after all. However, the centrality of difference and finitude in the buddy relationship creates an unbridgeable distance between participants that paradoxically produces an openness to alterity, a receptivity to otherness, and a respect for the foreignness in the friend and the self. Avoiding or assimilating such alterity is impossible here: With finitude foregrounded and ever in-between, differences cannot be subsumed into an identity. What emerges is an ethics of nonrecognition—I can't see myself in the other, I can't subsume the other into myself—which leaves the radical foreignness of both parties in tact and unharmed.[26] Such nonviolative relationality affords an opportunity to cultivate foreignness, to nurture unseen selves and unusual intimacies. Foucault's remarks on the disorderly and unauthorized affective ties between soldiers at war illuminate these aspects of the buddy relation:

> During World War I, men lived together completely, one on top of another, and for them it was nothing at all, insofar as death was present and finally the devotion to one another and the services rendered were sanctioned by the play of life and death. And apart from several remarks on camaraderie, the brotherhood of spirit, and some very partial observations, what do we know about these emotional uproars and storms of feeling that took place in those times? One can wonder how, in these absurd and grotesque wars and infernal massacres, the men managed to hold on in spite of everything. Through some emotional fabric, no doubt. I don't mean that it was because they were each other's lovers that they continued to fight; but honor, courage, not losing faith, leaving the trench with the captain—all that implied a very intense emotional tie. It's not to say: "Ah, there you have homosexuality!" I detest that kind of reasoning. But no doubt you have there one of the conditions, not the only one, that has permitted this infernal life where for weeks guys floundered in the mud and shit, among corpses, starving for food, and were drunk the morning of the assault. ("Friendship" 139)

The openness encouraged in the buddy relation, like the soldiers' "storms of feeling," holds the capacity to provoke affective ties that exceed practical utility and institutional codes. Something as paltry and restrictive as "sexuality" cannot define or contain the multiformity of desires, hatreds, loves, and ambivalences that might arise between these friends. Indeed, self-identity, sexual and otherwise, is for all intents and purposes checked at the door upon entering into a buddy relation; one leaves the world behind to join Nietzsche's "brotherhood of death," to share in Guibert's "common thanatological destiny." The political potential of such sharing is not to be overlooked.

Paolo Virno's essay, "The Ambivalence of Disenchantment," helps clarify the radical implications of the acceptance of finitude at the core of the buddy relationship. Like Hardt and Negri, Virno draws connections between contemporary labor practices and the common modes of feeling he finds in a diverse range of experience amid the biopolitical landscape. "Uncertain expectations, contingent arrangements, fragile identities and changing values" (15), though once considered unserviceable for capital, create a new breed of worker in the post-Fordist age. Feelings of alienation and disenchantment, once thought to carry revolutionary potential, have been integrated into the workplace as cynicism and opportunism. Nomadic uprootedness, now a quite common if not necessary way of life in a global economy reliant on migrant labor, benefit-less temp work, and pension-less careers, dims possibilities of forging revolutionary attachments through labor practices. Virno wonders, however, whether there might be a "neutral kernel" (24), an ambivalence, at the heart of this bleakness. He writes:

> Opportunism, cynicism, and fear define a contemporary emotional situation marked precisely by an abandonment to finitude and a belonging to uprooting, by resignation, servitude, and eager acquiescence. At the same time, they make that situation visible as an irreversible fact on whose basis conflict and revolt might also be conceived. (33)

Because capitalism has incorporated uprootedness and alienation into its productive processes, because the proletariat as a political class has been altered dramatically in its location and composition, Virno, again like Hardt and Negri, rethinks the traditional Marxian dialectic of class struggle. He begins with an acceptance of the present's irreversibility. Refusing to locate salvation in the past or future, Virno seeks revolutionary potential in the immanence of contemporary disenchantment. The ambivalence he locates here turns on belonging-as-such: What unites "the software technician, the autoworker at Fiat, and the illegal laborer" are feelings of belonging to volatile contexts, to the opportunism of labor, to adaptability itself (18). With the general intellect at the center of production, subjectivity is irrevocably uprooted and multiple, belonging not to a determinate something but rather to belonging-as-such. In this attachment Virno sees the emergence of community forms predicated not on shared essences, property relations, or exclusivity. The only hope for transforming the capitalist status quo lies in leaving behind traditional conceptions of community and embracing an "abandonment to finitude."

This abandonment—a disavowal of any and all flights into transcendence, be they religious, New Age, or philosophically dialectical—is precisely what engenders an intense attachment to belonging itself. Virno explains: "The abandonment to finitude is inhabited by a vigorous *feeling of belonging*. This combination may seem incongruous or paradoxical. . . . And yet, alienation, far from eliminating the feeling of belonging, empowers it. The impossibility of securing ourselves within any durable context disproportionately increases our adherence to the most fragile instances of the 'here and now'" (31). Distinct from the existential imperative to put finitude to work in the service of life, that is, to subsume death into life so as to live more authentically, Virno's abandonment to finitude is not necessarily a conscious philosophical position and by no means guarantees revolutionary action. Rather, it is one of the nonconscious affective consequences of the perceptual surplus and structural fleetingness of the postmodern landscape and workplace. Cynics and opportunists—shape-shifters, masters of adaptability, subjectivities belonging only to the vicissitudes of the market—succeed financially precisely because their belonging-to-uprootedness adheres to the ever-mutating yet seemingly immovable capitalist present.

However, belonging-as-such, in its ambivalence, can be put to work in the service of radical political projects: "youth movements and new labor organizations," for instance, that seek to "abandon their roles and throw off their oppressive chains rather than confront them openly" (31). These movements, among others, punk subcultures and Italian autonomism, choose "defection and 'exodus' over any other form of struggle" (31).[27] Autonomists, discussed briefly in Chapter 3, abandon not only transcendent Marxian goals but also their very identities as workers; punks, at least in their more "crusty" incarnations, likewise refrain from squaring off with authority and instead turn their backs, forsaking hope in the present and future alike. And yet, in the experience of defection these deserters actively affirm and invent new forms of life. Cynicism and nihilism may be these groups' constitutive ground, but in the movement of exodus from the present ways of being are fashioned, common habits surface, and the hazy horizons of a political project might be delineated. As Foucault described in "The Subject and Power," the movements of which Virno speaks are struggles for subjectivation: they seek to overcome biopolitically administered identity at any cost, often without conscious knowledge of exactly why or of what lies beyond. Indeed, the Foucault who in interviews extricated himself from Socratic dialogue in order to experiment with new ideas, the Foucault who abruptly rerouted his study of sexuality because he found that "after all, it was best to sacrifice a definite program to a promising line of approach" ("Preface," *Essential, V1: Ethics* 205) himself adumbrated such exodus. Disengaging from dialectical frameworks that ultimately reproduce dominant discursive terms and logics involves thinking and living experimentally. The boundaries of the "place" toward which these defectors travel are ever shifting; the project uniting them reveals itself only in the unfolding of the journey.

It is here where I find a connection between the ethics of the AIDS buddy system and the politics of later AIDS activism: in leaving behind traditional transcendent conceptions of friendship, the buddy system paved the way for a politics of friendship as shared estrangement. Moreover, the transformation of previous buddy system models, the disengagement from sexual identity, and the rethinking of friendship—all of which amounts to an experimental defection from the present—can be understood as the radical gesture of exodus that allows for the constitution of a political project. The complicated affects produced in the buddy relation (discomfort, frustration, love), the impersonal ethics encouraged (nonrecognition, openness to alterity, respect for absolute difference), and the constitutive abandonment to finitude (engendering intense feelings of belonging, belonging-as-such) find expression in ACT UP's inventive activist tactics, including die-ins (a form of protest in which activists play dead in charged public spaces, most famously Saint Patrick's Cathedral), and the Ashes Action (a protest in which ACT UP members threw the ashes of dead friends and lovers on to the White House lawn). None of this of course was necessarily intentional, planned, or inevitable: The political program and strategy became clear only in the flight from dominant frameworks of meaning and relating.

From the historian's perspective, this narrative might seem dubious, simplistic; but at the risk of transforming a complex history into a teleological narrative, at the risk of rewriting a history that has been so meticulously researched, I am making connections between the impersonal ethics of the buddy system and the radical politics of AIDS activism to stress the political viability of an ethical/political program that turns on shared estrangement. In the course of doing so, an essential paradox comes to light: How can a relation that bespeaks the anarchical contingency of all relationality in any way comprise an ethical framework, ground a political program, or establish the terms of a social contract replete with rights and duties? Just as affect always exceeds emotion, the asubjective force of friendship likewise creates a surplus uncontainable by political forms and institutions. In this surplus lies the potential to do, make, say, and think differently. Although friendship is by design incapable of cohering in an epistemological object deemed "society" or "politics," we must nonetheless seek out those social and political forms that best accommodate or approximate the antisocial nature of friendship. Only in these forms might we break away from the inherently inequitable and vicious hierarchies of identitarian difference. This is all to say that the impossibility of instituting friendship in something like the AIDS buddy system must be affirmed as a contradiction: Instead of throwing the proverbial baby out with the bathwater we must tarry within this essential paradox and valorize those communal forms that acknowledge and respect the impossibility of sociality as such. In the next chapter, I explore friendship as shared estrangement in connection with AIDS activist practices, and contemplate how we might resuscitate this relational model for contemporary queer politics. To set the stage for that discussion, and to bring to a close my critique of Hardt and Negri's project, a brief word on love.

Hardt and Negri seek in their multitude the politicization of love. Love quite literally has the final word in *Multitude* and the authors link constituent power with premodern Christian and Judaic conceptions of love to tease out their contemporary political potential. They write:

> We need to recuperate the public and political conception of love common to premodern traditions. Christianity and Judaism, for example, both conceive love as a political act that constructs the multitude. Love means precisely that our expansive encounters and continuous collaborations bring us joy. There is really nothing necessarily metaphysical about the Christian and Judaic love of God: both God's love of humanity and humanity's love of God are expressed and incarnated in the common material project of the multitude. (351–52)

Hardt and Negri's recourse to theological texts here, quite *à la mode* in contemporary Continental Philosophical circles,[28] is indicative of a broader Christian undercurrent in their project. Not only, as Sylvère Lotringer astutely observes, do the authors use the historical rise of Christianity as an analogy for revolutionary desire in *Empire* ("Foreword," 14), but the very telos of their multitude—to "push through Empire to come out the other side" (*Empire* 218)—serves as the heavenly afterlife that organizes the becoming of—indeed, the very being of—the multitude. Again, in Lotringer's words, "The telos, in other words, precedes the multitude and for the most part replaces it" (15). Christian love thus suits Hardt and Negri's project: Just as the nun denies herself earthly, sexual delights so as to prove her devotion to Christ, their multitude transcends the tedious politics of sexuality and unites in an idealized love to reach "the other side." The authors of *Multitude* fail to divest love of its burdensome history as the bourgeois home of proper sexual expression and as the transcendent romantic solution to messy, worldly matters. Unlike the AIDS buddy system that turned to friendship to delink sexuality from truth and, hence to deprive sexual identity of its social power, Hardt and Negri neglect to consider exactly how sexuality figures into their concept of love—its material manifestation and its political form thus remain hazy at best. Although the authors claim to be lending name to an already-existing multitude (various movements for social justice), and the affect that binds it (love), these names in fact mold and determine a mythical multitude's actions and relations. In the end, what we have here is arguably Marcuse's famous mantra, "Make Love, Not War," *sans* the sexual inflection—for the multitude's love is positive, active, "pure" in the Christian sense . . . but not necessarily of this world.

To be fair, the authors have complicated their theory of love after the publication of *Multitude*, pointing to the problems involved in adapting its premodern theological conceptions. In a lecture entitled, "Love in the Multitude" given at the University of Minnesota, Hardt traces a genealogy of love's depoliticization: in the Christian tradition, the separation between *eros* and *agape* (the former private and selfish, the latter public and charitable) and the destruction of difference in the transcendent unity of the love bond; in bourgeois society, the privatized entrapment of love (in the couple, the family, the nation, etc.) and the romantic reification of our powerlessness in relation to it (love "happens" like a lightning bolt, we "fall" in it, it comes from elsewhere, sneaks up on us, etc.). In the last installment of the Empire trilogy, *Commonwealth*, the authors seek to disentangle love from these corrupt forms and put it to work as (a) a social experiment in difference that affirms singularities in a common world; (b) the exercise of joy with the recognition of an external cause; and (c) a communal endeavor which increases collective power and realizes individual potential (182–87). Love, like the multitude, then, is positive and above all active: It is "productive" (180), "an ontological motor" (195), politically compositional (184), indeed, "the power of love is the constitution of the common and ultimately the formation of society" (195). Passive affections—for example, love's opposites (tolerance and indifference) and evil (the corruption of love to such an extent that its active power is obstructed)—require transformation. Following Spinoza's understanding of ideas and affects to the letter, the authors fail to complicate the gendered hierarchies at work therein: According to

Spinoza, inadequate ideas lead to passivity and increased susceptibility to the passions; passive affections must become active affects in order to be productive; affections must transform from a state of being acted on to a condition that increases the body's ability to act (Spinoza, 40–41). Although obvious from the vantage point of feminist theory, the value hierarchies emergent in this active–passive conception of love and its opposites are never problematized in Hardt and Negri's work. Is Spinozan love beyond gender and sexuality? Is active love masculine and tolerance/indifference passive and effeminate? If evil is merely "bad love," love in which productivity is stymied, is the material form of that love non-productive, i.e., non-procreative, promiscuous . . . homosexual? Furthermore, is there anything to be said for, as Leo Bersani asks in "Is the Rectum a Grave?," a power gleaned from passivity?

For Bersani's part, anal sex—historically and discursively linked with femininity, male homosexuality, and the abdication of power—brings about a certain *empowering* ego destruction. In "Rectum," Bersani reads Freud's *Three Essay on the Theory of Sexuality* against the grain to argue that masochism lies at the very foundation of a developing sexuality. The shattering of psychic structures, according to Bersani, is the precondition for the establishment of a sexual relation to others. And with this shattering comes *jouissance*. The male sexual subject's originary masochism, however, must be disavowed in the social realm as the (patriarchal) self is valueless unless active and autonomous. The relevance of queer male anal sex to Bersani's argument, then, concerns its social and discursive link to "losing one's manhood" and self debasement—anal sex at once fantasmatically re-enacts the ecstatic ego exploding of the subject's originary masochism as well as a metaphorical fucking of the sadistic, masculine ego ideals internalized by the gay male subject. It is this gay male bodily practice—not the parody of masculinity by the leather daddy nor the mockery of it by the camp queen—that serves as both the inspiration for the fantasmatic revulsion and physical violence perpetrated against queers in the social realm and, simultaneously, a potential site of queer resistance to the ever-seductive identification with/love of the ur-masculine ideal:

> If the rectum is a grave in which the masculine ideal (an ideal shared—differently—by men *and* women) of proud subjectivity is buried, then it should be celebrated for its very potential for death. AIDS has literalized that potential as the certainty of biological death, and has therefore reinforced the heterosexual association of anal sex with a self annihilation originally and primarily identified with the fantasmatic mystery of an insatiable, unstoppable female sexuality. It may, finally, be

> in the gay man's rectum that he demolishes his own perhaps
> otherwise uncontrollable identification with a murderous
> judgment against him. (222)

This, of course, is not to say that gay male anal sex is inevitably a site of queer resistance. Rather, it is a material practice that invites a fantasmatic destruction of normative masculine ego-ideals, a practice that potentially gives life to a queer self who, nurtured in the ecstatic pleasures of the anus, turns traitor against violent, patriarchal manhood.

Can Hardt and Negri's theory of love account for such a practice? Or, does love lift us up to a never-never-land unconcerned with such "dirty" acts? In discussing the "pseudocopulation" of male wasps, the authors make a nod to the political potential of "cruising and serial sex common to gay male communities" (*Commonwealth*, 187). Following Deleuze and Guattari, they describe the promiscuous sexual behavior of wasps (who "fuck" certain orchids not for nectar or survival but for pleasure) to highlight an unproductive form of love "based on the encounter of alterity but also on the process of becoming different" (187). They find in this coupling the very form of love that animates the biopolitical economy—immaterial labor, the production of affects—and applaud the wasp-orchid assemblage for its metaphorical indifference to (capitalist) efficiency and output. And the gay men who likewise direct biopower toward such unproductive, joyful ends? "This is not to say that cruising and anonymous sex serve as a model of love to emulate for Guattari (or Genet, Wojnarowicz, or Delany), but rather that they provide an antidote to the corruptions of love in the couple and the family, opening love up to the encounter of singularities" (187). When it comes to defining the material role of sexuality in a political model of love, the authors once again back away. What they offer in the right hand, they take away with the left: Promiscuous serial sex is useful as a metaphor but not to be emulated as a political model; it's fine for wasps, but humans, apparently, can do better. To claim, moreover, that the three mentioned gay male writers do *not* consider promiscuity an emulative model of love, let alone articulate its political potential, is either the result of bad reading or a deliberate whitewashing of their work.[29] In the end, Hardt and Negri fail to address the normative sexual standards that might emerge in their multitude's politicization of love. Overemphasizing the conceptual active-ness of the affect while simultaneously dismissing the ethical and political potential of actual, *human* practices of unproductive love, they unwittingly reveal the gendered and heteronormative realities of their idealized political project.

By contrast, if, as Foucault argues, sexuality is instrumental to the conceptualization and implementation of biopower for administrative purposes, then perhaps it is *through* sexuality that we might, like wasps and orchids, create alternative biopolitical assemblages. That is to say, if sexuality has been so useful for *biopotere*, the affects produced in unproductive sex practices may be vital to *biopotenza*. In the AIDS buddy system, we see the delinking of sexuality from truth via the institution of friendship as desire-in-uneasiness. In these friendships, as in Bersani's account of anal sex in a time of AIDS, both literal and fantasmatic deaths loom large. Such deaths, however, serve not as a limit to friendship; instead, just as a new self is valorized in Bersani's ego-exploding sex act, finitude becomes friendship's life-giving bedrock.

Chapter 5

Common Sense and a
Politics of Shared Estrangement

If, in essence, the goal of this book is to make some sense of Foucault's strategically vague proclamation that the "development towards which the problem of homosexuality tends is the one of friendship," then the task of this final chapter is to draw some connections between homosexuality in its historical specificity and a politics of friendship. I have thus far outlined the relational terms of a Foucaultian friendship of shared estrangement—guided by an ethics of discomfort, provoking an openness to alterity—and, however anti-institutional, indeed *antisocial*, called attention to its efficacy in the AIDS buddy system. The abandonment to finitude at the heart of the buddy relation, I suggest, produces an affective surplus—intense feelings of belonging, belonging-as-such—that can be directed toward non- or anti-institutional ends, namely, political activism. In the ubiquity of death, in friendships that refuse to transcend death, a radical politics lies in wait. However, I want to supplement this possibly too tidy narrative with a question: What does any of this have to do with homosexuality? If, as I argued in Chapter 3, the actualization of the Foucaultian friend requires the overcoming of homosexuality, that is, a movement of subjectivation that delinks sexuality from self-identity, why might this anti-identitarian gesture occur in homosexual communities? Is there a specifically queer component to the story of friendship's politicization as shared estrangement? A sexual or sensual component? Taking up Foucault's gauntlet, then, I explore in this chapter the ways a friendship as shared estrangement is explicitly linked to homosexuality and what friendship might do to solve, as Foucault deems it, this "problem."

For this reason, among others, I concluded the last chapter with a brief discussion of Leo Bersani's "Is the Rectum a Grave?," an essay that locates an anti-identitarian self-shattering—the dissolution of the (illusorily) masterful, patriarchal ego and of coherent sexual identity—in a specifically gay male sex act. Bersani, whose work from the seminal "Rectum" onward has been arguably a love–hate letter to Foucault,[1] wants to argue that there is indeed something unique to queer desire and sexual behavior that lends itself to the impersonal relationality we encountered in Foucault's friendship. If Foucault eschews the complexities of desire in order to focus on the difficulties and potentialities of pleasure,[2] Bersani embraces the abject social position homo-desire has been made to occupy and glimpses in its antisocial relational forms (cruising, nonmonogamy) the beginnings of a nonidentitarian community. Nevertheless, even if the travel routes are different, the conceptual destinations for Foucault and Bersani lie within spitting distance of one another, if not mark the very same spot. Although Bersani takes Foucault to task for his "facile evocation of the happy gay couple [as more socially and psychically disruptive than, say, the cruising butch bottom] and the idealizations of S/M as a privileged practice in de-genitalizing and expanding the field of the body's pleasures" ("A Conversation," *Rectum* 182), although he seeks to complement Foucault's work on relationality with a psychoanalytically conceived unconscious, the two thinkers share the belief that queer practices and communities are privileged sites for instantiating a post-identitarian politics. Foucault's numerous calls for gays to create an ethics and a culture not founded on scientific conceptions of identity resonate with Bersani's theory of nonidentitarian sameness, "homo-ness," which I explore in some detail later. Even though psychoanalysis appears to be the impassable barrier lying between these two thinkers, it becomes in the end a tool deployed by Bersani to realize what is arguably a Foucaultian goal. In short, with homo-ness Bersani is able to answer Foucault's questions: "How can a relational system be reached through sexual practices? Is it possible to create a homosexual mode of life?" ("Friendship" 137).

With this in mind, I leave aside both Foucault's conflicted relationship with psychoanalysis and Bersani's frustrations with the "gay daddy," as he nicknames Foucault,[3] in order to locate the common conceptual ground between them and to mine what is useful from both projects. A Foucault–Bersani formulation regarding friendship, for instance, might read as follows: If the becoming of homosexuality is friendship, if friendship is a relation that emphasizes impersonality, a relation guided by an ethics of discomfort that consequently opens onto an anti-identitarian politics, then it is in the immanence of homosexuality—in the relational terms of homosexual sociality—that we might locate and pursue this becoming. With conceptual help from Bersani and other antirelational thinkers (e.g., Tim Dean, Heather Love, Lee Edelman, William Haver), I explore in this chapter the work of David Wojnarowicz to articulate the politics of friendship as shared estrangement emergent in homosexual (anti)sociality and AIDS activism. Unlike Hardt and Negri who desexualize biopower (let alone the multitude and the love that binds it), Wojnarowicz recognizes the importance of sexuality for *biopotere* and, through sexual practice, seeks to dismantle it. For him, sex, affect, and politics are indivisible.

His diaries, published in part as *In the Shadow of the American Dream*, foreground the importance of rethinking sexuality as a marker of truth. In particular, the entries from the mid- to late-1980s, chronicling his involvement in AIDS activism, include meditations on sex and affect, life and death that reveal the uniqueness and power of his political vision. With his concept of "sense," a word that appears excessively in postcoital reflections (of which there is no shortage in the diaries), Wojnarowicz offers a strategy of resistance unwedded to the identitarian logic of biopolitical governance. Building on Foucault's insight that the discursive link between sexual desire and self-identity is a formidable tool of control that ultimately ends up repressing movements of collective revolt, Wojnarowicz's notion of sense ruptures this link and deterritorializes, or "communizes," affect. A slippery and polyvalent term in his usage, sense emerges at the point of indistinguishibility between life and death, between private emotion and common affect, and between rational understanding and a "body-knowledge" gleaned from sexual/sensual encounters. The ethics emergent in Wojnarowicz's various carnal escapades involves a breakdown of intersubjectivity, a delinking of sexual desire and truth, and, later, an understanding of death's immanence to life. These practices and knowledges, all of which he seems to rediscover in his activism, not only give insight into a singular political awakening but also offer a primer of sorts for contemporary queer activist strategy.[4] That is to say, understood in relation to Foucault's writings on biopolitics, Wojnarowicz's sense opens onto a politics against sexuality and for the common.

Locating an antirelational ethics in same-sex sexual encounters and experiences, an ethics which holds the capacity to realize a post-identitarian politics, is, as we have seen already with Bersani, tried-and-true queer strategy. Indeed, so much ink has been spilled recently over this very strategy that the various projects incorporating it have been given a name: "the antisocial turn" in queer studies, as coined by Judith Halberstam.[5] This intellectual movement of sorts comprises a semi-coherent body of anti-assimilationist queer scholarship emerging in response to at least three historical turns of event:

1. The blinding visibility of gays and gay issues in American pop culture, politics, and media.

2. The heteronormativizing of gay politics and culture (marriage, families, and, in the United States, the military).

3. The increasing homonormativity of an all too acquiescent gay community for which normative, bourgeois gender and relational standards become requirements for *all* queers seeking social legitimacy.

Inaugurated, according to Halberstam, with Bersani's "Rectum" and moving through the work of Edelman, Dean, Love, and Halberstam herself, the antisocial turn emphasizes negative affective states (shame, grief, hopelessness, failure), antihumanist relational models (impersonality, nonidentitarian sameness, nonrecognition), and its emissaries warn against the political redemption of queer history and affect, sexual or otherwise. Transforming shame into pride, despair into hope, that is, alchemizing the emotional wretchedness of the pre-Stonewall era or the feelings of helplessness and frustration of the early AIDS crisis into a bright future of gay weddings and families is the trade of a homonormative political agenda: Moneyed, white, gender-appropriate, property-owning, conspicuous consumers, or those who aspire to such status, need only apply. Rather than subsuming the ugly feelings of the past into a gay proud and positive present, Heather Love, for example, urges queers to embrace a politics that allows for trauma and psychological damage as such. For her, "there are ways of feeling bad that do not make us feel like fighting back" (*Feeling Backward*, 14). Instead, we must resist the moment of transcendence, of dialectical supersession, that transforms the misery of the queer past into a martyrdom for the present; we must "make a future backward enough that even the most reluctant among us might want to live there" (163).

Furthermore, and also relevant to my discussion of Wojnarowicz, Judith Halberstam has taken to task a handful of the above writers from the "gay white male patriarchy" who extol the "heroic" antisociality in the "gay male canon" (Genet, Warhol, Proust, Gide, etc.), but conveniently ignore "the quite dismaying archive of anti-social, masculinist, transphobic sexism as articulated by German homophiles" ("The Anti-social Turn," 152). Such homophilic masculinism, celebrated in prewar Germany and sympathetic with, if not essential to, Nazism, reminds us—if we still need reminding when 25 to 30 percent of self-identified gay Americans vote Republican[6]—that same-sex behavior and/or desire by no means translates into "good" politics, that antisociality can cut both ways, toward a fascist nihilism or toward post-identitarianism, and that antirelational ethics may, in the end, be irredeemable for any progressive political program.

At the risk, then, of glorifying once again the "gay male canon," at the risk of redeeming an at-best ambivalent "sense" for a contemporary queer politics, I argue that Wojnarowicz's contribution to the literature of queer sexual affect is unique in that it not only reveals the ethical potential of antirelationality, as the above writers theorize, but explicitly archives the transformation of this ethic into political action. Indeed, his memoirs and diaries can be read as training manuals of sorts in a politics of shared estrangement. Not unlike the AIDS buddy system, Wojnarowicz's work is instructive for gleaning the political potential of antirelational forms. The origins of Wojnarowicz's political sensibility can be located, however, in sexual encounters; the new subjective and relational models he "senses" in anonymous sex erupt in his activism and political art. If Wojnarowicz learns to distrust subjective interiority and sexual identity in his sentimental education at the Chelsea Piers, it is in AIDS activism that he puts such lessons to work. In the recognition of the "common thanatological destiny" he shares with a multitude of AIDS casualties, Wojnarowicz opens himself up not only to the individual stranger, as he did at the piers, but to the very idea of strangeness itself.

Sense and Sexuality

"Sense" in Wojnarowicz's usage is utterly overdetermined: In its repetition it becomes a catchword for matters pertaining to the perceptual (data gathered through the five senses), the rational (a conscious understanding), the emotional (a feeling or mood), the signifiable (concerning the meaning or gist of something), and a sensibility (a mode of being). In the following passage, seemingly written in a frenzy after an anonymous sexual encounter with a Texan at the Chelsea Piers, we see all of these "senses" at play:

> Realizing with the Texan man, the sense he evoked in the meeting, the senses I've been left with that are a bit unsettling, unsettling in their intoxicating beauty, in their rarity, the sense that I'd gladly give this stranger my soul my life my time in movement in living for the rest of my life, would live with him immediately, the giving away of preoccupation or routine to be finely held in the mind and rough hands of a stranger, this produced in the meeting a series of movements along a darkening hall, the heavy sound of footsteps, the casual swagger of a character turning on the silent balls of his feet, the motion toward me erasing the definition of 'stranger' making us less than strangers, the cocking of his head to the side, healthiness of the light in his eyes, the broad face, nose. How it is I'd give my life for/to him, not a sense of ego or egolessness, my life being very important to me in my personal freedoms, but like riding in a truck through the images of Texas, the badlands, the rolling vistas the buttes the cactus and fine sands of timelessness, the ever-present rouge line on metal, the continuous dusk at our feet, the guns over the visors, the

> bullets in the dashboard, the riding motion of the senses. (*In the Shadow* 127–28)

And soon after this cowboy road-trip fantasy, Wojnarowicz laments the inadequacy of words in relaying his experiences:

> [I]n the construction of words is the inherent failure to obtain the living sense of the desire. So although I've lived forms of movement that approach or start to come close to the scenes I desire, still when all is said and done, just as in the construction of these words I have still not touched the edge of it. (129)

The rawness of the language, the lack of grammatical structure, and the nearly punctuation-less, run-on sentences bespeak an inspired, if somewhat adolescent, urgency to communicate ideas and feelings before they pass into neurological ether. At the same time I find in Wojnarowicz's style a more studied attempt, apparent throughout his writings, to extricate some truth from the snares of linguistic and grammatical structure. A literary approach akin to Genet's excessive prose (repeatedly referenced in Wojnarowicz's diaries) or even Nietzsche's poetic aphorisms, Wojnarowicz's style works to wrest life from the gallows of language, urging the escape of a perhaps extra-discursive, affective force from language's proverbial prison house. But although his manic and surrealistic prose reads well as an attempt to escape the death grip of language, the author himself deems his efforts a failure.[7] What goes unacknowledged in this passage, however, is the way in which the word "sense" in all of its semantic richness and polymorphous perversity arguably escapes the mortification of language as it mutates and reanimates at every turn. One moment a function of the mind, another of the body, at once the most intimate of personal feelings and the most public of shared sentiment, "sense" here approaches meaninglessness, non-sense, in its very affective excess. The "living sense of desire" that Wojnarowicz feels unable to communicate in his diaries indeed comes to life in a word that resists a singular meaning. The result, what I am calling a "common sense," emerges through the production of "a series of movements" that give rise to an extra-linguistic form of communication at the interstices of Self and Other—an affective sensibility emanating from the sexual encounter but irreducible to one or the other lover.

And here the very "identityless-ness" of the Texan man becomes important. In anonymity, Wojnarowicz is allowed to enter into the man's life with an intensity that personal knowledge might never afford. The experience with the Texan's nonidentity motivates Wojnarowicz to articulate, however inarticulately, a new understanding of the self ("not a sense of ego or egolessness") and the Other ("erasing the definition of 'stranger' "). Foucault, as we have seen, designates Wojnarowicz's experience the movement of desubjection to subjectivation: the undoing of socially, historically determined selves and the creation of new ones. The affects, indeed, the sense, produced in the fabrication of pleasure between identity-less bodies provokes Wojnarowicz to imagine not only a new life, but also subjective and relational forms not founded on commonality, property, or intersubjectivity. Michael Warner in *The Trouble with Normal* gives credence to such forms in discussing the world-making capacities of public sex culture. He writes:

> When gay men or lesbians cruise, when they develop a love of strangers, they directly eroticize participation in the public world of their privacy. Contrary to myth, what one relishes in loving strangers is not mere anonymity, nor meaningless release. It is the pleasure of belonging to a sexual world, in which one's sexuality finds an answering resonance not just in one other, but in a world of others. (179)

Warner's remarks on the "resonance" between participants and the feelings of "belonging" provoked in anonymous sex are amplified in the work of Tim Dean. For Dean, the resonance and belonging in cruising are decidedly anti-intersubjective; in impersonal intimacy we can locate anti-identitarian ethical principles. Placing an emphasis on the cultivation of alterity in anonymous sex, Dean asks, "Why should strangers not be lovers and remain strangers?" (*Unlimited Intimacy* 212) His answer runs counter to the Christian relational ethic: instead of "loving thy neighbor as thyself," the ethic emergent in cruising "insists that the other's strangeness be preserved rather than annihilated through identification" (212). Machinic rather than humanist, antisubjective as opposed to intersubjective, the intimacy in these exchanges fosters an openness to alterity because identity is not at stake. When sex is merely the "plugging in of parts," as Guy Hocquenghem puts it,[8] when neither personality nor personhood are on the line, an openness to experimentation, newness, and difference is encouraged. Wojnarowicz's reflections attest to this; he is willing, after all, to begin anew with the Texan man, to let go of all "preoccupation or routine to be finely held in the mind and rough hands of a stranger." But why? According to Dean, what propels the anonymous encounter is a fascination with the foreignness of both the sex partner and the unknown in the self. What makes Wojnarowicz and the Texan man "less than strangers," then, is precisely their mutual love of and respect for strangeness: an attraction to the inarticulable, irreducible foreignness of the self and the other. Wojnarowicz reveals his disinterest in romantic fusion, in becoming identical with the man ("How it is I'd give my life for/ to him, not a sense of ego or egolessness, my life being very important to me in my personal freedoms") and insists that their singular strangeness be valued. Although such sexual behavior certainly involves risk—potential exposure to sexually transmitted diseases, to bodily harm and violation, even to the ruse of coherent self-identity—its greatest benefit lies in a capacity to produce a less violent, less cannibalizing self who welcomes the stranger within and without. To encounter foreignness, both externally and internally, and respect it as such; to mingle with others and refuse the violent act of intersubjective assimilation; to care for those in whom one finds nothing of oneself; such impersonal ethics respect difference at an ontological level and pave the way for communal forms unwedded to the dialectic of identity and difference.[9]

Bersani's concept of nonidentitarian sameness, that is, homo-ness, further helps articulate the subjective and relational models Wojnarowicz senses in his encounters. However much a "salutary devalorizing of difference" (*Homos* 7), homo-ness rests on a concept of infinite difference *in* sameness: a radical ontological alterity that has been suppressed by heteroized sociality—and for good reason. In his more recent work, Bersani essentially leaves behind dialectical psychoanalytic models of subjectivity (grounded in a necessarily sublatable lack), adopting instead conceptions of self and relationality more informed by monist philosophical traditions. Homo-ness arguably becomes substance whose singular form contains a multiplicity of difference that finds extension in diverse subjects. Difference in Bersani's estimation is not a trauma that needs to be overcome, but rather a "nonthreatening supplement to sameness" (7). Encountering foreignness in another unfolds the internally differentiated self and enriches its singularity. Any claim to coherent self-identity is therefore an attempt to wish away the fundamental, anarchical heterogeneity of homo-ness, which in turn seeks to unite singularities in social forms antithetical to the prejudicial hierarchies of identitarian difference. Homosexuality, according to Bersani, is "a privileged vehicle for homo-ness" in its social construction as a "love of the same" (10). If the other were loved as an extension of the self, would not then the boundaries between Self–Other and subject–object be porous, if not indistinct? Would this love, pushed to its logical endpoint, amount to a disinterest in the vicious and destructive ego, a self-divestiture, or a narcissism so profound that the world is reformulated *as* the self? How would we know for sure where "I" begin and "you" end? At the root of the (literally) superficial differences that have been a fount of antagonism (skin color, anatomy, preference for certain anatomies) lies a multiplicitous sameness that resists identity and seeks instead to bring together those who have nothing (superficially) in common. Bersani's project since "Rectum," then, has been a retheorization not only of the "gay community" but of community itself—from the ground up. Its goal lies in the following question: What if we were to stop believing in the inherent value of cultural identities and their affixed relational forms ("Gay Betrayals" 37–39)? What distinguishes his work from a traditional—and, as we have learned, dangerous—universalizing humanism is that it is in no way anthropocentric: When the world in its vastly different modes is ultimately the self extended outward; when we cease defining and defending ourselves against the world and learn to live within it; when we become uninterested in our identities, our "ego or egolessness," and more attuned to the innumerable repetitions of ourselves outside ourselves, an "ecological ethics" might emerge: "one in which the subject, having willed its own lessness, can live less invasively in the world" ("Sociability and Cruising" 62). This ethical relation requires perceptual training in recognizing the sameness, one could say the immanent heterogeneous oneness, at the heart of the world. Such training, according to Bersani, takes place as much in the study of art as in anonymous cruising. Both practices offer an education in impersonal intimacy; both encourage us to look for ourselves in another only to discover that representations and resemblances inevitably fail. The pleasure of finding always inaccurate replications of ourselves in art and in others allows us, however, to relate affectionately, nonviolently, to difference. And whereas artistic training can teach us about communication between human and non-human entities, "correspondences of forms within a universal solidarity of being" ("Psychoanalysis," *Rectum* 142), cruising puts us in step with the rhythm of sociality itself, revealing the extensibility of the subject and the exogeny of being.

By way of example, imagine yourself, for a moment, arriving at a gathering of acquaintances and friends.[10] You are excited about what the evening holds in store, happy to be out and about, but before settling into a conversation of any substance you flitter among attendees and chat with one person or another. Not looking to divulge anything too personal at this point, you instead enjoy the fleeting gratification of introductions and small talk with a variety of guests. Association and separation, the cadence of this sociality, provides a pleasure that investing oneself prevents. In fact, the delight here comes from willfully choosing not to be entirely oneself, from not getting tied down, from being reduced, as Bersani notes, to an "impersonal rhythm" ("Sociability and Cruising," *Rectum* 47). In this rhythm, we are attuned not only to the movement of desire and affection between humans but to the ebbing and flowing of tides, the rising and setting of suns, indeed, the impersonal rhythms of geological time. "[T]he pleasure of the associative process itself, of pure relationality," Bersani writes, "which, beyond or before the satisfaction of particular interests, may at once be the grounds, the motive, and the goal of all relations" (46). Not surprisingly, Bersani relates the pleasure of this associative process to cruising: In deliberately avoiding relationships that lead to attachment or possessiveness, in frolicking here and there without personal investment—that is to say, in creating relations undefined by property—one reduces the self to an impersonal rhythm and subtracts power from the destructive ego. In this gesture of self-subtraction, however, one is simultaneously intuiting and inventing relational forms uncontainable by hierarchies of social difference. By falling in step with the rhythm of sociality itself, one "senses" the radical heterogeneity, the nonidentitarian sameness, indeed, the common-ness of being.

William Haver illuminates the link between "bodies and pleasures" and the creation of the common in a recent lecture on Foucault and Genet. "The common," Haver writes, "is constituted in *and* as the very movement of circulation of all that refuses ownership, all that passes under the radar and off the grids of biopower" ("Reading Foucault's Genet Lectures" 7). Like Bersani, Haver finds this movement in cruising, this time in Genet's reminiscences of promiscuity in *The Prisoner of Love* as well as in Foucault's late work (in which he discerns "something suspiciously like nostalgia for the disreputable, furtive back-alley encounters that Gay Liberation was soon to disavow" [7]). Haver, however, pushes Bersani's insights by placing emphasis on cruising's biopolitical stakes. If the body's pleasures are the effect of an anarchical and asubjective affectivity, that is, if they are singular instances of a general circulation of affects within an infinitely variegated homo-ness, then the prohibition and/or privatization of this affectivity's free flow amounts to foreclosing the common. According to Haver, the enactment of the common in bodies and pleasures is not a sharing of private emotions or subjective desires; the common is movement, always becoming, never finite, impossible to share, grasp, or "rule in the name of" in every way that private property is. The common is also not an eruption of a preexisting state of being but rather the singular event of its happening, a coincident intuition and invention. In shedding the skin of a proprietary identity in anonymous sex, for instance, one intuits the possibility of a common and ushers it into being. The intuition (sense) and invention (sensualization) are co-implicated: in Haver's words, "[T]here is no common apart from a sense of the common, and conversely, . . . there is no sense of the common apart from the sensuousness of the common" (3). Sense and sensuousness are thus transductive: they operate as ideal and material relay points in the conversion to the common. "[A]ll sense assumes sensuousness as its own condition of possibility, and sensuousness always bears sense within itself. There is no sense apart from its sensuous provocation, and there is no senseless materiality" (3). In an earlier work Haver argues that the erotic is the very ground of sociality—the excessive supplement of the subject/object relation that transgresses the boundaries of all social relations—and hence the possibility of politics itself (*The Body* 132–34). In "Reading," however, the erotic and the common are equiprimordial if not interchangeable: simultaneously sensuous and sensible, at least in the form of intuition, the common always involves bodies and senses. And just as the common in its becoming cannot congeal into a political form ("We can never legislate, rule, or govern in the name of the common" ["Reading" 8]), the erotic in its perpetual movement always exceeds sexual identity and practice.

So, after this detour through various theories concerning the anti-identitarian ethical potential of bodies and pleasures, two conceptual characteristics of Wojnarowicz's "sense" are evident. The first is basic: As Haver discovers in Genet, I find in the sense Wojnarowicz detects in anonymous sex the coincident intuition and invention of the common. Sense in its various appearances in Wojnarowicz's writing is always a hunch, a sneaking suspicion, that a self other than the ego exists and that a community other than one founded on identity and property is possible. This hunch also is empirical proof of these forms: Sensing it in the anonymous encounter, Wojnarowicz wills the common into existence. Indeed, the very word, "sense," in its polyvalence, in its internal differentiation, in its excess of meaning, might be the ideal signifier for an unrepresentable common-ness that is always different from itself. Moreover, and this is my second point, in sense the seeds of Wojnarowicz's activist life can be located. For starters, a recognition of the always teeming erotic, moving through but not concretized in sex practices, gives lie to sexuality. Loving the stranger, the Texan man among many, affords Wojnarowicz affective access to the erotic that frees him from the shackles of sexual identity. The affects produced in these encounters encourage cooperative and consensual interactivity over a private comprehension of self-truth. As such, sense can be understood as the concurrent, noncognitive, affective recognition of the unsignifiable erotic and the common sensuousness that surges through the entrapped pleasures of normative relationality. Just as living labor always exceeds its concretization in labor practices, as Negri showed us, sense likewise works to overcome a deadened sexuality—the first step, according to Foucault, in resisting the administration of life in biopower.

Indeed, the centrifugal movement of subjectivation Foucault saw in anti-authoritarian struggles—those beginning with self-identity only to defect from it, dispense with it, and create experimental forms of life beyond it—is nothing but the event of the common. In Wojnarowicz's writing, this movement is chronicled: The sense of the common emergent in the sexual encounter reappears in his oppositional politics. This connection is made evident in a metaphor of a surfacing, explosive corporeal interior that Wojnarowicz employs in describing both the sex act and the HIV-positive body. A concept of exogenous being, the unfolding of subjective interiority onto the world, unites the two events of the common and reveals the development from an impersonal ethics to a radical politics. Regarding the former sense, Wojnarowicz relays the story of a rendezvous with "rough trade" in "Doing Time in a Disposable Body":

> The sweetness of the sad lips of the criminal face lowering itself around my dick and the quiet sucking motion that I guide him into. It is not just that violence fades into sweetness; it's looking at the flesh of the body and recognizing that it is a restraint that keeps the blood inside the form; where the blood of the body creates a pressure so that it would spray out in every direction if it were not for the skin holding it back; it's sensing the history of that body and the temporariness of it all. (*Memories* 28–30)

The sense gleaned here concerns not only the traces of the man's embodied history ("scars," "blue-ink tattoos," and "coal-scratched rubbings made in prison cells" [28]) and the end of that history, his mortality, but also the "temporariness" of the fleshly container's ability to effectively keep "the blood inside the form." The body here is "disposable" in its finitude and in its eventual incapacity to confine its viscera: It is only a matter of time before that body is food for worms, certainly, but even before then its insides will explode violently outward. This is to say, the temporariness "of it all" includes the ephemerality of the man's sweetness, the sex act itself, and, importantly, the skin that keeps the man hermetically sealed. Just as that body will die and that man will become violent again (which he does; Wojnarowicz must fight him off to escape), that flesh too will give way and blood will spray. On a conceptual level, then, Wojnarowicz intuits in this sexual encounter the proximity of finitude and exogeny. The body decays, this much is obvious, but in the fleetingness of the sexual encounter corporeal boundaries become porous, the blood pulsing within becomes part of the world, and a subjective interiority is, literally, exposed. If Wojnarowicz and the Texan man had a mutual love for the foreignness in the self and other, that foreignness here becomes an unknowable finitude. In recognizing and respecting finitude, in becoming an impersonal friend of it, being becomes exogenous. Wojnarowicz senses in anonymous sex the absolute foreignness of individuals, even the simple fact that each will die her or his own death, but that very separation becomes grounds for relation—it is precisely the relation of nonrelation that unleashes difference from its captivity in self-identity. Recognizing in anonymous sex the simultaneity of a "common thanatological destiny" and the exogeny of being, Wojnarowicz senses a communal and political form uncontainable by any institution or identity.

Sense becomes explicitly political in a brief piece Wojnarowicz wrote shortly before his death due to complications from AIDS. I quote it in part here:

> . . . I wake up every morning in this killing machine called america and I'm carrying this rage like a blood-filled egg and there's a thin line between the inside and the outside a thin line between thought and action and that line is simply made up of blood and muscle and bone and I'm waking up more and more from daydreams of tipping amazonian blow darts in "infected blood" and spitting them at the exposed necklines of certain politicians or government health-care officials or those thinly disguised walking swastikas that wear religious garments over their murderous intentions or those rabid strangers parading against AIDS clinics in the nightly news suburbs there's a thin line a very thin line between the inside and the outside. (*Close* 161)

This angry outburst, like the preceding passage, concerns the precarious, fleshly envelope and its volatile innards. This time, however, there is nothing but a "very thin line" between his "infected blood" and the politicians, lawmakers, religious leaders, health care officials, and other bigots who demonize PWAs, and for whom Wojnarowicz wishes death. The barrier itself is "simply made up of blood and muscle and bone" and what seeks to escape is multiple: Furious thoughts that will transform into homicidal behavior, compressed rage into violent political resistance, and, as the corporeal blockade begins to erode, "a thirty-seven-foot-tall one-thousand-one-hundred-and-seventy-two-pound man" (162). What Wojnarowicz observed in a sex partner—pressure, porous flesh, violence, finitude—he now finds in himself, this time in the form of nihilistic rage and murderous desire. This nihilism, however, is a reaction to the social containment of the common he once sensed in sex encounters.

Wojnarowicz's rage is directed at precisely those figures who attempt to harness the common in the name of sovereignty, those who force it into political forms. The temporariness of the event of the common is important: In a flash its movement is not arrested. The common captured, however, begets monsters: Sensuous joy mutates into seething rancor and beings who once opened themselves to the world now turn against it in defense. Just as the drowning victim often unwittingly accelerates his own demise, so we turn against ourselves, one another, and the world when we lose sense of the common. It is only in a collective activism that Wojnarowicz rediscovers the sense to which he earlier had access.[11]

Wojnarowicz's political sense is thus formed in reaction to the violent suppression of the ontological heterogeneity of the common in a homophobic and homo-ness-phobic society. When this heterogeneity is forced to become identical, when the becoming of the common is made to congeal in subjective, relational, or political forms (sexual identity, compulsory monogamy, the state), being-in-common transforms into absolute alienation. The exogenous being whose pulse syncs up with the impersonal rhythms of the world in anonymous sex morphs into the isolated monster whose blood burns within. The nonidentitarian mingling of bodies and pleasures in the sex act mutates into a destructive and nihilistic intersubjectivity. The government that in its neglect proceeds to "murder [PWAs] on a daily basis for nine count them nine long years" (162) finds its home in, and is in fact the source of, Wojnarowicz's homicidal fantasies. Indeed, those institutional forms that arrest the becoming of being-in-common to mark an identifiable subject and administer a manageable population set the stage for a war of all against all.

Only in the recognition of the nonidentical sameness of the other, only in acknowledging the solidarity in a finitude that is absolutely singular and unsharable, only in becoming hospitable to the strangest of all strangers within and without—that is, only in a politics of shared estrangement—might a reactive nihilism be circumvented. The transformation of alienated nihilism to collective resistance comes in an abandonment to a never-shared but radically common finitude. The term *shared estrangement*, then, is ultimately oxymoronic: It involves no intersubjective *partage*, no cannibalization of the other by the self; it is precisely *not* recognizing the self in the Other and not sharing common ground. It is instead an acknowledgment—affective, conscious, or otherwise—of an ontologically differentiated homo-ness, a recognition of the common-ness and singularity of finitude. The politics of shared estrangement in AIDS activism, then, concerns not only the solidarity of PWAs and their caregivers in response to the federal, medical, religious, and media neglect and demonization of AIDS in the early days of the crisis.

David Wojnarowicz, "A Painting to Replace the British Monument in Buenos Aires," 1984.

It is likewise more than the political harnessing of the rage, frustration, and helplessness experienced in witnessing the demise of friends and lovers left to die. More profoundly, it involves a radical abandonment to finitude, a becoming-friend of finitude, through which one intuits and enacts the anarchical common-ness seething in the infinite distance between singularities.

Common Sense

With "sense" Wojnarowicz initially gives name to the eruption of the common in the anonymous sex act. In this experience, the boundary between Self and Other is revealed as illusory and the ruse of subjective interiority is exposed. Being becomes exogenous: In the recognition of the absolute foreignness of finitude, it moves in sync with the world's impersonal rhythms, becomes receptive to its immeasurable variation, and is immersed in the flow of an ever-becoming common. However, when the common can no longer be sensed, when it is captured and forced into sovereign political forms, the "thirty-seven-foot-tall one-thousand-one-hundred-and-seventy-two-pound man" threatens to burst through the skin to begin a killing spree. What prevents him from murdering politicians, doctors, and priests is the solidarity in finitude, the recognition of the common-ness in estrangement, he finds in collective resistance. In locating a life-giving force in an unsharable death, Wojnarowicz activates the politics he senses in the erotic.

The "thirty-seven-foot-tall" man is arguably the subject of a piece by Wojnarowicz entitled, "A Painting to Replace the British Monument in Buenos Aires" (1984), and it is here where we can see Wojnarowicz's nihilism morph into political collaboration.[12] The painting depicts a man-monster burning from within, volcanic in its composition, barely held together, if at all, by a lava-like skin. With fiery, biblically apocalyptic horses racing beneath, the ogre glares with the eyes of Empire (British and American flags). Accordingly, it is dead set on destruction, reaching for the titular monument in the lower right-hand corner to lay waste to it. At the risk of reading AIDS "into" this painting, that is, at the risk of making all art by PWAs reveal something about AIDS, I understand the work to be forging connections between nihilism and the capture of the common in imperialism and global capitalism, as well as between AIDS activists and the mothers of those who disappeared during the Dirty War.

Painted on an Argentinean street poster marketing what seems to be a horseracing track, the piece incorporates two thoroughly commodified forms of public art—the cartoon and the advertisement—and puts them together in a critique of capitalism and colonialism. The monster upon first glance can be interpreted as the bearer of this critique: As a hybrid U.S.–British ambassador, it represents the violence of imperial power; in defacing and destroying an advertisement, an enemy of global capital. In the context of those passages discussed earlier regarding the explosive blood and porous skin of various bodies, however, the monster becomes many more beasts. It is the surfacing being of Wojnarowicz's angry tirade: the PWA on a homicidal rampage. It is the nihilist reacting violently to the capture of the common in colonialism and capitalism, a beast turning against the world and seeking revenge against those political and economic forms that arrest the becoming of being-in-common. It also is the figure materializing in anonymous sex acts, wherein subjective interiors burst forth and boundaries between subject and the world disintegrate. We have here, then, a monster with multiple goals and motivations. Erupting in murderous desire, he not only turns against sovereign power, but at the same time makes a gesture of political solidarity. In replacing a monument built by British colonialists to honor their victory over Argentina, he forges a political relation between PWAs and the colonized, and between grieving, rageful AIDS activists and protesting, mourning Argentinian mothers.

The monument in question sits on the Plaza de Mayo, the main *rambla* in the center of Buenos Aires. Soon after the Dirty War, a small obelisk was placed over the monument, covering it entirely, to commemorate the loss of the Argentinian disappeared. Each Thursday afternoon the mothers of the disappeared march up and down the plaza, grieving openly (Taylor *x*).[13] The painting, then, not only draws connections between the global devastation wrought by AIDS and Empire, but also evokes the uncontainability of affective power, the radical universalism of a rage provoked by grief. It creates a link between the mothers' mourning practice and the ACT UP protests in which Wojnarowicz both participated (die-ins) and inspired (the Ashes Action). In short, it turns nihilism into collective resistance by activating the unsharable common-ness of finitude.

Furthermore, the very idea of disappearance is a recurring theme in Wojnarowicz's memoirs. In *Close to the Knives*, he writes:

> When I was a teenager I had a recurring fantasy that began after my first motorcycle ride. . . . I saw myself riding this machine faster and faster and faster toward the edge of a cliff until I hit the right speed that would take me off the cliff in an arcing motion. At that instant when my body and the machine cleared the edge of the cliff and hit the point in the sky where I was neither rising nor falling—somewhere in there: once my body and the motorcycle hit a point in the light

and wind and loss of gravity, in that exact moment, I would suddenly disappear, and the motorcycle would continue the downward arc and explode into flames somewhere among the rocks at the bottom of the cliff. And it is in that sense of void—that marriage of body-machine and space—where one should most desire a continuance of life, that I most wish to disappear. (40–41)

In writing of a liminal zone between two motions ("neither rising nor falling") and at least two realms (earth and sky; presence and absence), Wojnarowicz calls into question a strict division between life and death—a division quite necessary to biopolitical sovereignty. His longing to disappear is a longing to become-other ("the marriage of body-machine and space"), propelled by an acknowledgment of death's immanence to life. In welcoming death, in wishing to disappear at the moment when he should most crave life, Wojnarowicz essentially becomes a friend of finitude. If finitude is the unknown, the unknowable, the complete stranger, then welcoming it into one's life, inviting it to cohabit, is a gesture of absolute hospitality. Now, both the Texan man and finitude become "less than strangers." As with the Texan, Wojnarowicz does not engage finitude on an intersubjective level—one can never dialectically engage with death; it is utterly opaque and remains so. Befriending this stranger within, however, lends itself toward a politics of friendship as shared estrangement. This relation encourages respect for a difference that can never be the same—an ontological difference that cannot be subsumed into an identity. In this event, one makes oneself infinitely susceptible to variation, radically open to difference both within and without. One forges a relation of nonrelation with oneself and others: The absolute singularity and radical common-ness of finitude becomes the bedrock of friendship. In Maurice Blanchot's words: "Such is, such would be the friendship that discovers the unknown we ourselves are, and the meeting of our own solitude which, precisely, we cannot be alone to experience ('incapable by myself alone, of going to the limits of the extreme')" (*Unavowable Community* 25). It is this gesture—befriending death and respecting its absolute difference—that founds a community of singularities that cannot be contained by political forms invested in hierarchies of identitarian difference. Wojnarowicz's most radical *political* gesture, then, is not suicide or martyrdom for a cause; it is developing a relationship with death that confounds the very logic of biopower.

To better understand this radical gesture, it is necessary to analyze more closely the *bios* and *necros* of biopower. In Foucault's estimation, this "life" is first and foremost the opposite of death: "Now it is over life, throughout its unfolding, that power establishes its dominion: death is power's limit, the moment that escapes it; death becomes the most secret aspect of existence, the most 'private'" (*HoS, V1*, 138). As long as death is made to mean the opposite of life, it perpetually hangs like a menacing storm cloud over the heads of a people. When conceived as life's limit—rather than as immanent to it—death makes us all its subjects: Living becomes an exercise in avoiding death, outsmarting it, foregoing its arrival. Sovereign power—in a word, *biopotere*, the power wielded by political forms that capture the common, that arrest the becoming of being-in-common—requires a conception of death as life's opposite. Death is relegated to the category of pure negation and constitutes the normative framework of life's value. In other words, if biopower invests life with the utmost value—promising a heaven on earth, a life worth living—it is death that determines this value. Sovereign power, therefore, operates on the principle of *making* live or *letting* die; it does not turn away from death, but mobilizes it in the service of normative life management.[14]

Exploring the etymological roots of the "bios" in Foucault's concept of biopower, Giorgio Agamben reveals in *Homo Sacer* that a modern definition of "life" is, in fact, a conflation of two premodern categories: naked life (*zoe*), "the simple fact of living common to all living beings" and *bios*, "the form or way of living proper to an individual or group" (1). Naked life functions as the constitutive exclusion of Classical politics—for Aristotle's *polis*, "the good life" requires a certain disavowal of naked life.[15] In biopower, however, *zoe* disappears in the *bios* of the citizen: these once necessarily separate realms become indistinct. Modern sovereignty rests on the furtive inclusion of naked life in the political realm. The state of exception—that "time out of time" when the sovereign, simultaneously inside and outside the law, declares nothing outside its domain—becomes unexceptional when naked life becomes the placeholder for sovereignty, when birth and citizenship are bound as one. The termination of a citizen's biological life is permissible provided the political concept of naked life is not sacrificed. For in the age of biopower, naked life is no longer a category sublated by politics; instead it dwells in the body of every citizen and authorizes a form of sovereignty, in various state guises, more ruthless and insidious than any Aristotle could have imagined (1–12).

If biopolitical disciplinarity functions through lived behavioral norms that aid in the reproduction of sovereign power, it likewise benefits from a normative conception of death. Taking into account Lee Edelman's claim in *No Future* that queerness plays the fantasmatic role of the death drive in a politics of reproductive futurism,[16] we can see that the "death" so important to biopower is not only physiological but also imbued with a sexual, relational, and communal essence. When AIDS emerges on the biopolitical landscape, for example, the normative criteria of biopower's "life" come to the fore. In the last chapter, I noted the Reagan administration's decidedly genocidal response to AIDS—one that divided the country into a "general" (natural, lawful, heterosexual) population and (monstrous, dangerous, queer) risk groups. Such an understanding of the syndrome makes clear that those lives initially affected by AIDS—gay men, IV drug users, prostitutes, by and large racial minorities—are utterly dispensable, unworthy of biopower's "life" because of their very form of life. AIDS' deaths from this vantage point are only tragic when they terminate a "life worth living," a life productive for capital and the state, a form of life consonant with the normative standards on which the perpetuation of sovereign power depends. Wojnarowicz clearly comprehends this characteristic of biopower by calling into question the strict division between life and death. In so doing, he forms a relationship with death unsanctioned by sovereign power: he reclaims from the sovereign the power to make live and let die.

In a diary entry from 1988 written shortly after his best friend and artistic mentor Peter Hujar died from AIDS-related complications, Wojnarowicz notes the importance yet ultimate ineffectiveness of memorial services. Writing in capital letters, he notes:

> THE THING THAT'S IMPORTANT ABOUT MEMORIALS IS THEY BRING A PRIVATE GRIEF OUT OF THE SELF AND MAKE IT A LITTLE MORE PUBLIC WHICH ALLOWS FOR COMMUNICATIVE TRANSITION, PEELS AWAY ISOLATION, BUT THE MEMORIAL IS IN ITSELF STILL AN ACCEPTANCE OF IMMOBILITY, INACTIVITY. TOO MANY TIMES I'VE SEEN THE COMMUNITY BRUSH OFF ITS MEMORIAL CLOTHES, ITS GRIEVING CLOTHES, AND GATHER IN THE CONFINES OF AT LEAST FOUR WALLS AND UTTER WORDS OR SONGS OF BEAUTY TO ACKNOWLEDGE THE PASSING OF ONE OF ITS CHILDREN/PARENTS/LOVERS BUT AFTER THE MEMORIAL THEY RETURN HOME AND WAIT FOR THE NEXT PASSING, THE NEXT DEATH. IT'S HEALTHY TO MAKE THE PRIVATE PUBLIC, BUT THE WALLS OF THE ROOM OR CHAPEL ARE THIN AND UNNECESSARY. ONE SIMPLE STEP CAN BRING IT OUT INTO A MORE PUBLIC SPACE. DON'T GIVE ME A MEMORIAL IF I DIE. GIVE ME A DEMONSTRATION. (*In the Shadow* 206)

This passage gives pause less for its ACT UP sloganeering and its caps-lock boldness—all of these qualities are typical of Wojnarowicz's late style—but rather for two curious fragments that demand further investigation: "one simple step" and "if I die" from the consecutive sentences, "One simple step can bring it [grief] out into a more public space. Don't give me a memorial if I die." The latter phrase, "if I die," must first be understood in its biographical context: Written at a moment in the author's life when memorial services were *de rigueur* due to the devastation wrought by AIDS on his New York community of friends and lovers, the implied meaning here seems, "If I too die from AIDS, like Peter, my memorial service should be a demonstration." Not surprising, especially coming from a man who was both an inspiration for and a participant in ACT UP actions, yet the unconscious of this likely slip reads more interestingly. The making contingent of the inevitable in the phrase "if I die" speaks to an incomprehensibility or even a willed amnesia concerning the inescapability of death—a forgetting, that is, possibly crucial to survival and continued creativity amid death's ubiquity. Nietzsche perhaps best describes this forgetfulness, what he calls an *active* forgetfulness, in the aphorism, "The Thought of Death," discussed in Chapter 1. I repeat it here for the sake of convenience:

> How strange it is that this sole certainty and common element [i.e., death] makes almost no impression on people, and that nothing is further from their minds than the feeling that they form a brotherhood of death. It makes me happy that men do not want at all to think the thought of death! I should like very much to do something that would make the thought of life even a hundred times more appealing to them.

For Wojnarowicz, living through the early days of AIDS panic, witnessing countless AIDS deaths, himself succumbing to AIDS-related complications in 1992, this forgetting is not or not only a deliberate ignorance, but also an acceptance of death's immanence to life. Although life might become "a hundred times more appealing" when death is omnipresent, in the age of AIDS a clear separation between the two realms becomes a fantasy no longer sustainable.[17] As opposed to dialectically subsuming death into life so as to "seize the day," Wojnarowicz rethinks the binary formulation of the two terms. In actively forgetting the inevitability of death, he simultaneously welcomes this stranger and thereby makes a decisive break with sovereign power. Deciding "if" he is going to die—that is, if he will *choose* to die as opposed to accepting that fact as a foregone conclusion—Wojnarowicz reclaims from the sovereign its authority over biopolitical investment and necropolitical abandonment. If death is power's limit, if the sovereign uses this limit to establish the normative standards by which a life must be lived, then in making death one's own, in creating a complicity between life and death, one disintegrates the boundary between the two realms and defects from the dominion of *biopotere*. When sovereign power can no longer be derived from death, a radical politics of life can commence.

Wojnarowicz's call for a demonstration instead of a memorial service illuminates the terms of such a politics. The "one simple step" needed to transform private grieving into public outrage involves not only the destruction of the walls that house the rooms in which memorial services take place, but likewise the destruction of the conceptual barriers between private and public. Mourning, according to Freud in "Mourning and Melancholia," is the proper way for the living to come to terms with the dead. Although a struggle arises when the libido must withdraw its cathexion to the (deceased) love-object, in the end, "reality gains the day" (166), the ego is restored, libidinal energy is eventually transferred to a new object, and the griever returns to the world to live again.[18] However changed the mourner in Freud's scenario, the world remains the same. To mourn privately is a necessary step to return to "life as usual"; death must be dealt with in private (the home, the chapel) so that public life remains orderly, manageable. For Wojnarowicz, a public funereal demonstration, then, would productively disrupt such order: rather than an "acceptance of immobility, inactivity," his protest/death march calls attention to the uniqueness of one particular life and the common-ness of finitude as such. This fantasized demonstration is not an occasion to commemorate a martyr; the sacrifice of life for a cause only confirms the terms of sovereign power for which death is the limit. If martyrdom teaches us that one must die in order to resist or become inaccessible to sovereign power, then politics becomes mired in death and the sovereign reigns supreme. In befriending finitude so as to loosen sovereign power's grip on life, Wojnarowicz becomes neither saint nor martyr; he instead transforms life's morbidity into a politics of constituent potentiality. Such a friendship involves neither a lusty death wish nor a dialectical subsumption through which death becomes a dreadful, ordering and organizing principle. Rather, as we glimpsed in Foucault's apartment in Chapter 1, this relationship requires an ethics of impersonality. To welcome finitude as an unknowable foreigner, to relate precisely at the point of nonrelation, encourages a strangeness, an openness, a becoming exogenous; indeed a very different relationship to death than the one commanded by sovereign power.

But how to cultivate such a relation? Giorgio Agamben once again becomes helpful here, this time in assessing the radicality of Wojnarowicz's political vision. In "Form-of-Life," an essay that predates *Homo Sacer* and is in some ways a *précis* of it, Agamben emphasizes the political potentialities of the essay's eponymous concept. As in *Homo Sacer*, Agamben begins by noting the two distinct definitions of life found in Classical philosophy: *zoe* (naked life) and *bios* (form of life). In modern biopower, naked life is mortified in juridical-social identities and becomes "the invisible sovereign that stares at us behind the dull-witted masks of the powerful, who, whether or not they realize it, govern us in its name" (8). From the perspective of sovereign power, forms of life are secondary to naked life, worthwhile inasmuch as they fulfill their biopolitical "destiny." This biological life, however, is an ahistorical abstraction ("life" and "death" have no intrinsic meaning from a scientific standpoint [7–8]) and exists nowhere but in its effects. Naked life always and only exists in forms of life: it is a concept only tangible in its material manifestations. Modern sovereign power takes control over naked life by making it indistinguishable from citizenship and biopolitically administered identity.

When unified with its form, that is, not mortified in its biopolitical vocation, however, naked life is a becoming of forms of life, or, in Agamben's lexicon, a "form-of-life." Thought-as-experience/experiment—a communal practice, an activity in which *bios* is only its own *zoe*—is Agamben's example of a form-of-life. He writes:

> Only if I am not always already and solely enacted, but rather delivered to a possibility and a power, only if living and intending and apprehending themselves are at stake each time in what I live and intend and apprehend—only if, in other words, there is thought—only then can a form of life become, in its own factness and thingness, *form-of-life*, in which it is never possible to isolate something like naked life. (9)

Echoing Foucault, whose concept of the care of the self also involves both thought-as-experiment/experience and the relinking of forms of being with being-in-common, Agamben posits form-of-life as the ground of a politics of potentiality. In contrast to the ambivalence that suffuses the concept in *Homo Sacer*, form-of-life in this essay has a thoroughly positive value. In this later work, Agamben illustrates the conflicting modes form-of-life might take. Both Adolf Hitler and *Flamen Diale* ("one of the greatest priests of classical Rome" [182]), for example, embody the coincidence of *zoe* and *bios*: The former juridically, in the way the political and physical bodies collapse into one; the latter joyfully, his naked life indistinguishable from the cultic functions it performs, his private and public lives identical.

Agamben's rendering of an *ambivalent* form-of-life in *Homo Sacer* gives pause, especially when considered alongside his critique of Antonio Negri's concept of constituent power. Not unlike Butler in her understanding of Foucault's power, Agamben claims that Negri's constituent power is always part of constituted power and that the very separation of constituent and constituted is groundless (43). It seems, however, that Negri's distinction between *biopotere* and *biopotenza* finds its conceptual double in Agamben's juridical (Hitler) and joyful (*Flamen Diale*) forms-of-life. Conversely, although Hardt and Negri distance themselves from Agamben in interpreting *Homo Sacer*'s naked life as "the negative limit of humanity" (*Empire*, 366), or, in a word, death, Negri's concept of living labor resonates with Agamben's concept of form-of-life in the earlier essay. Somewhere between "Form-of-Life" and *Homo Sacer*, that is to say, Agamben's naked life *immortalis* becomes naked life *moribunda*. Because *Homo Sacer* is written from the standpoint of sovereign power, constituent power is deadened, merely a variation of constituted power. In "Form-of-Life," however, Agamben conceives power from the opposite pole: Thought is a living labor, a potentiality that redoubles, not depletes, itself in cohering with practices; there is always, then, a surplus of possibility when naked life is joined with its form. Negri's words, ironically, best describe what I am understanding as form-of-life in Agamben's essay. He writes:

> In undergoing the process of actualization, potentiality re-potentiates itself, re-creates itself to the second power: far from being mortified, potentiality thus becomes more powerful precisely by actualizing itself. But such an ontology of potentiality is nothing other than Marxian ontology: the productive act does not decree the death of labor; the productive act, rather, is that act which exalts and accumulates labor—and once it does that, one can then take off once again, starting from a new and higher level. ("It's a Powerful Life" 180)

In "Form-of-Life," a naked life joined with a form is not exhaustive but expansive; in this essay Agamben has not yet given up on a naked life that incessantly produces when joined with its form. Although *Homo Sacer*'s "form-of-life" is arguably the logical extension of the concept in "Form-of-Life," it might be simply one of many elaborations of this early version; at worst, *Homo Sacer* betrays the concept's potential.

So, what if Agamben's early notion of form-of-life had been taken in a different direction? What if it remains the positive ground for a politics of potentiality? And what, in the end, does this have to do with Wojnarowicz and AIDS activism? In a word, Agamben helps us understand AIDS activism as a form-of-life in which *zoe* coheres in *bios*: a set of practices within which living itself is at stake. Befriending finitude in the mode of shared estrangement is none other than the invention of a form-of-life. AIDS activists compel finitude to collaborate with a way of life, linking naked life with a form. Like *Flamen Diale* whose public and private selves are indistinguishable, AIDS activists make their deaths, that most private phenomenon in biopower, a matter of public record and concern. From die-ins, a form of protest in which activists become corpses in charged public spaces such as churches or high traffic thoroughfares, to the Ashes Action, a demonstration at which ACT UP members threw the remains of their friends and lovers on the White House lawn, ACT UP transforms the morbidity of naked life into the ground of constituent power. In doing so they reveal not only the ways in which naked life is exploited by sovereign power, but also that naked life is a source of renewal, potentiality, and possibility—laboring to live reveals living labor. From the standpoint of AIDS activism, naked life is not the corporeal powerlessness manipulated by *biopotere* but a finitude to befriend. Moreover, making death immanent to life ushers in what Spinoza calls an "absolute freedom": a freedom of boundless becomings and limitless energies emergent in conquering the fear of death (*Ethics* 290–98). Hazy fantasies of an afterlife imagined to console mortal anxieties ironically make death something to fear—heaven or hell?; will I make it, will I not?—and prevent a frank reconciliation between the two realms. In a radical abandonment to finitude, however, there is no choice but to live deliberately or die trying: In overcoming the fear of death, we become most dangerous, most creative, or both at once.

Only when death is understood as immanent to life does a progressive politics of living have a chance. Public AIDS mourning rituals and protests are arguably the political manifestation of such an understanding. If, on an individual level, the befriending of finitude foils the biopolitical imperative to preserve an absolute separation between life and death, then writ large, in the form of collective resistance, it holds the capacity to disrupt "life as usual" and consequently to undermine sovereign power's life management. From this perspective, die-ins, in which AIDS activists make privatized death public, are arguably the result of such friendships. In staging their own deaths, in, essentially, living their deaths, activists are liberated, dangerous, artistic. When finitude is welcomed simultaneously as absolute stranger and friend, living passionately, as Wojnarowicz's life writings demonstrate, is nothing to fear.

In AIDS activism, the death inherent in *zoe* is transformed from individual morbidity to collective potentiality. Insofar as public AIDS mourning rituals make death communal and political, they render visible the forms of life against which normative life is defined in biopower. If death is necessarily relegated to the private sphere, such rituals bring death out of the closet in order to expose the biopolitical manipulation of life. Another fantasy of Wojnarowicz's from *Close to the Knives*:

> I imagine what it would be like if, each time a lover, a friend, or a stranger died of this disease, their friends, lovers, or neighbors would take the dead body and drive with it in a car a hundred miles an hour to washington d.c. and blast through the gates of the white house and come to a screeching halt before the entrance and dump their lifeless form on the front steps. It would be comforting to see how those friends, neighbors, lovers, and strangers mark time and place and history in such a public way. (122)

On October 11, 1992, Wojnarowicz's dream became reality in the Ashes Action.[19] Chanting "Bringing death to your door/We won't take it anymore," ACT UP members stormed the White House gate armed with urns containing the remains of friends and lovers. Citing Wojnarowicz as an inspiration for this "political funeral," these rageful mourners threw the remains, urns and all, over the heads of the ever-present police force and onto the South Lawn, ashes flying in every direction. This blatant refusal to keep death tucked away in the private sphere is emblematic of ACT UP's most radical gesture: the transformation of naked life's morbidity into a politics of constituent potentiality—the invention of a form-of-life. Comparing this action with the AIDS Memorial Quilt, one participating activist declares: "The AIDS Quilt has become the acceptable face of AIDS death in the US; its focus is New Age religiosity rather than social or political explication." Repudiating all such flights into transcendence with the Ashes Action, ACT UP reveals that bare life has been exploited in modern biopower: The life that is a source of power has been veiled in a death cloak. Symbolic of a radical abandonment to finitude wherein life itself is at stake in living, the Ashes Action serves as merely one example of the kind of politics that can emerge when death's finality is incorporated as a source of potentiality. Indeed, Wojnarowicz's life writings are nothing if not manifestos of the political potency of befriending finitude in both the sex act and activism. Exploding the conceptual boundaries between Self and Other, between self and world, and between a public life and a private death, his "common sense" remains vital to a queer constituent power.

Epilogue

Whatever Friends

In the end, what can be done with a concept of friendship as shared estrangement? Can the multitudinous "we" referred to in the queer mantra "We are Everywhere" mobilize around a representational politics of friendship? Impossible, both conceptually and practically. In these dark days when an institution as wholesome, state empowering, and economy boosting as gay marriage is still believed to be, by more than a handful of America's priestly lawmakers, the slippery slope that will lead to excesses such as bestiality and incest, the more widespread yet less tangible relation of friendship stands no chance in the halls of political representation. Yet what seems on the surface friendship's greatest weakness is in fact its greatest strength: Its very unrepresentability points toward a politics beyond representation. Giorgio Agamben in *The Coming Community* emphasizes the political power of unrepresentability and summons a community of "whatever-being," a community of what I understand to be friends:

> What the State cannot tolerate in any way, however, is that the singularities form a community without affirming an identity, that humans co-belong without any representable condition of belonging (even in the form of a simple presupposition). The State, as Alain Badiou has shown, is not founded on a social bond, of which it would be an expression, but rather on the dissolution, the unbinding it prohibits. For the State, therefore, what is important is never the singularity as such, but only its inclusion in some identity, whatever identity (but the possibility of the whatever itself being taken up without an identity is a threat the State cannot come to terms with). (38)

It goes without saying that patriarchal, homosocial friendships are the vehicles through which contemporary governmental and corporate

149

organizations perpetuate their reign of terror. This model of friendship and its concomitant violence and exclusivity is precisely the "social bond" Aristotle located at the heart of the *polis*. As Agamben notes here, and as Foucault noted elsewhere, what such patriarchal friendships suppress and fear most are the excessive, asubjective, affective intensities surging through them. A state can only manage identifiable subjects and deadened relational institutions: those empty shells that arrest the becoming of being and forcefully prevent the coming of being-in-common. The "whatever" that is a "threat the State cannot come to terms with" is none other than the infinitely variegated sameness that Bersani and Dean find in cruising and non-monogamy, that Wojnarowicz sensed in his sex and his activism, that the AIDS buddy network put to work in the service of caregiving, and that AIDS activists transformed into a politics of shared estrangement. If it is the case that the radical heterogeneity seething beneath identifiable subjects and representable communities is snuffed out in the name of "belonging," then the legalization of gay marriage, however celebrated as a path toward greater social diversity, is merely another instance of the common captured.

Like Bill's withheld AIDS cure in *To the Friend*, marriage taunts us with the possibility of salvation, a cure of sorts to a politics of fear and exclusion. But just as Guibert at the end of that novel learns to withdraw from Bill's game, the queer community might similarly recognize the pitfalls of keeping our eyes locked on the marital prize. Medieval pronouncements concerning marriage's sanctity are merely classic examples of tried-and-true rhetorical bait and switch: They make us just outraged enough to remain docilely locked within the discursive framework of the "marriage debate," while distracting us from more radically immanent, more politically menacing, whatever friendships. Gay marriage will eventually be legalized in the United States because capital knows no morality: If it's good for both the economy and for the state—creating manageable consumers and citizens—it will be hard-pressed to fail. Judith Butler's remarks on the use of identity for rights and representation come to mind here:

> As much as it is necessary to assert political demands through recourse to identity categories, and to lay claim to the power to name oneself and determine the conditions under which that name is used, it is also impossible to sustain that kind of mastery over the trajectory of those categories within discourse. This is not an argument against using identity categories, but it is a reminder of the risk that attends every such use. (*Bodies* 227–28)

The fight for gay marriage is doubtless situated within the conundrum of reifying the very categories that have historically constrained and disciplined same-sex desire. Its success will only fortify the link between truth and sexuality, a link that has proven immensely useful to the state. But as gay rights activists lobby for marriage, a Faustian pact in which our souls are not the only thing on offer, friendships that call into question traditional, dialectical conceptions of belonging, community, and liberation can, and should, also be nurtured.

If the "development towards which the problem of homosexuality tends is the one of friendship," it is because friendship is always a becoming and refuses to cohere into an identity. By contrast, if homosexuality is a "problem" it is precisely because it arrests the becoming of being—sexological categories apprehend a heterogeneous common longing to assemble singularities in anti-identitarian communities. The friend intuits and enacts this common: it is a fleeting placeholder for the asubjective affectivity moving through ontologically variegated singularities; it is the figure that cultivates an internally differentiated sameness and opens itself and others to the infinite variation of being. The friend thus welcomes the stranger: makes it familiar while respecting and fostering its foreignness. In befriending absolute foreignness—an irreducible, inarticulable foreignness in the form of finitude—the friend sets the stage for a politics of shared estrangement: a politics that undercuts the sovereign's capacity to make live or let die, a politics that confounds the very logic of *biopotere*.

I hear the corporeal music made by this community of whatever friends in a 1992 Bob Ostertag composition entitled "All the Rage." A collaboration among Ostertag, the Kronos Quartet, and David Wojnarowicz (whose "A Painting to Replace the British Monument in Buenos Aires" appears on the disc's cover), "All the Rage" is a manipulated recording of a gay rights rally accompanied by a string concerto and a spoken-word poem concerning gay-bashing, bashing back, and AIDS mourning. The title of the work speaks not only to the affects produced in the AIDS activism of that era, but also to the "trendiness" of the syndrome at that time. From the red ribbons donned by celebrities to the use of AIDS to sell products (e.g., a Benetton advertisement featuring a Christ-like AIDS patient on his death bed),[1] the endless media spectacle generated by AIDS was an attempt to represent the syndrome so as to domesticate it, to overexpose it so as to resolve the crisis in identitarian representation it effected. The colloquial, clichéd title, then, is at least three things at once:

1. A cutting, satirical reference to the "chic" media spectacle of AIDS.

2. An acknowledgment of the rage this spectacle produces.

3. An homage to the affect that underscores the composition
   and AIDS activism itself.

In the cover art, as I analyzed in Chapter 5, all of these furies are visualized, and more.

Although instrumental to the conception of the project, Wojnarowicz died of complications due to AIDS before the release of "All the Rage." Bob Ostertag, an American composer of electronic/experimental music, wrote the piece after recording a riot in San Francisco in October 1991. The riot was a response to the veto of a bill designed to protect gays and lesbians from discrimination. In the piece, Ostertag weds manipulated recorded sound with notated music and a libretto. The result is a composition which lies at the generic interstices of modern classical/avant-garde music and spoken-word performance. Like that point of indistinguishibility, that in-between, Wojnarowicz so often tried to conceive, "All the Rage" constitutes a liminal space of its own. Although locatable in a tradition of American experimental music (Steve Reich's "Come Out" leaps to mind), "All the Rage"—both the cover art and the composition—is a *bricolage* of aesthetic forms that coheres into a unique whole. Just as Wojnarowicz paints on a found Argentinian advertisement, Ostertag composes over the found sound of a crowd's screams, chants, and rumblings.[2] The music of the body thus grounds the composition and threatens to overtake the notated music and lyrics throughout. The various corporeal noises—wails, grunts, voices, shrieks—seem to belong to nobody and everybody: They are anonymous, singular, and radically common. But who are these protesters? How many are there? Tens? Hundreds? Thousands? The very unidentifiableness of the crowd confounds, yet its visceral music persists.

In a lecture given to the Music Teachers National Association in 1957, John Cage spoke of music's future. In one of his more anecdotal moments he remarks:

> There is no such thing as an empty space or an empty time. There is always something to see, something to hear. In fact, try as we may to make a silence, we cannot. For certain engineering purposes, it is desirable to have as silent a situation as possible. Such a room is called an anechoic chamber, its six walls made of special material, a room without echoes. I entered one at Harvard University several years ago and heard two sounds, one high, one low. When I described them to the engineer, he informed me that the high one was my nervous system in operation, the low one my blood in circulation. Until I die

there will be sounds. And they will continue following my
death. One need not fear about the future of music. (*Silence* 8)

The musicked body predates what we call music: In fact, it presignifies
music as a signifying system. For Deleuze and Guattari, music is of primary
significance in helping to articulate philosophy. Their idea that meaning
originates in bodies, rather than being imposed on them necessarily or
solely through discourse, aids in interpreting Ostertag's composition. The
rage welling up in his recorded riot is a music all its own and common
to all. The music of affect, like Wojnarowicz's sense, resists representation
because it is so radically common. Producing infinite, ametrical rhythms
that precede the regulatory concepts of harmony, melody, and meter,
the musicked body orchestrates prior to mediation by linguistic or visual
discourses; musical affect is excessive of the semiotic codes that make
it meaningful. Existing prior to thought, the musicked body may be
understood as stimulating thought, even initiating it. The immediacy of
corporeal affect produces a "sonic space-time," an interval between music
and meaning, in which the body simply is musicked, in which alternative
modes of thinking, hearing, and perceiving—grounded in, rather than
imposed upon, the body—are made possible.[3] Writing on the proximity
of music, affect, and finitude, Deleuze and Guattari note: "Music is never
tragic, music is joy. But there are times it necessarily gives us a taste for
death; not so much happiness as dying happily, being extinguished"
(*Thousand Plateaus* 299).

The spoken-word component of "All the Rage," far from subtle,
supplies linguistic signification to the affects that emerge through the
music.[4] The libretto grounds the piece, offering an accessible counterpart
to the anonymous yelps and at times frenzied, at times elegiac string
accompaniment. Non-narrative, the words become yet another instrument,
another voice in this sea of voices, distinctive and forceful. The lyrics are
most interesting in their more onomatopoetic moments, when they mimic
the musicked body and slip into a repetitive stammer: "Beating. Beating
breaking and beating and breaking and beaten and beating and breaking
and beating and beating." Yet as stirring as these irate barbs and saddening
vignettes are, their power pales in comparison to the nonlinguistic musical
aspects of the piece. Although "All the Rage" refers to a particular historical
event, the riot we hear does not represent it. Indeed, the composition has
everything and nothing to do with its historical referent. The manipulation
of the tape—a single voice repeatedly chanting "Go for it!," another, "Burn
it down!," looped whistles, digitally enhanced window smashing, and so
on—calls into question the riot's very reality. Far from the conventions of

realism used in documentary film and news clips, this "representation" resists representation: No matter how many times we listen, we will never know how many people were there, what they looked like, or even if the event occurred at all. The whatever friends responsible for this racket remain anonymous and invisible, refusing to consolidate into a community of belonging, refusing to affirm a manipulable identity.

As reportage and advertising have proven, representations of AIDS and AIDS deaths domesticate this radically unrepresentable syndrome and make it serviceable for capital. In an age where the image designates value, in Debord's coinage, "the society of the spectacle," representability is always commodifiable. Although "All the Rage" refers to a specific event, it points toward a politics beyond representation: a gathering of whatever friends, a community of being-in-common uncontainable in identitarian hierarchies. Its affects converge with and form new compositions with the sadness of the mothers of the disappeared, with the violence of Empire, with the furious joy of activists. And of course rage: rage as the affect of infinite mourning, rage as the symphony of the musicked body. The very repeatability of the recording puts us in a different relation with the dead: We listen and the dispersed crowd regroups; we stare and Wojnarowicz and the millions of lives lost to AIDS reanimate. Like the Argentine mothers, our mourning is perpetual. Like the world in the midst of a pandemic, we are inconsolable. Although an artifact of a bygone era, this symphony is hardly finished.

Notes

Introduction

1. In addition to Deleuze and Guattari's musings on friendship and thought in *What is Philosophy?* (2–6; 102–107), my reflections on the provenance of friendship as shared estrangement also are indebted to Eleanor Kaufmann's *The Delirium of Praise*. See especially Chapter Four, "Madness and Repetition: The Absence of Work in Deleuze, Foucault, and Jacques Martin," 62–83.

2. A cropped close-up of the photo appears on the cover of Gallimard's collection of Guibert's photography, *Photographies*, as well as on the cover of Guibert's posthumously published novel, *Blindsight*. The image also appears, among other places, in Pierre Borhan's *Man to Man: A History of Gay Photography* 218.

3. Raymond Macherel argues that in placing "*L'ami*" at the beginning of *Le seul visage*, Guibert, whose reputation as a writer had already been established, announces himself as a photographer. Macherel interprets Guibert's inserted hand, the focal point of the image, as the mark of a photographer's presence. The hand calls attention to the photographer's power to direct our gaze and to determine, via the depression of a shutter release by the other "invisible hand," exactly what and how we see. Octavio Moreno Cabrera builds on Macherel's thesis, asserting that Guibert's gesture foregrounds a problem inherent to the medium: The outstretched hand highlights the gap between subject and object, between viewer and viewed, and renders the photographic gaze tactile, violating, potentially violent. I discuss in the pages to come the implications of both these authors' observations for a Guibertian theory of friendship. See Raymond Macherel, *La tentation d'image(s): Ecriture et photographie dans l'oeuvre d'Hervé Guibert* 16–20; and, Octavio Moreno Cabrera *La photo écrite et le roman flashé: Modes de relation de l'image photographique et du texte littéraire dans l'oeuvre d'Hervé Guibert* 108–11.

4. For analytical purposes, I call these figures by name at the outset of my interpretation, only to complicate such naming in note 6.

5. Viewing "*L'ami*" alongside Guibert's male nudes (see, e.g., "T., 1976" and "*Sans-titre, 1979–1980*" in *Photographies*), as well as in the biographical context of the photographer's sexual self-identification, it is understandable why many

have concluded that this photograph concerns gay identity, homosexual desire, etc. Curiously, however, "*L'ami*," and not the more "homosexual" male nudes, is the only of Guibert's photos featured in Borhan's *Man to Man: A History of Gay Photography*, an anthology featuring almost exclusively nudes and same-sex sex acts. Raymond Macherel similarly argues that the photo presents Guibert as a subject of (homosexual) desire, but he complicates the matter. On the one hand, the arguably forceful hand gesture, the shirtless chest on which the hand rests, the intimate lighting, and so on, seem a declaration of sexual identity. On the other hand, this photo is complex and polyvalent, more than just a "gay-positive" image. For Macherel, it renders visible the circulation of desire itself:

> *Cette photo est donc bien plus que ce que le regard commun veut bien y voir c'est-à-dire la revendication d'un désir homosexuel. En rendant visible ce qui est de l'ordre de l'invisible, <<L'ami>> exprime certains des enjeux essentiels de l'acte photographique et fixe toute la tension mobile de désir, tension entre la vise et la retenue, entre la pudeur et l'impudeur, entre le regard suspendu et le moment de l'étreinte.* (20)

> [This photo is thus much more than what everybody wants to see, that is to say, the reclamation of homosexual desire. In making visible the unseen, "*L'ami*" explores some of the essential stakes of the photographic act and captures all the mobile tension of desire, tension between yearning and restraint, between shame and shamelessness, between the suspended gaze and the moment of the embrace. (translation mine)]

Like Macherel, I resist the urge to limit my interpretation of the photo to the biographical and the "homosexual" so as to allow the photograph to speak more openly.

   6. Although biographical context and the size of the reaching hand justify the assumption that we are viewing the limb of one anatomically male Hervé Guibert, the hand itself is not unequivocally masculine. Specifically, it reveals little or no body hair and the arm to which it is attached is clothed in what could be, in conventional sartorial semiotics, a woman's blouse. Guibert, however, frequently photographed his outstretched limbs, usually a hand, sometimes a foot or two: see "*Sans titre, 1981*," and a shot almost compositionally identical to "*L'ami*," "*Sans titre, 1982*." Thierry, in various states of undress, is also a frequent subject in Guibert's photographs, usually referred to as "T." The chest hair and morphology match the Thierry of "*Thierry, 1979*" (presented on the adjacent page in the Gallimard volume, *Photographies*). Given the biographical and textual evidence, it is finally safe to assume that the outstretched hand belongs to Guibert and the chest to Thierry. However, in what must have been a slip, or, more interestingly, a betrayal, Agathe Gaillard renamed "*L'ami*," "*T., L'ami*" in a posthumous 1994 retrospective of Guibert's work, "*Photographies*," at the Galerie Claire Fontaine in Luxembourg. Guibert himself never identified Thierry in his original title: both in his hand-written table of contents for *Le seul visage* ("*Liste des photos publiées dans*

Le seul visage," IMEC) and in the book itself, the photograph is simply *"L'ami."* Although this name change might at first glance seem insignificant, identifying Thierry as the friend arguably transforms what I understand to be a nascent theory of friendship into a mere biographical document. In short, the more specific title alters the meaning of "the friend," and, in turn, the concept of friendship, which is in fact averse to proper names.

7. Ralph Sarkonak, referring to Guibert's novel, *To the Friend*, describes the paradoxical relational dynamic between Guibert and Thierry (Jules in the novel) as a binding separation. After quoting a long passage from the novel concerning these characters' impending deaths from AIDS, Sarkonak writes: "It [the passage] describes Hervé and Jules making out not just in spite but in the face of the terrible syndrome that at once binds and separates them" ("Traces and Shadows" 190). I see this same dynamic visualized in *"L'ami,"* which, because it was taken well before Guibert knew he or Thierry were HIV positive, seems an integral component of Guibert's theory of friendship.

8. Frédérique Poinat, in *L'oeuvre siamoise: Hervé Guibert et l'experience photographique*, discusses the photo as a moment in a sexual/sensual narrative:

> *Le corps nu devient pratiquement une abstraction et pourtant un moment unique de tendresse et de désir. Il s'agit ici d'exprimer le sens du toucher et cette image, dans son flou et son modelé lumineux, va au-delà d'une caractéristique traditionelle du genre. Avant d'être une image gay, la photographie de Guibert isole un moment de tendresse entre deux corps masculins.* (100)

> [The naked body becomes almost an abstraction, and yet this is a special moment, full of tenderness and desire. It is here in expressing the sense of touch that this image, in its haze and its sculpted lighting, goes beyond the traditional conventions of the genre. Before being a "gay" image, Guibert's photograph isolates a moment of tenderness between two male bodies. (translation mine)]

Poinat also observes that *"L'ami"* is consistent with a photographic trend in the 1980s concerning a "plural discourse" of masculinity: in the works of, for example, Duane Michals, Ajamu, Nan Goldin, and so forth, male bodies are depicted not as the site of patriarchal phallic power, but as vulnerable, tender, and with multiple surfaces.

9. I refer to this iconic act of betrayal here to highlight the importance of betrayal itself for a Guibertian ethics of friendship. See ensuing discussion and note 16.

10. See, among other texts, Gilles Deleuze's "Desire and Pleasure" in which Deleuze notes: "The last time we saw each other, Michel told me, with much kindness and affection, something like, I cannot bear the word *desire*; even if you use it differently, I cannot keep from thinking or living that desire = lack, or that desire is repressed. Michel added, whereas myself, what I call pleasure is perhaps what you call desire; but in any case I need another word than *desire*"

(*Foucault and His Interlocutors* 189). I elaborate on Foucault's work on the ethics of pleasure in Chapter 2.

11. See Foucault, "The End of the Monarchy of Sex" (*Foucault Live* 217).

12. I borrow this phrase, "the administered life," from Adorno and Horkheimer's *Dialectic of Enlightenment* and from Adorno's *Minima Moralia*. In brief, their concept concerns the social and psychological effects following the shift from high capitalism to late capitalism and the predominance of the Culture Industry. The typical characteristic of the individual under late capitalism, in their view, is a damaged ego—ego-weakness and narcissism—resulting from repeated and inescapable exposure to products of the Culture Industry. Self-preservation becomes possible only by identifying and adapting to the whims of capital, by privileging the exchange value of commodities over use value. In other words, self-preservation is intimately entangled with self and social destruction that finds its extreme form in fascism, the conditions for which already exist under late capitalism. Although, of course, Foucault took umbrage at Frankfurt School theories of sexual liberation and instinctual rebellion (largely the ideas of Marcuse and Reich), I find some conceptual consonance between Adorno's administered life and Foucault's disciplinary society. It could be argued, in fact, that much of Foucault's late work entails adapting Adorno's concept to his own (biopower, governmentality, etc.) and thus imagining alternatives to the *biopolitically* administered life. For a discussion of the original concept, see Adorno and Horkheimer, *Dialectic of Enlightenment* ix–x, 38, 264; as well as Adorno's *Minima Moralia* 42, 117, 124.

13. See Montaigne, "Of Friendship" in *The Complete Essays of Montaigne* 135–44.

14. This phrase in the original is "*par un sort thanatologique commun.*" (*A l'ami* 102). Linda Coverdale translates it as "we would share the same fate in death" (*To the Friend* 91). I am partial to Emily Apter's "by a common thanatological destiny," however, because, as she notes, "*sort* means both destiny or lot, and spell or charm." ("Fantom Images" 96). In my reading, Guibert is surely making a pun here: these friends' common fate is simultaneously a curse and, as disturbing as it might seem, a blessing. Death is both the end and the foundation of their friendship. I build on the notion of finitude as friendship's bedrock in Chapter 2 when discussing Guibert's *To the Friend*.

15. One cannot overlook the possibility that Guibert's betrayals of Foucault were "crimes of passion," especially because he himself referred to them as such. My interest in raising the issue of a possible lover's vengeance, however, is not to set straight the biographical record, nor to psychoanalyze the treacherous acts, nor even to overemphasize the possible, likely, erotic charge between these friends. It is, rather, to point out that in a friendship as unusual as theirs and in theories of friendship such as theirs, sexual desire (and its discontents) is a red herring. Judging from their work on friendship and what we know of their relational lives, sex does not make or break a friendship—it is simply not the pivot around which the bond turns. Certainly, the betrayals may be borne of unrequited love (as evidenced in *To the Friend*, perhaps, by Hervé-the-protagonist's bitter jealousy toward Muzil's lover, Stéphane, and by Hervé's quite conflicted response to seeing

Muzil's secret bedroom after that character's death [105–107])—but the fact that Guibert incorporates betrayal into his concept of friendship reveals how important such an act is to the relation. For an index of the critical responses to Guibert's betrayal of Foucault's secrets, see Sarkonak, *Angelic Echoes* 205–206; and, Apter, "Fantom Images" notes 2–5, 96.

16. Guibert betrayed Roland Barthes in similar fashion. After Barthes's death Guibert published a quite heart-rending love letter Barthes wrote to him in 1977. See "Fragments for H.," in *"L'Autre Journal,"* Issue 4, Semaine du 19 au 25 mars, 1986.

17. *"Le 28 juillet 1983, Michel m'écrit un vrai texte dans une lettre"* in *"L'Autre Journal d'Hervé Guibert"* in *L'Autre Journal* 10, December 1985, 69.

18. In *Feeling Backward*, Heather Love provides a succinct and helpful history of friendship's valorization in feminist and queer scholarship. Although friendship has certainly provided solace for those denied state-sanctioned forms of relation, and while it is appealing to conceive of friendship as a relation that musses binary-logicked understandings of relationality (homo–hetero, male–female, etc.), Love ultimately argues that such renderings of friendship sublate all that is troublesome in the relation into an idealized form. Such strategy, moreover, is consonant with a "gay-positive" political vision that ignores or subsumes the misery of the queer past into a hetero- and homonormative agenda. Love's interest lies, rather, in teasing out the political potential of the uncomfortable aspects of friendship, of the ugly feelings in affection, and of the hopelessness of impossible intimacies. Although she argues that Foucault understands friendship "as a utopian space beyond the constraints of marriage and the family" (75), a claim that I seek to disprove, she nonetheless highlights his less idealistic renderings of the relation: The desire-in-uneasiness that, according to Foucault, draws friends together, for example. My reading of Foucault's friendship thus charts similar terrain, yet one of my goals is to show how such disturbing relational models have already been put to work politically in the form of AIDS caregiving and activism. For more on friendship's important role in feminist and queer history and scholarship, see Love, 75–81.

19. Genet's influence on Guibert's writing is evident both in subject (homosexuality, violence, saints, betrayal, etc.) and style (excessive prose, florid description, religious metaphors, etc.). Sarkonak finds similarity between Guibert and Genet in that both conceived of writing as a limit experience. See *Angelic Echoes* 286.

20. Leo Bersani links betrayal to an "antimonogamous promiscuity" in his essay "Gay Betrayals." For him, such relational betrayals contribute to a "radical anti-relationality that may be the prerequisite negativity for an anti-identitarian community" (*Is the Rectum a Grave? and Other Essays* 44). In other words, the practice of betrayal is part of an ethical model that lends itself to an anti-identititarian, anti-assimilationist queer politics. I analyze closely Bersani's subjective and relational models in Chapter 5 to articulate a concept of a post-identitarian "common sense" in David Wojnarowicz's work.

21. Quoted in Apter's "Fantom Images" 90. Original in Guibert's *L'image fantome* 170.

22. Considering that James Miller in *The Passion of Michel Foucault* devoted significant space to the discussion of the revealed secrets in this story, Guibert's remark should also be read as a criticism of the misguided psychoanalytic impulse motivating that biography.

23. For a discussion of homosexuality as the open secret, see, among other places, Eve Kosofsky Sedgwick, *The Epistemology of the Closet* 67–90.

24. Guibert, too, may be raising similar questions about spirituality in his work. As mentioned earlier, he, like Genet, displays a near obsession with religion and one can find parallels of Foucault's materialist spirituality in Guibert's photography. In "*La sacrastie*," for example, a bouquet of flowers sits on a windowsill, veiled by a wind-swept curtain. The flowing curtain calls to mind the liturgical vestments found in a sacristy, while the wind itself evokes the arrival or the presence of the Holy Spirit—the spirit made flesh, the spirit in the material world. Read in this context, "*L'ami*" could also be alluding to a religious practice, specifically, the Christian ritual of laying on of hands. In Roman Catholicism, the religious denomination most referenced in Guibert, this sacrament is used in ordination ceremonies to authorize a priest or deacon to administer sacraments, most importantly, the Eucharist. A bishop lays his hands on the head of a priest or deacon kneeling before him, a homoerotically charged scenario if ever there was one, symbolically invoking the Holy Spirit and transmitting its powers to the underling. "*L'ami*," then, might be interpreted as an ironic play, or even a queer jab, at this ritual. Given Foucault's insistence on the relinking of philosophy and spirituality and his intimation that friendship itself is part of a materialist spiritual practice, however, one could argue that Guibert too is taking this ritual seriously (transforming it into a secular rite) and making a similarly Foucaultian point: the friend is the one through which spirituality materializes, through which self-knowledge is linked with self-transformation. Which is to say: Practices of friendship are materialist spiritual practices.

25. A detailed discussion of *stultitia* and *sapientia* and the philosopher-guide's various forms can be found in *Hermeneutics* 130–64.

26. See Judith Halberstam, "The Anti-social Turn In Queer Studies," *Graduate Journal of Social Science*, Vol. 5, Issue 2, 2008.

27. The legalization of same-sex marriage along with lifting the ban on the military's "Don't Ask, Don't Tell" policy are the two goals of Sullivan's polemic, *Virtually Normal*. Once these two obstacles are overcome, according to Sullivan, "we should have a party and close down the gay rights movement for good" (Kim, "Andrew Sullivan, Overexposed," web). For a sharp, scathing critique of *Virtually Normal*'s argumentative inconsistency and its promotion of a masculinist, neoliberal dystopia, see Lisa Duggan's *The Twilight of Equality* 55–66. In perhaps the funniest critical sound bite of the last decade, Duggan writes of Sullivan's gay political fantasy: "we get marriage and the military, then we go home and cook dinner, forever" (62).

28. Gandhi, *Affective Communities* 10. The mere mention of a "politics of friendship" brings to mind many an other contemporary thinker: Deleuze and Guattari, Alan Bray, Georges Bataille, Maurice Blanchot, Jean-Luc Nancy, and, of course, Jacques Derrida. Gandhi, for example, makes use of Derrida's concepts

of hospitality, cosmopolitanism, and forgiveness in articulating the politics of friendship emergent in Victorian anti-imperialist subcultures. The aforementioned thinkers, Gandhi's book, and Derrida's concepts are all immensely important to any philosophical/historical consideration of friendship; they doubtless inform my understanding of friendship as shared estrangement. However, in this project I resist engaging Derrida specifically, as his work on friendship has already generated an enormous amount of scholarship. Foucault's "queer" concept, on the contrary, has been—surprisingly, and to the detriment of the burgeoning literature on the subject of friendship—insufficiently studied. Thus, I am by and large concerned here with the uniqueness and significance of Foucault's intervention, particularly as it emerges in his later work on antiquity, ethics, subjectivity, and biopower. That said, Derrida's insistence on the "not yet" of friendship and the "to come" of absolute democracy suffuses my Foucaultian preoccupations throughout. Indeed, Derrida's parting questions in "Politics of Friendship" might well serve as an epigraph to this project:

> [I]s it possible . . . not to found, there where it is doubtless no longer a matter of founding, but to open up to the future, or rather to the "come" of a certain democracy (for democracy is to come: not only will it remain indefinitely perfectible, hence always insufficient and future, but belonging to the time of the promise, it will always remain in each of its future times, to come: even when there is democracy, it never exists, it is never present, it remains an unrepresentable concept), to the "come" of a certain democracy that would no longer be an insult to the friendship we have tried to think, beyond the homo-fraternal and phallogocentric schema? When will we be ready for an experience of equality that would be a respectful test of friendship, and that would at last be just, just beyond justice as law, that is, measure up to its immeasure? (387–88)

Chapter 1

1. 'Le 28 juillet 1983, Michel m'écrit un vrai texte dans une lettre,' in "L'Autre Journal d'Hervé Guibert" in L'Autre Journal 10, December 1985, 69. A partial translation of this letter appears in David Macey's The Lives of Michel Foucault 239–40. Special thanks to Charles Beezel for help with translation of the letter in its entirety.

2. Just one example of such discussion: At the 2004 "Sexuality after Foucault" conference hosted by the University of Manchester, England, there was a panel devoted specifically to Foucaultian friendship, moderated by Jeffrey Weeks who also presented his new work on the topic. The plenary speech by Didier Eribon likewise concerned Foucault's late emphasis on cultivating new forms of relations, specifically friendships. David Halperin, another plenary speaker, discussed what he argues is the antipsychoanalytic conception of subjectivity in Foucault and what it offers for queer politics and relationality. In short, friendship

is a hot topic, if not the next frontier, in Foucault studies, especially queer Foucault studies. Although the lectures above and books and articles below aid immensely in my own work, my main contention with the scholarship thus far is that, on the whole, it does not take seriously enough the philosophical and political implications of Foucault's concept. Without working through the ontological and ethical questions that Foucault's late work on subjectivity and friendship raises, one is left with precisely the pop-psychological or New Age conception of self and relationality that Foucault absolutely discouraged. That said, the following work specifically about Foucault and friendship is instrumental to my project: Didier Eribon's *Insult and the Making of the Gay Self*, David Halperin's *Saint Foucault*, Daniel T. O'Hara's "Michel Foucault and the Fate of Friendship," Charles J. Stivale's "The Folds of Friendship: Derrida-Deleuze-Foucault," and David Webb's "On Friendship: Derrida, Foucault, and the Practice of Becoming."

3. Foucault discusses de Sade and *My Secret Life* in *HoS, V1* 21–2; 148–50.

4. Specifically, Foucault mentions Guibert's first book, *La mort propagande*, published in 1977.

5. For a closer analysis of the historical roots of the confession in the Christian pastoral, see Foucault's "The Subject and Power" in *Essential, V3: Power* 326–48. Foucault also discusses the nascent confessional rituals at play in the practices of the self during the first two centuries A.D. in his 1982 seminar at *Collège de France*, *The Hermeneutics of the Subject* 355–70. Although present in the Hellenistic and Roman eras, the confession is modified in the fourth century A.D. toward a goal of self-renunciation as opposed to self-cultivation. I discuss this modification and the differences between Hellenist/Roman and Christian confessions in my section on *parrhesia*.

6. See Halperin, *Saint Foucault* 25–31. I paraphrase his insights for the remainder of this paragraph.

7. See especially, Barthes, *The Pleasure of the Text*.

8. In "Traces and Shadows," Ralph Sarkonak goes so far as to argue that Guibert merely transformed Foucault's work into fiction: "It is my belief that much of Guibert's work can be read as a fictionalization of Foucault's theories" (180). Based on my genealogy of the concept of friendship as shared estrangement in the Introduction, I assert that this theory emerges between the two. It would not be what it is without the unique contributions of each individual. For more details on the friends' mutual interest in each other's work, see David Macey's *The Lives of Michel Foucault* 471–80.

9. Foucault, "*Le gai savoir*," as quoted in Halperin, *Saint Foucault* 94.

10. Chapters 4 and 5 concern the political forms antirelationality and impersonality might take. My thoughts on impersonality and anti-intersubjectivity here and in forthcoming chapters are largely indebted to Leo Bersani and Adam Phillip's *Intimacies*, Bersani's collected essays in *Is the Rectum*, and Tim Dean's *Unlimited Intimacy*.

11. Foucault concludes *Fearless Speech* with this metaphor of the artist, borrowed from Plutarch's "On the Control of Anger." See *Fearless Speech* 166.

12. I find that history, to an extent, has proven Foucault's musings on the political potentiality of S&M a bit romantic. I relay the ideas here as they are

consistent with his arguments for the political importance of impersonality. For a critique of Foucault's writings on S&M from a psychoanalytic perspective, see Leo Bersani's *Homos* 77-112.

13. Foucault uses the metaphor of the chess game when discussing depersonalization in S&M in "Sexual Choice, Sexual Act" in *Essential, V1: Ethics* 151-52.

14. Foucault, "*Le gai savoir*," as quoted in Halperin, *Saint Foucault* 89.

15. I explore this idea of sameness—specifically, Leo Bersani's concept of homo-ness—in Chapter 5.

16. See Hardt, *Gilles Deleuze* vxii-xix; 40-55. Hardt describes this moment as the "zero hour" between pure negation and creation. Echoing Deleuze and Guattari's statement, he writes: "At the limit of this destruction, at midnight, the focal point, there is a transformation, a conversion from knowledge to creation, from savage negation to absolute affirmation, from painful interiority to joyful exteriority" (51). I discuss this movement—*pars destruens, pars construens*—in greater detail in Chapter 3.

17. Nietzsche's concept of active forgetting requires an absolute negation: leaving the past behind so as to fully experience the present. The passage quoted from Deleuze and Guattari's *What is Philosophy?* resonates with Nietzsche's thoughts on active forgetting:

> Forgetting is no mere *vis inertiae* as the superficial imagine; it is rather an active and in the strictest sense positive faculty of repression that is responsible for the fact that what we experience and absorb enters our consciousness as little while we are digesting it (one might call the process "inpsychation") as does the thousandfold process, involved in psychical nourishment—so-called "incorporation." To close the doors and windows of consciousness for a time; to remain undisturbed by the noise and struggle of our underworld of utility organs working with and against one another; a little quietness, a little *tabula rasa* of the consciousness to make room for new things, above all for the nobler functions and functionaries, for regulation, foresight . . .—that is the purpose of active forgetfulness, which is like a doorkeeper, a preserver of psychic order, repose and etiquette; so that it will be immediately obvious that there will be no happiness, no cheerfulness, no hope, no pride, no *present* without forgetfulness. (Nietzsche, *On the Genealogy of Morals* in *Basic Writings of Nietzsche* 493-94)

I discuss active forgetting in more detail in Chapter 2, specifically the necessity of "forgetting" or leaving behind traditional understandings of friendship in order to create new forms.

18. For a biographical account of Foucault's last days, see Macey 470-71.

19. My point here is *not* to fetishize the theme of death in Foucault's work or life, as James Miller does in *The Passion of Michel Foucault*. (For an astute critique of such fetishism, see David Halperin's "The Describable Life of Michel Foucault" in *Saint Foucault* 143-52.) Rather, I broach the issue here to set the

stage for a rethinking of finitude specifically in relation to biopolitics. In Chapter 5, I develop this insight in my discussion of David Wojnarowicz's understanding of death's immanence to life. Because death is biopower's limit, the limit that determines the normative standards of living, befriending finitude—not lusting after it or living in dreaded fear of it, but cultivating a relationship with it, treating it as an unknowable foreigner whose absolute alterity must be respected—might go some way in loosening the biopolitical sovereign's grip on life.

20. See Jarman *Blue* and Klein "IKB 79."

Chapter 2

1. See especially "Interview with Michel Foucault" conducted by D. Trombadori in *Essential, V3: Power* 239–97.

2. Foucault, "Polemics, Politics, and Problematizations" in *Essential, V1: Ethics* 113.

3. This quotation comes from the first GIP pamphlet as reprinted in Eribon, *Michel Foucault* 227.

4. Here I am referring to Foucault's recurrent remark that his historical/genealogical work is a "toolbox" from which one might fashion a weapon for a particular struggle. See specifically the 1974 essay "*Prisons et asiles dans le mécanisme du pouvoir*" in *Dits et Ecrits II* 523–24.

5. In Foucault's genealogy of sexuality, marriage occupies not only a privileged position in the deployment of sexuality, but also plays a key role in the "deployment of alliances." The latter concerns a pre-biopolitical strategy of social management "firmly tied to the economy in the role it can play in the transmission or circulation of wealth," and ultimately serves to "reproduce the interplay of relations and maintain the law that governs them" (*HoS, V1* 106). Although, historically speaking, pre-biopolitical and instrumental to the fabrication of sexuality, the deployment of alliances continues to be useful for social administration as it interpenetrates with the properly biopolitical deployment of sexuality, especially in the site of the family. See *HoS, V1* 106–12.

6. My thoughts on homosociality here are indebted to Eve Kosofsky Sedgwick's essential work on the topic. See especially *Between Men* 83–96.

7. From the unpublished drafts of an interview with Paul Rabinow and Hubert L. Dreyfus, "19 April 1983" 10.

8. I borrow this succinct formulation of Hegelian ontology from Hardt, *Gilles Deleuze* 2–4.

9. My interpretation of Foucault as a philosopher of immanence heavily relies on Deleuze, *Foucault* as well as Cesare Casarino's lectures on *The History of Sexuality, Volume II* in his Spring 2001 University of Minnesota seminar, "*Ecce Queer: Michel Foucault's History of Sexuality and the Futures of Queer Theory.*"

10. See also Halperin, "Is There a History of Sexuality?" 418–24.

11. Plato's turn to the subject of love, Foucault argues in the penultimate chapter of *The History of Sexuality, Volume Two*, evaluates the love of boys in relation to a search for truth and a renunciation of pleasures rather than as an

ethical dilemma concerning the love object. This shift foreshadows the Christian principles of "the sins of the flesh" and the various attempts to completely eradicate desire. The post-Platonic philosophers reorganize the arts of existence around a different axis—the care of the self, Foucault's concern in *The History of Sexuality, Volume III*. Although not my primary focus here, this step is important in understanding Foucault's grand-scale genealogy of the subject and truth in Western culture. For our purposes, it is sufficient to note that Plato's shift in emphasis transforms the open-ended arts of existence into a more stringent prescriptive code with a predetermined teleology.

12. Blanchot, *The Unavowable Community* 25. For Blanchot, the exposure to the death of another is the foundation not only of friendship but of communication and community *tout court*. It is only in the recognition of the absolute opacity of finitude in the self and the other—that is, a recognition of the simultaneous common-ness and singularity of finitude—that a true friendship begins. He writes: "And it is in life itself that that absence of someone else has to be met. It is with that absence—its uncanny presence, always under the prior threat of disappearance—that friendship is brought into play and lost at each moment, a relation without relation or without relation other than the incommensurable" (25). This incommensurable relation, however, can bring together those who have nothing in common; that is, friendships founded on incommensurability hold the capacity to realize "the community of those who have no community" (25), the anti-identitarian community established on a radical, ontological being-in-common. This insight is central to my understanding of Guibert's concept of friendship and I develop the concepts of being-in-common and anti-identitarianism in relation to AIDS caregiving and activism in Chapters 4 and 5.

13. There are numerous interpretations of "Foucault's" name, Muzil. For example, Jean-Pierre Boulé argues that Guibert is making a nod to Foucault's and Musil's similarly unfinished projects at their respective times of death: for Foucault, *The History of Sexuality* project, for Musil, *The Man Without Qualities* (*"A l'ami qui ne m'a pas sauvé la vie" and Other Writings* 5). Emily Apter refers to the name as "an obvious play on the Austrian author" without further explanation (85), and Ralph Sarkonak simply notes that Musil was "one of the novelist's favorite writers" ("Traces and Shadows" 182). I assert that the reference to Musil (specifically, his masterwork) also is significant because it calls attention to one of the key features of Foucaultian/Guibertian friendship: impersonality and identityless-ness. Moreover, transforming Foucault into a "man without qualities" gives Guibert the blank slate he needs to re-invent him. See my introduction and Chapter 1 for more concerning the role of impersonality in the invention of fictitious personas in friendship.

14. I explore the political implications of being-in-common especially in Chapter 5.

15. Indeed, such *homophilic* bonds, according to Aristotle, constitute the *polis* and mark the relations among citizens. Leela Gandhi locates a counterpoint to Aristotelian friendship in Epicurean *philoxenic* bonds: In their receptivity to visitors and foreigners, such friendships are potentially disruptive to state security. E.M. Forster builds on this Epicurean understanding of friendship in *Two Cheers*

for Democracy, claiming that he would betray his country before betraying his friend. According to Gandhi, Forster's friend is a "metaphor for dissident crosscultural collaboration" (10). Although there is certainly some conceptual resonance between this *philoxenic* friend and Guibert's, they part ways in placing different emphases on betrayal and finitude. For Gandhi's succinct and helpful genealogy of friendship in Western philosophy, see *Affective Communities* 27–33.

16. In addition to Heidegger, one cannot forget Carl Schmitt, also a Nazi supporter, for whom the friend/enemy binary is the conceptual bedrock of the political. See *The Concept of the Political* 25–37.

Chapter 3

1. Wittig, Monique. "The Straight Mind" in *The Straight Mind and Other Essays* 32.

2. I borrow this snapshot of the 1960s French intellectual climate from Michael Hardt's "Introduction: Hegel and the Foundations of Poststructuralism" (*Gilles Deleuze*, ix–xv). For a more detailed and complex account of this same history, see Schrift, *Twentieth-Century French Philosophy*.

3. Foucault, "Two Lectures" in *Power/Knowledge* 80.

4. According to Hardt's interpretation of Deleuze's oeuvre in *Gilles Deleuze*, studying these philosophers provided Deleuze with a nondialectical ontology, ethics, and politics, respectively.

5. This very basic overview of Hegelian ontology is purely schematic. Even in its simplicity, however, we can see Judith Butler's and David Halperin's indebtedness to a Hegelian interpretation of Foucault. For more complex and rigorous accounts of Hegelian ontological negation, see Hegel's own *Science of Logic* (especially, "Book One: The Doctrine of Being") and Jean-Luc Nancy's *Hegel: The Restlessness of the Negative*.

6. Hardt in *Gilles Deleuze* provides a nice summary of this concept: "The pure negation is the first moment of a precritical conception of critique: *pars destruens, pars construens*. The important characteristics are the purity and autonomy of the two critical moments. Negation clears the terrain for creation; it is a bipartite sequence that precludes any third synthetic movement" (xiii). Deleuze in *Nietzsche and Philosophy* conducts a more thorough investigation of the conversion from negation to affirmation: "This is the 'decisive point' of Dionysian philosophy: the point at which negation expresses an affirmation of life, destroys reactive forces and restores the rights of activity. The negative becomes the thunderbolt and lightning of a power of affirming. *Midnight*, the supreme focal or transcendent point which is not defined by Nietzsche in terms of an equilibrium or a reconciliation of opposites, but in terms of a conversion" (174–75). Deleuze also diagrams from a Nietzschean standpoint the varied results of the master–slave encounter (e.g., the triumph of active forces, the triumph of reactive forces) in a handy chart. See *Nietzsche and Philosophy* 146.

7. Here again there is resonance with Guibert's "L'ami." The emphasis on touch, skin, and surface in the photo, discussed in the introduction, seems now a

visualization of a Nietzschean divesture of homosexual essence. In other words, *l'ami* is born only after homosexual interiority is annihilated.

8. I refer here to Louis Althusser's essay, "*Une philosophie pour le marxisme: 'La ligne de Démocrite,'*" and specifically Cesare Casarino's discussion of this essay in *Modernity at Sea: Melville, Marx, Conrad in Crisis* 149–51.

9. Here I am building on Kathi Week's critique of Butler's reading of *Paris is Burning*. Arguing that drag families are more than a mere resignification of normative kinship models, Weeks writes:

> The drag performance can be conceived as a way of talking back that is in itself an individual practice. A house, on the other hand, is potentially more than a reiteration (with difference) of the traditional family: within these social spaces it enacts new modes of collectivity that more than an individual, can create and sustain alternative values, needs, and desires. The drag performances may help challenge the norm, whereas the kinship networks carry the potential to enact a transvaluation on the site cleared by this deconstructive practice. (145)

10. This sentence, in a nutshell, summarizes Michael Hardt and Antonio Negri's project in *Multitude*. I discuss how their collaborative work bears on a Foucaultian politics of friendship in the next chapter.

11. Michel Foucault, "The Subject and Power" in *The Essential Works of Michel Foucault, Volume Three: Power* 326–48.

12. I borrow this notion of positive political myth-making from Antonio Gramsci who applauded Machiavelli for having created a "concrete phantasy which acts on a dispersed and shattered people to arouse and organise its collective will" (*Selections from the Prison Notebooks* 125). Timothy Brennan also discusses the positive myth-making at work in Michael Hardt and Antonio Negri's *Empire* in his critical essay/review, "The Emperor's New Clothes." He writes: "Negri has long understood that politics today requires myth—that people need a common obsession to inspire them and that progress never happens through patient persuasion alone" (342). I see a similar rhetoric of myth-making at work in *Saint Foucault*.

13. See Foucault, *Essential, V1: Ethics* 163–74 and 141–56, respectively.

14. Said, *World, Text and Critic* 245; as quoted in Halperin, *Saint Foucault* 21.

15. Dews, "Power and Subjectivity in Foucault" 92; as quoted in Halperin, *Saint Foucault* 22.

16. Halperin does point the reader toward works that dispute Foucault's critics (namely, Keith Gandal, Mark Maslan, Ed Cohen, Judith Butler, and Joseph Rouse). However, his failure to produce an original interpretation of the ontological aspects of Foucault's theory of power leaves the reader with a distorted view of Foucault's "new politics."

17. Said 246; as quoted in *Saint Foucault* 21.

18. As nitpicking as this criticism might seem, the lyric referenced in this quotation is not from a Sex Pistols' song. It is, in fact, a lyric from Stiff Little Finger's "Suspect Device," released in 1979. The actual lyrics are "They take away

our freedom/ In the name of liberty," a comment on political strife in Northern Ireland.

19. In his own words: *"C'est ce groupe d'intellectuels hostiles au reaganisme mais hostiles également aux nouvelles formes de la politique, qui est visé en tout premier lieu dans Saint Foucault. Le livre fut écrit contre eux"* (13). [It is this group of intellectuals equally hostile to Reaganism and to new forms of politics who are targeted in the first place in *Saint Foucault*. The book was written against them. (translation mine)]

20. I refer here to Foucault's *Madness and Civilization* and *Discipline and Punish*.

Chapter 4

1. The *Empire* trilogy includes: *Empire* (Cambridge, MA: Harvard UP, 2000); *Multitude: War and Democracy in the Age of Empire* (New York: Penguin, 2004); and *Commonwealth* (Cambridge, MA: Harvard UP, 2009). I designate Hardt and Negri's project the "most productive" elaboration of Foucault's biopower because I essentially agree with their critique of the various adaptations of the concept by authors such as François Ewald, Roberto Esposito, and Giorgio Agamben. In essence, their critique concerns these authors' failure to grasp the dual nature of biopower: its capacity for normative management of populations (*biopotere*) as well as its potential for subjectivation: the production of alternative subjectivities (*biopotenza*). I discuss this distinction in detail in note 8. For more on their critique of biopower's theorists, see *Commonwealth* 56–63.

2. U.S. Department of Health and Human Services, "Adult Male Circumcision Significantly Reduces Risk of Acquiring HIV: Trials Kenya and Uganda Stopped Early," in *National Institutes of Health News on the Web*, December 13, 2006. http://www3.niaid.nih.gov/news/newsreleases/2006/AMC12_06.htm (accessed August 2010). I analyze this study in detail in this chapter.

3. In her definitive history of ACT UP, *Moving Politics: Emotion and ACT UP's Fight Against AIDS*, Deborah B. Gould divides AIDS activism into two phases: (a) 1980–1986—activism is marked by caregiving, service provision, lobbying, and candlelight vigils; (b) 1986–mid-1990s—founding of ACT UP, turn toward more direct-action activism, including die-ins, civil disobedience demonstrations, and the like. One goal of Gould's book is to explain the reasons for this shift in activist tactics. In addition to various historical events that galvanized gay and lesbian communities (including the *Bowers v. Hardwick* decision, which essentially criminalized gay sex on a federal level), Gould, guided by Raymond Williams' notion of "structures of feeling" and a Bourdieuian conception of "emotional habitus," argues that the historical "feeling states" circulating in gay communities played a significant role in the shift from "polite" to confrontational activism (46). By and large, I follow her historical schematic and discuss it in detail later in this chapter.

4. Gould notes that it was during these early days of AIDS caregiving that the term *lesbian and gay community* became more common (as opposed to the earlier *gay men* or *lesbians*). Of course, historically entrenched tensions between gay men and lesbians did not simply disappear during this time. Because

mainstream media, medical, and political establishments discursively constructed HIV as a "homosexual problem," however, many lesbians felt that they too were under attack and that it was important to rally behind a shared gay identity to combat AIDS-phobia and anti-homosexual sentiment. See Gould, 65–68.

5. Melinda Cooper convincingly refutes this claim in her book, *Life as Surplus: Biotechnology and Capitalism in the Neoliberal Era*. In a masterful analysis of the enmeshed development of biotech industries and neoliberal economic policy, she argues that as a result of various processes of financialization and debt creation in the 1980s and 1990s, the United States does indeed occupy a privileged position in terms of global capital flows and imperial power. She writes:

> [T]he life sciences have played a commanding role in America's strategies of economic and imperialist reinvention. Over the past few decades, the U.S. government has been at the center of efforts to reorganize global trade rules and intellectual property laws along lines that would favor its own drug, agribusiness, and biotech industries. (4–5)

For more on the United States as the focal point of economic and imperial power in the age of Empire, see Cooper, Chapter One, "Life Beyond the Limits," 15–50.

6. See Roach, *Cultural Critique*, Issue No. 48, Winter, 2001.

7. See Marx, *Grundrisse* 693–706.

8. The distinction between a biopower "from above" (*biopotere*) and "from below" (*biopotenza*) in Hardt and Negri's formulation is crucial in understanding the anti-authoritarian political forms emergent in biopolitics. *Biopotere* delineates a constituted power and *biopotenza* a constituting one. Cesare Casarino describes these forms in the following way: "*Potenza* [*pouvoir* in French] can often resonate with implications of potentiality as well as the decentralized or mass conceptions of force and strength. *Potere* [*puissance* in French], on the other hand, refers to the might or authority of an already structured and centralized capacity, often an institutional apparatus such as the state" (Casarino and Negri, "It's a Powerful Life: A Conversation on Contemporary Philosophy" 181). I find this distinction especially useful for articulating the politics emergent—the biopower "from below"—in the AIDS buddy network.

9. Here again, the absence of any discussion of the global politics of AIDS reveals the shortcomings of Hardt and Negri's analysis. For example, South Africa's 1997 Medicines and Related Substances Control Amendment Act authorized the Mandela administration to bypass Big Pharma patent protections in order to make available antiretorvirals to its citizens. Consequently, the United States, ever invested in Big Pharma, threatened sanctions. Adam Sitze deems Mandela's Act a key moment in the history of the global multitude. He writes: "Though many *altermondialistes* cite Seattle as the first significant victory over the ostensibly anonymous and abstract forces of multinational capital, we must not forget that, two months earlier, seven hundred highly motivated and highly organized people forced the USTR [U.S. Trade Representative] to announce, against a supposedly invincible Big Pharma lobby, that 'the trade dispute was resolved and that the

U.S. government would cease pressuring South Africa on the issues of compulsory licensing and parallel imports' " (779–80). At this point one must question why Hardt and Negri fail to discuss this important *altermondialiste* victory, let alone offer it as a prime example of their multitude's power. Since the victory reveals that there are in fact national focal points in the age of Empire, namely, the United States and its Big Pharma business interests, does it draw too many lines in their unstriated biopolitical global landscape? Because AIDS itself is so overdetermined by the category of sexuality, does ignoring its history and politics allow the authors to unseat sexuality as biopower's central *dispositif*?

10. Sylvère Lotringer, "Foreword: We, the Multitude," *A Grammar of the Multitude* 12.

11. It goes without saying that sexuality, however important, is merely one factor in the biopolitical determination of valuable forms of life, lives deemed worthy of living, saving, and investing in. Indeed, as Adam Sitze notes in "Denialism," from the standpoint of capital both African PWAs and free antiretrovirals are expendable because neither creates surplus value. He writes: "To the extent that essential medicines cannot generate capital, capital renders them inessential, withholding them from the vast majority of people they are designed to treat. Conversely, by refusing to commit to the health of people living with HIV/AIDS unless those people satisfy a condition extraneous to health (the capacity to produce surplus value), capital separates people with HIV/AIDS from what they could do with ARV [antiretroviral] treatments" (775–76). I focus exclusively on the politics of sexuality in this particular case study, then, not to ignore the numerous factors at play in determining the allocation of HIV/AIDS treatment and research funding, but instead to emphasize the conceptual power sexuality continues to hold in the logic of prevention. Furthermore, the NIH trial highlights the limitations of Hardt and Negri's analysis of global biopolitics, in which sexuality disappears in a generalized concept of *bios*.

12. Quoted passages from U.S. Department of Health and Human Services, "Adult Male Circumcision." Details regarding rates of U.S. HIV incidence can be found at http://www.cdc.gov/hiv/topics/surveillance/incidence.htm (accessed August 2010).

13. Grover, Jan Zita, "AIDS: Keywords," *AIDS: Cultural Analysis, Cultural Activism* 28–29.

14. Analyzing the West's involvement in South African HIV prevention, Melinda Cooper notes: "[T]he tools of Western public health are wholly unsuited to dealing with the specificities of the disease in Africa, where heterosexual transmission has always dominated; the imposition of the Western model of AIDS prevention in South Africa amounts to the pursuit of apartheid-era public health policies by other means" (69). What goes unexamined in Cooper's analysis is a discussion concerning the Western invention and enforcement of the very categories "heterosexual" and "homosexual." I raise the question of these categories' applicability to the African AIDS crisis to draw further attention to the apartheid-style politics the homo–hetero binary engenders.

15. McNeil, Jr., Donald G. "Circumcision Halves H.I.V. Risk, U.S. Agency Finds," *New York Times*, December 14, 2006, <http://www.nytimes.com/2006/12/14/health/14hiv.html> (accessed June 15, 2008).

16. See Watney, *Policing Desire*; Patton, *Inventing AIDS*; and Waldby, *AIDS and the Body Politic*.

17. Even George Bush's PEPFAR (The President's Emergency Plan for AIDS), praised as "the single most beneficent achievement of this beleaguered White House," by the most liberal of *New York Times* columnists, Frank Rich, ultimately secured Big Pharma's patent rights for antiretrovirals ("The Gay Old Party Comes Out," *New York Times*, October 15, 2006, web). On the surface a humanitarian project devoid of profit-driven motives and instituted only after many years of hard work by AIDS activists, PEPFAR in fact works to make sub-Saharan Africa ever more, forever more, dependent on U.S. pharmaceutical corporations. As Sitze notes, "Even though Bush's speechwriters included in his 2003 State of the Union address an unusually candid remark regarding the 'immense possibility' offered by generic HIV/AIDS treatments, PEPFAR's only notable achievement since then has been how quickly it has thrown the immense powers of the U.S. executive branch behind Big Pharma's suppression of that very possibility" (778). Concerning the immanence of HIV/AIDS and global capital, see Sitze, 776–79. For more on neoliberal capitalist delirium—the investment in biological futures and the concomitant devaluation of actually existing life—see Cooper, 24–49.

18. Like Hardt and Negri, Brian Massumi builds on Deleuze and Guattari's and Spinoza's concepts of affect. See Massumi, *Parable for the Virtual: Movement, Affect, Sensation*; Gilles Deleuze and Félix Guattari, *A Thousand Plateaus: Capitalism and Schizophrenia*, and Spinoza, *Ethics*, "Part Three: On the Origin and Nature of the Emotions." For helpful summaries of Massumi's and Deleuze and Guattari's work on affect, see Gould, 18–30, and Shouse, "Feeling, Emotion, Affect."

19. As Gould's history of AIDS caregiving and activism does not include a discussion of the affective turn in labor practices, I raise the issue to supplement and build on her thesis. Without doubt, the "moving politics" of AIDS activism are likewise informed by, if not an indirect response to, the major economic shifts in the late-1970s: the embrace of neoliberal economic theory in the West (emphasizing individual accountability and privatization at any cost), the re-structuring of the American healthcare system with the passing of The Health Maintenance Organization Act of 1973 (emphasizing profit over care), and, as Hardt and Negri point out, capitalism's increasing investment in affect. I am arguing, then, that in addition to being shaped by what Gould understands as "*bad* feelings like shame about gay sexual difference and a corollary fear of ongoing social nonrecognition and rejection" (57), that is to say, in addition to being a bid for social respectability and acceptance, the buddy system also is a creative response to larger economic shifts and a genuinely democratic biopolitical response to the increasing incorporation of affect into labor practices.

20. Gould counters a teleological tendency in histories of AIDS activism "by treating the 1981–86 period with its own integrity, valuable in its own right, rather than seeing it as 'not ACT UP' or as simply laying he ground for ACT UP's entrance onto the historical stage (although it certainly did that)" (56). I too hope to avoid such a tidy narrative, but will run the risk for validating it (as Gould does in the parenthetical conclusion to the quoted sentence) by arguing that the affects nurtured in AIDS service provision, specifically, the experience of friendship as shared estrangement in the buddy system, informed ACT UP actions such as

die-ins and the Ashes Action. Additionally, whereas Gould seeks to describe the emotional habitus that delineated the political horizon in the various stages of AIDS activism—that is, seeking to understand why certain forms of activism occurred at certain times while other options were foreclosed—I am more interested in focusing on the ethical terms and affective dimensions of the buddy friendship in order to tease out the fecund political dynamic occurring therein.

21. For more on early AIDS service organizations and the social acceptance of homosexuality, see Gould, 85–100.

22. A statement made in 1985 by Margaret Heckler, director of the Department of Health and Human Services, reveals the Reagan administration's eugenic approach to solving the AIDS crisis: "We must conquer AIDS before it affects the heterosexual population, the general population. We have a very strong public interest in stopping AIDS before it spreads outside the risk groups, before it becomes an overwhelming problem" (as quoted in Paul Ranogajec, "Letter from the Editor: A Shameful Budget," web). For more on the Reagan administration's denialist response to AIDS, see Gould, 49–51.

23. This structural similarity is not coincidental. Many of the early ASOs and activist strategies are indebted to, if not derived directly from, self-help, consciousness-raising models used in the women's health movement and various feminist political organizations. For more on the grassroots models that informed ASOs, see Patton, 9–17.

24. See Montaigne, "Of Friendship" in *The Complete Essays of Montaigne* 138–39; Aristotle, *Nicomachean Ethics* 140–8; Plato, "Phaedrus" in *Symposium and Phaedrus* 60–65.

25. In Foucault's words: "Now it is over life, throughout its unfolding, that power establishes its dominion: death is power's limit, the moment that escapes it; death becomes the most secret aspect of existence, the most 'private' " (*HoS, V1* 138). In Chapter 5, I complicate Foucault's distinction between public = life/private = death in a discussion of the relationship between biopolitics and finitude.

26. In *Unlimited Intimacy*, Tim Dean discovers similar ethical principles in cruising and impersonal sex, but argues that an ethics of non-recognition are not necessarily the province of sex practices. Such ethics, then, can and should emerge in other social and cultural sites as well. I discuss Dean's work more extensively in the next chapter, but here I would like to note that the buddy relation—by the books, strictly nonsexual—can be understood as one of those sites beyond sexual practice in which an impersonal ethics emerges.

27. Given the historical moment about which Virno writes (1980s) and the described political strategy of the youth movements and labor organizations (defection, exodus), I surmise here that Virno is referencing punk subcultures and the Italian autonomist movement, perhaps among others.

28. See Giorgio Agamben's *The Time That Remains: A Commentary On The Letter To The Romans*; Alain Badiou's *Saint Paul: The Foundation of Universalism*; and Slavoj Žižek's *The Fragile Absolute: Or, Why is the Christian Legacy Worth Fighting For?*

29. The political salience of David Wojnarowicz's model of unproductive sexual promiscuity is the topic of the next chapter.

Chapter 5

1. In "A Conversation with Leo Bersani," among other essays, the author reveals that while Foucault has been "immensely important" to him, he has "mixed feelings" about Foucault's work itself (182). Bersani's ambivalence in the end concerns Foucault's dismissal of psychoanalysis: Among other things, Foucault understood psychoanalysis as an integral component in the deployment of sexuality, as the heir to Christian confession, and as a tool of heteronormativity in postwar France and America. The status Foucault has been granted as the founding father of queer studies, however, unduly sidelines Bersani's important early work on the psychic life and social effects of queer subjects and practices. In the recent antisocial turn in queer studies, discussed in this chapter, Bersani's work, in all of its complexity and contentiousness, seems to be getting its due. As fate would have it, queer theory, appropriately enough, has two daddies. For more on the tensions and complicities between Bersani and Foucault, see "Fr-oucault and the End of Sex" in *Rectum* and Chapter Three, "The Gay Daddy," in *Homos* 77–112.

2. Tim Dean, in a February 2010 lecture at Brown University, "Why is Pleasure 'a Very Difficult Behavior'?," explores the titular comment made by Foucault in a 1983 interview, "The Minimalist Self:" "I think pleasure is a very difficult behavior. . . . I would like and I hope I'll die of an overdose [Laughter] of pleasure. Because I think it's really difficult and I always have the feeling that I do not feel *the* pleasure, the complete total pleasure and, for me, it's related to death" (*Politics, Philosophy, Culture*, 12). Unlike Bersani, who, in "Fr-oucault" argues that a psychoanalytic account of the death drive is useful in understanding how the development of the relational modes deriving from pleasure can be blocked (137), Dean focuses instead on the "double helix" of power/pleasure in Foucault's work. He argues that part of the reason pleasure is so "difficult" for Foucault is because it opens the self-contained subject up to potential intimacies, violations, and risks. In short, in becoming infinitely more susceptible to pleasure, as Foucault urged, Dean argues that we also become infinitely more susceptible to power and manipulation. Such susceptibility can be, on the one hand, ecstatic and transformative, but, on the other, invasive, violent, and deadly. Moreover, Foucault's friendship, both "the sum of everything through which they [the intergenerational friends] can give each other pleasure" and, at the same time, a relation founded on a "desire-in-uneasiness," likewise reveals how enmeshed difficulty and pleasure are, how pleasure might even be ontologically indebted to difficulty ("Friendship" 136). A version of Dean's conference lecture will appear as "The Biopolitics of Pleasure" in a forthcoming special issue of *South Atlantic Quarterly* entitled "Future Foucault," edited by Jacques Khalip.

3. "The Gay Daddy" is the title of Chapter Three of *Homos* in which Bersani critiques Foucault's desexualization of homophobia and pleasure.

4. My argument here is indebted to Douglas Crimp's seminal essay, "How to Have Promiscuity in an Epidemic" (*AIDS: Cultural Analysis, Cultural Activism* 237–71). For Crimp, promiscuity teaches experimentation, creativity, and adaptation: precisely the skills needed to develop effective HIV-prevention

campaigns and to care for HIV-positive friends and lovers. Although I am more interested in the ways Wojnarowicz's promiscuity engenders an openness to foreignness, an openness that manifests politically in befriending finitude, Crimp's essay remains an important reference point for my work.

5. See Halberstam, "The Anti-Social Turn in Queer Studies," *Graduate Journal of Social Science*, Vol. 5, Issue 2, 2008.

6. This percentage of course fluctuates due to the unreliability of polling data and varies according to source (e.g., the president of the Log Cabin Republicans claimed that 27 percent of GLBT-identified Americans voted for Republican presidential candidate John McCain in 2008, whereas a Harris poll showed only 16 percent of GLBT voters went for McCain). According to the *Windy City Times*, which bases its claim on polling data from the National Election Pool (a coalition of ABC, CBS, CNN, Fox, NBC, and the Associated Press), "in the last several presidential elections, the percentage of LGB voters supporting the Democrat has hovered around 70 to 75 percent" (Keen, "Obama's Win and the Gay Vote," web).

7. In *The Body of This Death*, William Haver interprets Wojnarowicz's frustration with language (for inadequately capturing his "sense") as an insight into not only the *limits* of the discursive but the very constitution of discursivity. That is to say, for Haver, what Wojnarowicz butts up against in his frustration with language is finitude itself, "which is radically unsignifiable, which can never become signification but is nevertheless the ground of *signifiance* as the possibility for, and the process of bringing into being, any signification whatsoever" (123). Sense, for Haver, necessarily occludes finitude in order to become intelligible, significant. I interpret Wojnarowicz's sense, however, as the recognition of affective excess— finitude is not its foundation, but, rather, an ontological, asubjective affective fullness. Haver himself seems to move away from his Heideggerian reading of sense in a conference presentation, "Reading Foucault's Genet Lectures," given at Brown University in February 2010. I discuss this later, more Spinozist lecture to help articulate the political potential of Wojnarowicz's concept of sense.

8. See Hocquenghem, *Homosexual Desire*, especially Chapter Four, "Capitalism, The Family and the Anus" 110–12. Hocquenghem sees revolutionary potential in same-sex anonymous sex because, unlike the phallic vertical hierarchies fostered in normative heterosexual relations, "homosexual groupings" (in Turkish baths, to use his example) are structured horizontally, more equitably. In such groupings, Hocquenghem finds "the traces of this state of primary sexual communism" (111).

9. See Dean, *Unlimited Intimacy*, especially Chapter Four, "Cruising as a Way of Life" 207–12.

10. A similar example is used by Georg Simmel in his 1910 essay, "The Sociology of Sociability," the essay through which Bersani develops his concept of homo-sociability. Although Simmel's example of the social butterfly at the party is utterly desexualized, Bersani finds the same impersonal rhythm of sociability in the act of cruising, specifically bathhouse cruising. For Bersani's elaboration of Simmel's concept, see "Sociability and Cruising," *Rectum* 45–48; for bathhouse cruising as training in impersonal intimacy, see 59–62.

11. Because Wojnarowicz uses almost identical language, metaphors, and scenarios in articulating the "sense" in sex and in activist embodiment, we can trace

a line, not necessarily causal, between these two "senses." In other words, it is not that the common materializing in sex necessarily engenders the common harnessed in political activism; rather, the very same common is accessed in both, and the rush, the sense, in experiencing it is the same. In this passage Wojnarowicz's rage can be understood as a reaction to the foreclosing of the common in a hetero-ized form of sociality that suppresses the sense he gleaned in anonymous sex.

12. A copy of the painting appears in Wojnarowicz, *Fever* 44. The painting also serves as the cover art for "All the Rage," a collaboration among composer, Bob Ostertag, musicians, The Kronos Quartet, and, in role of visual artist, Wojnarowicz himself. I discuss this collaboration in the epilogue.

13. Thanks to Cecily Marcus for relaying her experiential account of this weekly event.

14. I am indebted to Adam Sitze's essay, "Denialism," for aiding in my articulation of death's value to biopower. Sitze discusses a biopolitical strategy in the work of South African AIDS activist Zackie Achmat salient for my interpretation of Wojnarowicz's reconceptualization of life and death. See especially, Sitze, 790–96.

15. For Agamben, Aristotle's *polis* requires a concept of naked life as an excluded inclusion. The separation of the two definitions of life (*zoe* and *bios*) is thus the fundamental activity of sovereign power. In this sense, Agamben re-periodizes Foucault's conception of biopower and argues that Western politics is biopolitical from its inception. I ultimately disagree with him here: As I argued in the last chapter, for Foucault the invention of sexuality is fundamental to the formation of biopower in the sense that it provides the linchpin between individualizing and totalizing techniques of social management.

16. Lee Edelman argues in *No Future: Queer Theory and the Death Drive* that the constitutive ground of modern politics is the promise of a reproductive futurism embodied in the figure of the Child. The protection of innocent life, a value so unquestioned that it becomes morally unquestionable, is the only politically responsible position. And yet, the fantasy of the future affixed to the Child delineates and authenticates a vision of social order that necessarily excludes queerness (as nonprocreativity, as unproductiveness). In Edelman's words, the terms of reproductive futurism "impose an ideological limit on political discourse as such, preserving in the process the absolute privilege of heteronormativity by rendering unthinkable, by casting outside the political domain, the possibility of a queer resistance to this organizing principle of communal relations" (2). Edelman's polemic thus embraces the queer force of negativity, disavows futural hope, and puts stock in a self- and social-negating *jouissance*. In this sense, my "friend of finitude" finds a kindred spirit in Edelman's anti-futural queer.

17. I owe this insight to Alexander Garcia Düttman's *At Odds with AIDS: Thinking and Talking about a Virus*. Of living with HIV in the early days of the crisis he writes: "One no longer lives and has not yet died, because one has died already and nevertheless lives on, because life and death merge beyond recognition" (2). I explore the political potential of this form of subjectivity below.

18. In melancholia, by contrast, Freud argues that libidinal energy is not directed toward another love object but withdrawn into the ego itself, wherein an identification with the abandoned object is established. The subject regresses to a narcissism (a narcissistic identification with the lost object), and thereby

has a tendency toward sadism and mania. The distinguishing mental features of melancholia are "a profoundly painful dejection, abrogation of interest in the outside world, loss of capacity to love, inhibition of all activity, and a lowering of self-regarding feelings that finds utterance in self-reproaches and self-revilings, and culminates in a delusional expectation of punishment" (165).

19. Video footage of the Ashes Action is available in the AIDS Activist Video Preservation Project in the New York Public Library. All quotations in this paragraph come from various protesters seen and heard in that footage.

Epilogue

1. See Benetton Group's 1992 advertisement, "David Kirby—A 'Pietà.' "

2. Ostertag, Liner Notes, "All the Rage."

3. For more on the musicked body, affect, and heterotopia, see Gary C. Thomas, "Men at the Keyboard: Liminal Spaces and the Heterotopian Function of Music" in *Beyond the Soundtrack.*

4. The libretto, written by Sara Miles and performed by Eric Gupton, reads as follows:

> The first time someone said queer and I knew they meant me, I'm swinging a stick as I walk past the stoop, eating a popsicle, glancing up and the world breaks open with the single word exploding out of the sentence, my life sentence, the wrong thing I did somehow, the wrong thing I am, queer. The first time someone I know was killed for it. Back before most of the men I know were dying, Vernon's down by the river one evening and a guy drives by with a semi-automatic rifle and opens fire, screaming 'Faggots die.' The first time someone really tries to kill me. With a knife like they tried to kill Julio, a baseball bat they did Jo, a bottle like Vickie, a two by four like Matt, a fist a fist a fist a foot and a fist. The first time I watched a friend die. Back when only some government knew what was spreading and they kept quiet. Phil; lying by the window scared and surprised, and the priest says Victor can't come in here because he's not family. The first time I think this can't keep going on maybe I should die too. Like Bruce in the hospital on his last birthday, thirty-one, in a wheelchair with a party hat and a useless IV drip. Manuel mad, spitting blood in the kitchen, because he can't afford the drugs. Jerry going blind and the insurance company tries to cancel his policy. Vince going blind and his folks refuse to talk to him. Diane tossing in pain and no one will hold her hand. Tim propped up in the waiting room, Raul starving at home, Gregory in the back seat of a car, racing, racing towards his death. The first time I say I love you to a man I haven't said it to before, and I'm mad that it took me this long, and I'm queer as hell, and I can feel my heart again just like the first time. Beating. Beating breaking and beating and breaking and beaten and beating and breaking and beating and beating.

Bibliography

Adorno, Theodor W. *Minima Moralia: Reflections on a Damaged Life*. Trans. E. F. N. Jephcott. London; New York: Verso, 2005.

Agamben, Giorgio. *The Coming Community*. Minneapolis: University of Minnesota Press, 1993.

———. "Form-of-Life." *Means without End*. Trans. Vincenzo Binette and Cesare Casarino. Minneapolis: University of Minnesota Press, 2000. 3–12.

———. *Homo Sacer: Sovereign Power and Bare Life*. Stanford: Stanford UP, 1998.

———. *The Time That Remains: A Commentary On The Letter To The Romans*. Stanford: Stanford UP, 2005.

Althusser, Louis. "*Une philosophie pour le marxisme: 'La ligne de Démocrite.*' " *Sur la philosophie*. Paris: Gallimard, 1994.

Apter, Emily. "Fantom Images: Hervé Guibert and the Writing of "sida" in France." *Writing AIDS: Gay Literature, Language, and Analysis*. Eds. Murphy, Timothy F., and Suzanne Poirier. New York: Columbia University Press, 1993.

Arac, Jonathan. *After Foucault: Humanistic Knowledge, Postmodern Challenges*. New Brunswick: Rutgers UP, 1988.

Arato, Andrew and Eike Gebhardt, eds. *The Essential Frankfurt School Reader*. Oxford: Blackwell, 1978.

Aristotle. *Nicomachean Ethics*. Cambridge: Cambridge UP, 2000.

Ashes Action. Dir. Jim Hubbard. AIDS Activist Video Preservation Project. New York: New York Public Library, 1993.

Badiou, Alain. *Saint Paul: The Foundation of Universalism*. Stanford: Stanford UP, 2003.

Barthes, Roland. "Fragments pour H." *L'Autre Journal* 4 (Semaine du 19 au 25 mars, 1986): 81–2.

———. *The Pleasure of the Text*. Trans. Richard Miller. New York: Hill and Wang, 1975.

Baudrillard, Jean. *Forget Foucault*. New York: Semiotext(e), 1987.

Bellour, Raymond. "H.G./F." *Grand Street*. 10.3 (1991): 78–81.

Benetton Group. "David Kirby—A 'Pietà.' " Advertisement. 1992. *The Commercial Closet*. <http://www.commercialcloset.org/cgi-bin/iowa/portrayals.html?record=559> (accessed August 2010).

Bernauer, James. *Michel Foucault's Force of Flight: Toward an Ethics for Thought*. Atlantic Highlands, NJ: Humanities Press International, 1990.

Bernauer, James and David Rasmussen. *The Final Foucault.* Cambridge, MA: MIT Press, 1988.

Bersani, Leo. *The Culture of Redemption.* Cambridge, MA: Harvard UP, 2000.

———. *Homos.* Cambridge: Harvard UP, 1995.

———. *Is the Rectum a Grave?: And Other Essays.* Chicago: University of Chicago Press, 2010.

———. "Is the Rectum a Grave?" *AIDS: Cultural Analysis, Cultural Activism.* Ed. Douglas Crimp. Cambridge, MA: MIT Press, 1987. 197–222.

Bersani, Leo, and Adam Phillips. *Intimacies.* Chicago: University of Chicago Press, 2008.

Blanchot, Maurice. *Friendship* Trans. Elizabeth Rottenberg. Stanford: Stanford UP, 1997.

———. *The Unavowable Community.* Trans. Pierre Joris. New York: Station Hill Press, 1988.

———. *Une voix venue d'ailleurs.* Paris: Gallimard, 2002.

Borhan, Pierre, and Gilles Mora. *Man to Man: A History of Gay Photography.* New York: Vendome Press, 2007.

Boulé, Jean-Pierre. *Guibert: "A l'ami qui ne m'a pas sauvé la vie" and Other Writings.* Glasgow: University of Glasgow Press, 1995.

———. *Hervé Guibert: L'entreprise de l'écriture de du moi.* Paris: l'Harmattan, 2001.

Boyne, Roy. *Foucault and Derrida: The Other Side of Reason.* London: Unwin Hyman, 1990.

Bratich, Jack Z., Jeremy Packer, and Cameron McCarthy, eds. *Foucault, Cultural Studies, and Governmentality.* Albany: State University of New York Press, 2003.

Brennan, Timothy. "The Emperor's New Clothes." *Critical Inquiry* 29.2 (2003): 337–67.

———. *Wars of Position: The Cultural Politics of Left and Right.* New York: Columbia UP, 2006.

Brown, Michael P. *RePlacing Citizenship: AIDS Activism and Radical Democracy.* New York: The Guilford Press, 1997.

Butler, Judith. *Bodies that Matter: The Discursive Limits of "Sex."* New York: Routledge, 1993.

———. *Gender Trouble: Feminism and the Subversion of Identity.* London: Routledge, 1990.

———. *The Psychic Life of Power: Theories in Subjection.* Stanford: Stanford UP, 1997.

———. *Subjects of Desire: Hegelian Reflections in Twentieth-Century France.* New York: Columbia UP, 1987.

Cabrera, Octavio Moreno. *La photo écrite et le roman flashé: Modes de relation de l'image photographique et du texte littéraire dans l'oeuvre d'Hervé Guibert.* Memoir de DEA, Universidad de Salamanca, soutenu le 26 septembre 2003 sous la direction de Mme. Amelia Gamoneda Lanza. Le fonds de Guibert, Caen, France: Bibliothèque de l'IMEC.

Cage, John. "Experimental Music." *Silence.* Hanover, NH: Wesleyan UP, 1961.

Casarino, Cesare. "The Biopolitical Turn." Minneapolis: University of Minnesota Seminar, Fall 2004.

———. "*Ecce* Queer: Michel Foucault's History of Sexuality and the Futures of Queer Theory." Minneapolis: University of Minnesota Seminar, Spring 2001.

———. *Modernity at Sea: Melville, Marx, Conrad in Crisis.* Minneapolis: University of Minnesota Press, 2002.

Casarino, Cesare, and Antonio Negri. *In Praise of the Common: A Conversation on Philosophy and Politics.* Minneapolis: University of Minnesota Press, 2008.

———. "It's a Powerful Life: A Conversation on Contemporary Philosophy." *Cultural Critique* 57 (Spring 2004): 151–83.

Clarke, Eric O. *Virtuous Vice: Homoeroticism and the Public Sphere.* Durham, NC: Duke University Press, 2000.

Cook, Deborah. *The Subject Finds a Voice: Foucault's Turn Toward Subjectivity.* New York: P. Lang, 1993.

Cooper, Melinda. *Life as Surplus: Biotechnology and Capitalism in the Neoliberal Era.* Seattle: University of Washington Press, 2008.

Crimp, Douglas. "How to Have Promiscuity in an Epidemic." *AIDS: Cultural Analysis, Cultural Activism.* Ed. Douglas Crimp. Cambridge, MA: MIT Press, 1987. 237–71.

———. *Melancholia and Moralism: Essays on AIDS and Queer Politics.* Cambridge, MA: MIT Press, 2002.

Crossley, Nick. *The Politics of Subjectivity: Between Foucault and Merleau-Ponty.* Aldershot, England: Avebury, 1994.

Cvetkovich, Ann. *An Archive of Feelings: Trauma, Sexuality, and Lesbian Public Cultures.* Durham, NC: Duke University Press, 2003.

Davidson, Arnold, ed. *Foucault and His Interlocutors.* Chicago: University of Chicago Press, 1997.

Dean, Mitchell. *Governmentality: Power and Rule in Modern Society.* London: Sage, 1999.

Dean, Tim. *Beyond Sexuality.* Chicago: University of Chicago Press, 2000.

———. "The Biopolitics of Pleasure." *South Atlantic Quarterly*, special issue, "Future Foucault." Ed. Khalip, Jacques (forthcoming, 2012).

———. *Unlimited Intimacy: Reflections on the Subculture of Barebacking.* Chicago: The University of Chicago Press, 2009.

———. "Why is Pleasure 'a Very Difficult Behavior'?" Conference Presentation. Future Foucault: On the Anniversary of Bodies and Pleasures Conference. Providence: Brown University, February 26, 2010.

DeBord, Guy. *The Society of the Spectacle.* Trans. Donald Nicholson-Smith. New York: Zone Books, 1995.

de Lauretis, Teresa. "The Essence of the Triangle or, Taking the Risk of Essentialism Seriously: Feminist Theory in Italy, the U.S., and Britain." *Differences: A Journal of Feminist Cultural Studies* 1 (Summer 1989): 3–37.

Deleuze, Gilles. *Foucault.* Trans. Seán Hand. Minneapolis: University of Minnesota Press, 1988.

———. *Negotiations 1972–1990.* Trans. Martin Joughin. New York: Columbia University Press, 1995.

———. *Nietzsche and Philosophy.* Trans. Hugh Tomlinson. New York: Columbia University Press, 1983.

Deleuze, Gilles and Félix Guattari. *A Thousand Plateaus: Capitalism and Schizophrenia*. Trans. Brian Massumi. Minneapolis: University of Minnesota Press, 1987.

———. *What is Philosophy?* Trans. Hugh Tomlinson and Graham Burchell. New York: Columbia University Press, 1994.

Derrida, Jacques. "Cogito and the History of Madness." *Writing and Difference*. Trans. Alan Bass. Chicago: University of Chicago Press, 1978. 31–64.

———. "Politics of Friendship." *American Imago: Studies in Psychoanalysis and Culture* 50.3 (1993): 153–91.

———. *Politics of Friendship*. Trans. George Collins. London: Verso, 1997.

Derrida, Jacques and Anne Dufourmantelle. *Of Hospitality*. Trans. Rachel Bowlby. Stanford: Stanford UP, 2000.

Detel, Wolfgang. *Foucault and Classical Antiquity: Power, Ethics and Knowledge*. Trans. David Wigg-Wolf. Cambridge: Cambridge UP, 2005.

Dews, Peter. "Power and Subjectivity in Foucault." *New Left Review* 144 (1984): 72–95.

Diamond, Irene and Lee Quinby. *Feminism and Foucault: Reflections On Resistance*. Boston: Northeastern UP, 1988.

Dreyfus, Hubert L. and Paul Rabinow, eds. *Michel Foucault: Beyond Structuralism and Hermeneutics*. 2nd ed. Chicago: University of Chicago Press, 1983.

Duggan, Lisa. *The Twilight of Equality?: Neoliberalism, Cultural Politics, and the Attack on Democracy*. Boston: Beacon Press, 2003.

Edelman, Lee. "Ever After: History, Negativity, and the Social." *South Atlantic Quarterly* 106. 3 (Summer 2007): 469–76.

———. *No Future: Queer Theory and the Death Drive*. Durham, NC: Duke UP, 2004.

Eng, David L. and David Kazanjian, eds. *Loss: The Politics of Mourning*. Berkeley: University of California Press, 2002.

Eng, David L. with Judith Halberstam and José Esteban Munoz. "Introduction: What's Queer about Queer Studies Now?" *Social Text* 84–5: 23.3–4 (Fall–Winter 2005): 1–17.

Eribon, Didier. *Insult and the Making of the Gay Self*. Trans. Michael Lucey. Durham, NC: Duke UP, 2004.

Eribon, Didier. *Michel Foucault*. Trans. Betsy Wing. Cambridge, MA: Harvard UP, 1991.

Esposito, Roberto. *Bíos: Biopolitics and Philosophy*. Minneapolis: University of Minnesota Press, 2008.

Faderman, Lillian. *Surpassing the Love of Men: Romantic Friendship and Love between Women from the Renaissance to the Present*. New York: William Morrow and Co., 1981.

Flynn, Thomas R. *Sartre, Foucault, and Historical Reason*. Chicago: University of Chicago Press, 1997.

Follér, Maj-Lis, and Håkan Thörn. *The Politics of AIDS: Globalization, the State and Civil Society*. New York: Palgrave Macmillan, 2008.

Foucault, Michel. "Le 28 Juillet 1983, Michel m'écrit un vrai texte dans une letter." "L'Autre Journal d'Hervé Guibert." *L'Autre Journal* 10 (December 1985): 69.

———. *The Archaeology of Knowledge*. Trans. A.M. Sheridan Smith. New York: Pantheon Books, 1972.

———. *The Birth of Biopolitics: Lectures at the Collège De France, 1978–79*. Trans. Graham Burchell. New York: Palgrave Macmillan, 2008.

———. *Discipline and Punish: The Birth of the Prison*. Trans. Alan Sheridan. New York: Vintage, 1977.

———. *Dits et Ecrits, II*. Eds. Daniel Defert and François Ewald. Paris: Gallimard, 1994.

———. *Dits et Ecrits, IV*. Eds. Daniel Defert and François Ewald. Paris: Gallimard, 1994.

———. *The Essential Works of Michel Foucault, Volume One: Ethics: Subjectivity and Truth*. Ed. Paul Rabinow. New York: The New Press, 1997.

———. *The Essential Works of Michel Foucault, Volume Two: Aesthetics, Method, and Epistemology*. Ed. James D. Faubion. New York: The New Press, 1998.

———. *The Essential Works of Michel Foucault, Volume Three: Power*. Ed. James D. Faubion. New York: The New Press, 2000.

———. *Fearless Speech*. Ed. Joseph Pearson. New York: Semiotext(e), 2001.

———. *Foucault and His Interlocutors*. Ed. Arnold I. Davidson. Chicago: University of Chicago Press, 1998.

———. *Foucault Live: Interviews 1966–84*. Ed. Sylvère Lotringer. New York: Semiotext(e), 1996.

———. *The Hermeneutics of the Subject*. Trans. Graham Burchell. Ed. Frédéric Gros. New York: Palgrave Macmillan, 2005.

———. *The History of Sexuality, Volume One: An Introduction*. Trans. Robert Hurley. New York: Vintage Books, 1990.

———. *The History of Sexuality, Volume Two: The Use of Pleasure*. Trans. Robert Hurley. New York: Vintage Books, 1990.

———. *The History of Sexuality, Volume Three: The Care of the Self*. Trans. Robert Hurley. New York: Vintage Books, 1986.

———. *Madness and Civilization: A History of Insanity in the Age of Reason*. Trans. Richard Howard. New York: Vintage Books, 1973.

———. *The Order of Things: An Archaeology of the Human Sciences*. New York: Vintage Books, 1994.

———. *Power/Knowledge: Selected Interviews and Other Writings, 1972–1977*. Trans. and Ed. Colin Gordon. New York: Pantheon Books, 1980.

———. *This is Not a Pipe*. Trans. James Harkness. Berkeley: University of California Press, 1983.

Foucault, Michel and Maurice Blanchot. *Foucault, Blanchot*. New York: Zone Books, 1987.

Foucault, Michel, Hubert L. Dreyfus, and Paul Rabinow. "19 April 1983." Caen, France: Bibliothèque de l'IMEC, Reference # D250(5), 1983.

Freccero, Carla. *Queer/Early/Modern*. Durham: Duke University Press, 2006.

Freeman, Elizabeth. "Time Binds, or Erotohistoriography." *Social Text* 84–5: 23.3–4 (Fall–Winter 2005): 57–68.

Freud, Sigmund. "Three Essays on the Theory of Sexuality." *The Freud Reader*. Ed. Peter Gay. New York: W.W. Norton and Co., 1989. 239–92.

———. "Mourning and Melancholia." *General Psychological Theory: Papers on Metapsychology*. New York: Collier Books, 1963. 164–70.

Gaillard, Agathe. *Hervé Guibert: Photographies*. (Catalog for posthumous exhibition of Guibert's photography at Galerie Claire Fontaine à Luxembourg (7 Place de Clairefontaine, L-1341 Luxembourg, 6–22 janvier 1994). Caen, France: Bibliothèque de l'IMEC, Le fonds Guibert, Boite 2, 1 f. ma.

Gandhi, Leela. *Affective Communities: Anticolonial Thought, Fin-De-Siècle Radicalism, and the Politics of Friendship*. Durham, NC: Duke UP, 2006.

Gane, Mike, ed. *Towards a Critique of Foucault*. London: Routledge, 1986.

Gane, Mike and Terry Johnson, eds. *Foucault's New Domains*. London: Routledge, 1993.

García Düttmann, Alexander. *At Odds with AIDS: Thinking and Talking About a Virus*. Stanford: Stanford UP, 1996.

Genet, Jean. *Prisoner of Love*. Trans. Barbara Bray. Hanover NH: Wesleyan UP, 1992.

Gramsci, Antonio. *Selections from the Prison Notebooks*. Trans. Quintin Hoare and Geoffrey Nowell Smith. New York: International Publishers, 1971.

Gros, Frédéric. *Foucault et la folie*. Paris: Presses universitaires de France, 1997.

Gould, Deborah B. *Moving Politics: Emotion and ACT UP's Fight against AIDS*. Chicago: University of Chicago Press, 2009.

Guibert, Hervé. *À L'ami qui ne m'a pas sauvé pas la vie*. Paris: Gallimard, 1990.

———. *Blindsight: A Novel*. Trans. James Kirkup. New York: George Braziller, 1996.

———. *L'image fantôme*. Paris: Les editions de minuit, 1981.

———. "Liste des photos publiées dans *Le seul visage*." Caen, France: Bibliothèque de l'IMEC, Le fonds Guibert, Boite 2, 1 f. ma.

———. "A Man's Secrets." Trans. Arthur Goldhammer. *Grand Street* 10.3 (1991) 66–71.

———. *La mort propagande*. Paris: LGF—Livre de Poche, 1992.

———. *Photographies*. Paris: Gallimard, 1993.

———. *Le seul visage*. Paris: Les editions de minuit, 1984.

———. *To the Friend Who Did Not Save My Life*. Trans. Linda Coverdale. New York: High Risk Books, 1991.

Gutting, Gary, ed. *The Cambridge Companion to Foucault*. Cambridge: Cambridge UP, 1994.

———. *Michel Foucault's Archaeology of Scientific Reason*. Cambridge: Cambridge UP, 1989.

Halberstam, Judith. "The Anti-social Turn in Queer Studies." *Graduate Journal of Social Science* 5.2 (2008): 140–56.

———. *In a Queer Time and Place: Transgender Bodies, Subcultural Lives*. New York: New York UP, 2005.

———. "Shame and White Gay Male Masculinity." *Social Text* 84–5: 23.3–4 (Fall–Winter 2005): 220–33.

Halperin, David. "Is There a History of Sexuality?" *The Gay and Lesbian Studies Reader*. Eds. Henry Abelove, Michèle Aina Barale, and David Halperin. New York: Routledge, 1993. 416–32.

———. "Monsters from the Id: Gay Sex, Psychoanalysis, and the Inner Life of Male Homosexuality." Keynote Address. Sexuality after Foucault Conference. Manchester, England: University of Manchester, November 28, 2004.

———. *Saint Foucault*. Oxford: Oxford UP, 1995.

———. *Saint Foucault* (Edition française). Trans. Didier Eribon. Paris: Epel, 2000.

Halperin, David M., and Valerie Traub. *Gay Shame*. Chicago: University of Chicago Press, 2009.

Han, Béatrice. *Foucault's Critical Project: Between the Transcendental and the Historical*. Trans. Edward Pile. Stanford: Stanford UP, 2002.

Hardt, Michael. *Gilles Deleuze: An Apprenticeship in Philosophy*. Minneapolis: University of Minnesota Press, 1993.

———. "Love in the Multitude." Keynote Address. Out of Time Conference. Minneapolis, MN: University of Minnesota, October 21, 2006.

Hardt, Michael and Antonio Negri. *Commonwealth*. Cambridge, MA: Harvard UP, 2009.

———. *Empire*. Cambridge: Harvard UP, 2000.

———. *Labor of Dionysus: A Critique of the State-Form*. Minneapolis: University of Minnesota Press, 1994.

———. *Multitude: War and Democracy in the Age of Empire*. New York: The Penguin Press, 2004.

Haver, William Wendell. *The Body of This Death: Historicity and Sociality in the Time of AIDS*. Stanford: Stanford UP, 1996.

———. "Reading Foucault's Genet Lectures." Conference Presentation. Future Foucault: On the Anniversary of Bodies and Pleasures Conference. Providence: Brown University, February, 26, 2010.

Hegel, G.W.F. *Science of Logic, Volume One*. Trans. W.H. Johnston and L.G. Struthers. New York: The MacMillan Company, 1929.

———. *Phenomenology of Spirit*. Trans. A.V. Miller. Oxford: Oxford UP, 1977.

Hekman, Susan J., ed. *Feminist Interpretations of Michel Foucault*. University Park, PA: Pennsylvania State UP, 1996.

Herring, Scott. *Queering the Underworld: Slumming, Literature, and the Undoing of Lesbian and Gay History*. Chicago: University of Chicago Press, 2007.

Horkheimer, Max and Theodor W. Adorno. *Dialectic of Enlightenment*. Trans. John Cumming. New York: Continuum, 1987.

Hoy, David Couzens, ed. *Foucault: A Critical Reader*. Oxford: Blackwell, 1986.

Hutter, Horst. *Politics as Friendship: The Origins of Classical Notions of Politics in the Theory and Practice of Friendship*. Waterloo, Ont.: Wilfrid Laurier University Press, 1978.

Inda, Jonathan Xavier, ed. *Anthropologies of Modernity: Foucault, Governmentality, and Life Politics*. Malden, MA: Blackwell, 2005.

Jarman, Derek. *Blue*. Zeitgeist Films, 1994.

Kant, Immanuel. *Foundations of the Metaphysics of Morals and What is Enlightenment?* Trans. Lewis White Beck. New York: Macmillan, 1990.

Kaufman, Eleanor. *The Delirium of Praise: Bataille, Blanchot, Deleuze, Foucault, Klossowski*. Baltimore: Johns Hopkins UP, 2001.

Keen, Lisa. "Obama's Win and the Gay Vote." *Windy City Times* 24.8, 5 November 2008: <http://www.windycitymediagroup.com/ARTICLE.php?AID=19735> (accessed August 2010).

Kim, Richard. "Andrew Sullivan, Overexposed." *The Nation on the Web*. 18 June 2001: <http://www.thenation.com/article/andrew-sullivan-overexposed> (accessed August 2010).

King, Preston T., and Heather Devere. *The Challenge to Friendship in Modernity.* London: Cass, 2000.

Klein, Yves. "IKB 79." 1959. Tate Modern, London. 1972. <http://www.tate.org.uk/servlet/ViewWork?workid=8143> (accessed August 2010).

Kordela, Aglaia Kiarina. *$urplus: Spinoza, Lacan.* Albany: State University of New York Press, 2007.

Lloyd, Genevieve. *Spinoza and the Ethics.* London: Routledge, 1996.

Lotringer, Sylvère. "Foreword: We, the Multitude." *A Grammar of the Multitude.* By Paolo Virno. New York: Semiotext(e), 2004. 7–19.

Love, Heather. *Feeling Backward: Loss and the Politics of Queer History.* Cambridge, MA: Harvard UP, 2007.

Macey, David. *The Lives of Michel Foucault.* New York: Vintage Books, 1993.

Macherel, Raymond. *La tentation d'image(s): Ecriture et photographie dans l'oeuvre d'Hervé Guibert.* Memoire de Maitrise sous la direction de Mme Ségolène Le Men et de Mr. Frédéric Lambert, Université Paris VII. Le fonds de Guibert, Caen, France: Bibliothèque de l'IMEC.

Mahon, Michael. *Foucault's Nietzschean Genealogy: Truth, Power, and the Subject.* Albany: State University of New York Press, 1992.

Marsden, Richard. *The Nature of Capital: Marx after Foucault.* London: Routledge, 1999.

Marx, Karl. *Grundrisse.* Trans. Martin Nicolaus. New York: Penguin, 1973.

Marx, Karl and Friedrich Engels. *The Marx–Engels Reader.* Ed. Robert Tucker. New York: W.W. Norton & Co., 1978.

Massumi, Brian. *Parables for the Virtual: Movement, Affect, Sensation.* Durham, NC: Duke UP, 2002.

McLaren, Margaret A. *Feminism, Foucault, and Embodied Subjectivity.* Albany: State University of New York Press, 2002.

McNay, Lois. *Foucault: A Critical Introduction.* New York: Continuum, 1994.

———. *Foucault and Feminism: Power, Gender, and the Self.* Boston: Northeastern UP, 1993.

McNeil, Jr., Donald G. "Circumcision Halves H.I.V. Risk, U.S. Agency Finds," *New York Times* 14 December 2006: <http://www.nytimes.com/2006/12/14/health/14hiv.html> (accessed August 2010).

The Milan Women's Bookstore Collective. *Sexual Difference.* Bloomington: Indiana UP, 1987.

Milchman, Alan and Alan Rosenberg, eds. *Foucault and Heidegger: Critical Encounters.* Minneapolis: University of Minnesota Press, 2003.

Miller, James. *The Passion of Michel Foucault.* New York: Anchor Books, 1994.

Montaigne. "Of Friendship." *The Complete Essays of Montaigne.* Trans. Donald M. Frame. Stanford: Stanford UP, 1948. 135–44.

Moore, Patrick. *Beyond Shame: Reclaiming the Abandoned History of Radical Gay Sexuality.* Boston: Beacon Press, 2004.

Moss, Jeremy, ed. *The Later Foucault.* London: Sage, 1998.

Mowitt, John. *Percussion: Drumming, Beating, Striking.* Durham, NC: Duke UP, 2002.

———. "Queer Resistance: Michel Foucault and Samuel Beckett's 'The Unnamable.'" *Symploke: A Journal for the Intermingling of Literary, Cultural and Theoretical Scholarship* 4.1-2 (1996): 135–52.

Musil, Robert. *The Man Without Qualities.* Trans. Sophie Wilkins. New York: Knopf, 1995.

Nancy, Jean-Luc. *Hegel: The Restlessness of the Negative.* Trans. Jason Smith and Steven Miller. Minneapolis: University of Minnesota Press, 2002.

———. *The Inoperative Community.* Trans. Peter Connor, Lisa Garbus, Michael Holland, and Simona Sawhney. Minneapolis: University of Minnesota Press, 1991.

Nardi, Peter M. *Gay Men's Friendships: Invincible Communities.* Chicago: The University of Chicago Press, 1999.

Nealon, Christopher S. *Foundlings: Lesbian and Gay Historical Emotion before Stonewall.* Durham, NC: Duke UP, 2001.

Nealon, Jeffrey T. *Foucault Beyond Foucault: Power and Its Intensifications since 1984.* Stanford: Stanford UP, 2008.

Negri, Antonio. "Twenty Theses on Marx: Interpretation of the Class Situation Today." *Marxism Beyond Marxism.* Eds. Saree Makdisi, Cesare Casarino and Rebecca E. Karl. New York: Routledge, 1996. 149–80.

Nietzsche, Friedrich. *Basic Writings of Nietzsche.* Trans and Ed. Walter Kaufman. New York: The Modern Library, 1992.

———. *The Gay Science.* Trans. Walter Kaufman. New York: Vintage Books, 1974.

———. *Thus Spoke Zarathustra.* Trans. R.J. Hollingdale. New York: Penguin, 1961.

O'Hara, Daniel T. "Michel Foucault and the Fate of Friendship." *boundary 2* 18.1 (1991): 83–103.

———. *Radical Parody: American Culture and Critical Agency After Foucault.* New York: Columbia UP, 1992.

O'Leary, Timothy. *Foucault: The Art of Ethics.* New York: Continuum, 2002.

Oksala, Johanna. *Foucault on Freedom.* Cambridge: Cambridge UP, 2005.

Ostertag, Bob and The Kronos Quartet. *All the Rage.* Elektra/Nonesuch, 1993.

Pakaluk, Michael. *Other Selves: Philosophers on Friendship.* Indianapolis: Hackett, 1991.

Paras, Eric. *Foucault 2.0: Beyond Power and Knowledge.* New York: Other Press, 2006.

Paris is Burning. Dir. Jennie Livingston. Off White Productions, 1991.

Patton, Cindy. *Inventing AIDS.* New York: Routledge, 1990.

Piggford, George. "'In Time of Plague': AIDS and its Significations in Hervé Guibert, Tony Kushner, and Thom Gunn." *Cultural Critique* 44 (Winter 2000): 169–96.

Plato. *Symposium and Phaedrus.* New York: Dover Thrift, 1993.

Poinat, Frédérique. *L'oeuvre siamoise: Hervé Guibert et l'experience photographique.* Paris: l'Harmattan, 2008.

Poster, Mark. *Critical Theory and Poststructuralism: In Search of a Context.* Ithaca: Cornell UP, 1989.

———. *Foucault, Marxism, and History: Mode of Production Versus Mode of Information.* New York: Blackwell, 1984.

Quinby, Lee. *Freedom, Foucault, and the Subject of America.* Boston: Northeastern UP, 1991.

Racevskis, Karlis, ed. *Critical Essays on Michel Foucault.* New York: G.K. Hall, 1999.

Rajan, Tilottama. *Deconstruction and the Remainders of Phenomenology: Sartre, Derrida, Foucault, Baudrillard.* Stanford: Stanford UP, 2002.

Rajchman, John. *Michel Foucault: The Freedom of Philosophy.* New York: Columbia UP, 1985.

Ramazanoğlu, Caroline, ed. *Up Against Foucault: Explorations of Some Tensions Between Foucault and Feminism.* London: Routledge, 1993.

Ranogajec, Paul. "Letter from the Editor: A Shameful Budget." *Common Sense on the Web* February 2002: <http://www.nd.edu/~com_sens/issues/old/v16/v16_n4.html#budget> (accessed August 2010).

Raymond, Janice G. *A Passion for Friends: Toward a Philosophy of Female Affection.* Boston: Beacon Press, 1986.

Reich, Steve. "Come Out." *Early Works.* Elektra/Nonesuch, 1987.

"Resistance." *The New Shorter Oxford English Dictionary.* Thumb Index Edition. Ed. Lesley Brown. Oxford: Oxford UP, 1993. 2562.

Revel, Judith. *Le vocabulaire de Foucault.* Paris: Ellipses Édition, 2004.

Rich, Adrienne. "Compulsory Heterosexuality and Lesbian Existence." *The Gay and Lesbian Studies Reader.* Eds. Henry Abelove, Michèle Aina Barale, and David Halperin. New York and London: Routledge, 1993. 227–54.

Rich, Frank. "The Gay Old Party Comes Out." *New York Times* 15 October 2006: <http://select.nytimes.com/2006/10/15/opinion/15rich.html> (accessed August 2010).

Roach, Thomas J. "Sense and Sexuality: Foucault, Wojnarowicz, and Biopower." *Nebula: A Journal of Multidisciplinary Scholarship* 6.3 (2009): <http://www.nobleworld.biz/nebulajmsarchives/nebula63.html> (accessed August 2010).

Roach, Tom. Review of *Empire,* Michael Hardt and Antonio Negri. *Cultural Critique* 48 (Winter 2001): 253–54.

———. "Impersonal Friends: Foucault, Guibert, and an Ethics of Discomfort." *new formations: A Journal of Culture/Theory/Politics.* 55 (Spring 2005): 54–72.

Rose, Nikolas. *The Politics of Life Itself: Biomedicine, Power, and Subjectivity in the Twenty-First Century.* Princeton, NJ: Princeton UP, 2006.

Rosemann, Philipp W. *Understanding Scholastic Thought with Foucault.* New York: St. Martin's Press, 1999.

Said, Edward W. *The World, the Text, and the Critic.* Cambridge: Harvard UP, 1983.

Saint-Amand, Pierre. "The Secretive Body: Roland Barthes's Gay Erotics." *Yale French Studies* 90 (1996): 153–71.

Sarkonak, Ralph. *Angelic Echoes: Hervé Guibert and Company.* Toronto: University of Toronto Press, 2000.

———. "Traces and Shadows: Fragments of Hervé Guibert." *Yale French Studies* 90 (1996): 172–202.

Sawicki, Jana. *Disciplining Foucault: Feminism, Power, and the Body.* New York: Routledge, 1991.

Schmitt, Carl. *The Concept of the Political*. Expanded ed. Trans. George Schwab. Chicago: University of Chicago Press, 2007.

Schrift, Alan D. *Twentieth-Century French Philosophy: Key Themes and Thinkers*. Malden, MA: Blackwell, 2006.

Sedgwick, Eve Kosofsky. *Between Men: English Literature and Male Homosocial Desire*. New York: Columbia UP, 1985.

———. *Epistemology of the Closet*. Berkeley: University of California Press, 1990.

Shapiro, Gary. *Archaeologies of Vision: Foucault and Nietzsche on Seeing and Saying*. Chicago: University of Chicago Press, 2003.

Shepard, Benjamin and Ronald Hayduk, eds. *From ACT UP to the WTO: Urban Protest and Community Building in the Era of Globalization*. London: Verso, 2002.

Sheridan, Alan. *Michel Foucault: The Will to Truth*. London: Tavistock, 1980.

Shouse, Eric. "Feeling, Emotion, Affect." *M/C: A Journal of Media and Culture* 8.6 (2005): <http://journal.media-culture.org.au/0512/03-shouse.php> (accessed August 2010).

Sitze, Adam. "Denialism." *South Atlantic Quarterly* 103.4 (Fall 2004): 769–810.

Smart, Barry. *Foucault, Marxism and Critique*. London: Routledge, 1983.

Spencer, Liz, and R. E. Pahl. *Rethinking Friendship: Hidden Solidarities Today*. Princeton, NJ: Princeton UP, 2006.

Spinoza. *Ethics*. Trans. and Ed. G.H.R. Parkinson. Oxford: Oxford UP, 2000.

Stiff Little Fingers. "Suspect Device." *Inflammable Material*. Restless Records, 1979.

Stivale, Charles J. "The Folds of Friendship: Derrida-Deleuze-Foucault." *Angelaki: Journal of the Theoretical Humanities* 5.2 (2000): 3–15.

———. *Gilles Deleuze's ABCs: The Folds of Friendship*. Baltimore: Johns Hopkins UP, 2008.

Strozier, Robert M. *Foucault, Subjectivity, and Identity: Historical Constructions of Subject and Self*. Detroit: Wayne State UP, 2002.

Sullivan, Andrew. *Virtually Normal: An Argument about Homosexuality*. New York: Vintage, 1995.

Sunder Rajan, Kaushik. *Biocapital: The Constitution of Postgenomic Life*. Durham, NC: Duke UP, 2006.

Taylor, Diana. *Disappearing Acts: Spectacles of Gender and Nationalism in Argentina's "Dirty War."* Durham, NC: Duke UP, 1997.

Thomas, Gary. "Men at the Keyboard: Liminal Spaces and the Heterotopian Function of Music." *Beyond the Soundtrack: Representing Music in Cinema*. Eds. Daniel Goldmark, Lawrence Kramer, and Richard Leppert. Berkeley: University of California Press, 2007. 277–92.

U.S. Department of Health and Human Services, "Adult Male Circumcision Significantly Reduces Risk of Acquiring HIV: Trials Kenya and Uganda Stopped Early," in *National Institutes of Health News on the Web*, 13 December 2006: <http://www3.niaid.nih.gov/news/newsreleases/2006/AMC12_06.htm> (accessed August 2010).

Virno, Paolo. "The Ambivalence of Disenchantment." *Radical Thought in Italy.* Eds. Paolo Virno and Michael Hardt. Minneapolis: University of Minnesota Press, 1995. 13–34.

———. "Notes on the 'General Intellect.'" *Marxism Beyond Marxism.* Eds. Saree Makdisi, Cesare Casarino and Rebecca E. Karl. New York: Routledge, 1996. 265-72.

———. *A Grammar of the Multitude.* Trans. Isabella Bertoletti, James Cascaito, and Andrea Casson. New York: Semiotext(e), 2004.

Visker, Rudi. *Michel Foucault: Genealogy as Critique.* Trans. Chris Turner. London: Verso, 1995.

Waldby, Catherine. *AIDS and the Body Politic.* New York: Routledge, 1996.

Waldby, Cathy, and Robert Mitchell. *Tissue Economies: Blood, Organs, and Cell Lines in Late Capitalism.* Durham, NC: Duke UP, 2006.

Watney, Simon. *Policing Desire: Pornography, AIDS and the Media.* Minneapolis: University of Minnesota Press, 1987.

Webb, David. "On Friendship: Derrida, Foucault, and the Practice of Becoming." *Research in Phenomenology* 33 (2003): 119-140.

Weeks, Kathi. *Constituting Feminist Subjects.* Ithaca: Cornell UP, 1998.

Wittig, Monique. *The Straight Mind and Other Essays.* Boston: Beacon Press, 1992.

Wojnarowicz, David. *Close to the Knives: A Memoir of Disintegration.* New York: Vintage, 1991.

———. *In the Shadow of the American Dream: The Diaries of David Wojnarowicz.* 1st ed. New York: Grove Press, 1999.

———. *Fever: The Art of David Wojnarowicz.* New York: Rizzoli Books, 1998.

———. *Memories That Smell Like Gasoline.* San Francisco: Artspace Books, 1992.

Žižek, Slavoj. *The Fragile Absolute: Or, Why is the Christian Legacy Worth Fighting For?* London: Verso, 2001.

Index